Read! Move! Learn!

Active Stories for Active Learning

by Carol Totsky Hammett and
Nicki Collins Geigert

1

EARLY CHILDHOOD

Read!
Move!
Learn!

Active Stories
for Active
Learning

Carol Totsky Hammett and
Nicki Collins Geigert

Read! Move! Learn!

© 2007 Carol Totsky Hammet and Nicki Collins Geigert
Printed in the United States of America.

Published by Gryphon House, Inc.
10726 Tucker Street, Beltsville, MD 20705
301.595.9500; 301.595.0051 (fax);
800.638.0928 (toll-free)

Visit us on the web at www.ghbooks.com

Cover: ©2007, Straight Shots Product Photography, www.get-it-shot.com.

Library of Congress Cataloging-in-Publication Data

Hammet, Carol Totsky, 19--
Read! move! learn! / Carol Totsky Hammet and Nicki Collins Geigert. illustrations, Kathy Farrell
     p. cm.
  ISBN-13: 978-0-87659-058-4
 1. Education, Preschool--Activity programs. 2. Education,
Preschool--Curricula. 3. Lesson planning. 4. School year. I. Title.

Gryphon House is a member of the Green Press Initiative, a nonprofit program dedicated to supporting publishers in their efforts to reduce their use of fiber sourced forests. For further information visit: www.greenpressinitiative.org

Bulk purchase

Gryphon House books are available for special premiums and sales promotions as well as for fund-raising use. Special editions or book excerpts also can be created to specification. For details, contact the Director of Marketing at Gryphon House.

Disclaimer

Gryphon House, Inc. and the authors cannot be held responsible for damage, mishap, or injury incurred during the use of or because of activities in this book. Appropriate and reasonable caution and adult supervision of children involved in activities and corresponding to the age and capability of each child involved, is recommended at all times. Do not leave children unattended at any time. Observe safety and caution at all times.

Every effort has been made to locate copyright and permission information.

Table of Contents

Keep the following in mind as you plan the activities in this book:

1. *Some activities require a large space. If you do not have a large space in your classroom, or the use of a gym or multipurpose room, consider using a hallway or taking the activity outdoors.*

2. *If the space is too small to accommodate all children at one time, divide the class into small groups that suit the space you have.*

3. *Tell the children to stretch out their arms, creating their personal space that does not touch anyone else.*

4. *If you do not have a gym or multipurpose room, push the furniture to one side of the room to maximize your open floor space.*

Introduction

Jack be nimble,
Jack be quick.
Jack jump over
The candlestick.

Is this familiar nursery rhyme an invitation for early childhood teachers to focus on literacy or on active learning with children? It's both! Young children love to move, and they learn most effectively through movement. By designing literacy lessons to engage children physically, you can add fun and excitement to the learning process by connecting lessons learned through movement to literacy. For example, as a child jumps to music, he is learning the following: rhythm, sequencing, coordination of movement, memory, and when to start and stop. These same skills are used when learning to read. *Read! Move! Learn!* provides activities that combine early literacy with activities that are fun. Our interests and experiences in early literacy development and movement education were the catalysts for creating a teacher resource that brings new energy and richness to story time.

Another reason we wrote *Read! Move! Learn!* is to address the issue of the health and wellness of young children, in particular the fact that many children lack the exercise they need to ensure good health, strength development, and coordination. Research suggests an alarming increase in childhood obesity caused, in part, by a lack of opportunities for children to participate in regular physical activity (Sanders, 2002). We are also very aware of the increased demands to prepare children to meet educational standards at younger and younger ages. David Elkind, an expert in childhood development, described this trend by stating that parents and schools are geared no longer toward child development, they are geared toward academic achievement (Elkind, 2001). Teachers are examining their daily schedules closely to find time to do more. The information and activities in this book will help you address these topics and successfully meet your challenges.

Let's begin by looking at what health experts tell us about exercise, nutrition, and what young children need. In 2005 former President Bill Clinton, in collaboration with the American Heart Association (Medical News Today, 2005), set up a joint alliance aimed at slowing the rate of increase in childhood obesity, with the school lunch program being one of the three areas targeted. Additionally, other groups such as GOPHER (Active and Healthy Schools, 2004), and Dr. Marion Nestle (Food

Marketing, 2006), have worked to bring about change not only to the school lunch program, but also to the entire school environment.

According to the National Association for Sport and Physical Education, along with the American Heart Association and The President's Council on Physical Fitness, there is a national goal to improve the health, nutrition, and physical activity levels of all children, including children with disabilities (NASPE, 2002, 2004). In 2005, the U.S. Surgeon General, Richard Carmona, spoke at the Early Childhood Conference hosted by the U.S. Department of Education Office of Special Education Programs on "The Value and Promise of Every Child." In his remarks, Carmona talked about developing the "health literacy" of all our nation's children, including children with disabilities, and stated that the healthcare crisis of childhood obesity could be tackled. He encouraged all sectors of our society to join the fight against childhood obesity by "teaching children to enjoy healthy foods in healthy proportions and by encouraging all children to be physically active for at least 60 minutes a day…not only in sports but also simple things like taking the stairs, riding their bikes, and just getting out and playing" (Carmona, 2005).

Accordingly, the National Association of Sport and Physical Education (2002) developed the following guidelines for all children:

▶ Infants (birth–12 months) need a safe area with unrestricted movement that provides space adequate enough to allow stimulating toys and room for activities that promote development of movement skills such as reaching, grasping, crawling, standing, rolling over, and so on.

▶ Toddlers (12–36 months) should be provided 30 minutes of accumulated planned opportunities for guided gross motor activity each day, such as climbing, dancing, and running, along with several hours of unstructured playtime that includes gross motor activity. The activities should include, for example, progressively appropriate opportunities to develop locomotor skills: walking, running, and jumping; body control skills: balancing, rolling, and weight bearing skills on the hands; and ball handling skills: throwing, kicking, and catching.

▶ Preschoolers (ages 4–5) should be provided at least 60 minutes a day of accumulated (many episodes) planned vigorous (fatigue producing within a short time) physical activity, including non-competitive games, balance stunts, simple tumbling, and dancing or movement to music.

Additionally, they need at least 60 minutes—and up to several hours—a day of unstructured activity that includes opportunities for safe climbing, balancing, sliding, hanging, and swinging. It is also important to remember that young children should not be sedentary for more than one hour at a time, unless they are sleeping.

► School-age children should be encouraged to move after two hours of sedentary activity (NASPE, 2004).

A lack of physical activity can lead to a lack of development of motor and cognitive skill competence (Block, 2001). Furthermore, lack of activity has been found to have a major effect on the health and well-being of young children, and when children are not healthy, their mental health suffers as well as their physical health (Elliott & Sanders, 2005). Healthy habits, developed early in childhood, can promote overall health, help to prevent childhood obesity, improve coordination, and establish exercise as part of a daily routine. Research is strongly suggesting that participation in moderate weight-bearing activities, on a regular basis, can increase bone density in school-age children (Laing, et al, 2005). Activities such as rope jumping, soccer, dancing, and recreational gymnastics are all found to be beneficial.

Turning our attention to early literacy development, we find teachers faced with the heart of the dilemma. A stronger focus on academics has found its way into many early childhood classrooms. We find more rigid instructional strategies being suggested, including more paper and pencil tasks. Playtime is being nudged out by more seat time. Administrators and center directors are taking a closer look at standardized assessment of young children and are requiring more time devoted to testing. Teachers are asking the question, "How do I meet the motor development needs of the children while, at the same time, meet new academic challenges?"

Best practices in literacy development suggest that teachers adopt a balanced approach to curriculum design and choice of teaching strategies. By this we mean that the "one-size-fits-all" philosophy does not provide you with the wide variety of strategies and the flexibility you need to reach every child. The collection of action-packed stories in *Read! Move! Learn!* provides unique tools and a fresh approach to help you engage children during story time.

Children between three to seven years have vast differences in listening, speaking, reading, and writing skills. Moreover, every classroom has children from different ethnic, cultural, and economic backgrounds. How a child approaches learning also varies. Although most children learn through all modalities, many children have preferences. Some children are strong auditory learners or visual learners—they take in everything they hear or see. Many children, however, prefer to use their tactile and kinesthetic abilities (touch and motion) to learn about their environment. We chose each book in *Read! Move! Learn!* to address all learning modalities, assisting you in bringing together a world of literature and a playground full of action.

We recognize that each year you, as teachers, will have a wonderfully unique group of children. To get the most out of *Read! Move! Learn!*, browse through the alphabetical list of books. We are confident that many of the titles can be found in your classroom or school library. Select stories based upon the interests of the children and the goals set for them in literacy and movement. Also consider your own interests. The enthusiasm you bring to Story Time will be contagious! Take some time to explore the spaces and places that are available for active lessons. Take inventory of the equipment you will need and make a list of what you can borrow, make, or purchase. Learn action vocabulary words and literacy terms that are unfamiliar to you, and check the Glossary (Appendix A) for definitions and explanations. The time utilized in preplanning will serve you well, resulting in engaging and fun activities that are easy to implement. With these best practices in place, you can explore active learning and literacy with your children, allowing them to become confident life-long movers and readers, benefiting from the best of both worlds.

Part One, "Connecting Literacy and Movement," discusses basic information about motor development, developing rhythmic and movement qualities, and early literacy concepts. Managing an environment where children are invited to move requires attention to details. We have included strategies that have worked well for us, in addition to thoughtful feedback from teachers with whom we have collaborated. Of particular importance is the discussion about adaptations and accommodations for children with diverse learning needs.

Part Two, "Read, Move, and Learn with Books," is the heart of the book. We have featured 74 children's books. Each selection includes a brief annotation, suggestions to engage the children during Story Time, information about literacy concepts to focus on as you read to the children, action vocabulary, and concepts to explore. In addition, each selection includes two or three activities created specifically to support the book's storyline and characters. These plans, depending on the storyline, suggest activities to enhance the development of motor skills such as hopping or jumping, and dramatic play skills. The activities encourage improvisation, interpretation, and creativity. Safety tips are included where appropriate. Because teachers often follow themes or topics when developing lessons, we listed additional books, categorized by themes, for your consideration. The ideas and activities in this book have all been tried and tested on children ages three to seven years old. When we field-tested the activities, the children were not shy about making suggestions, resulting in lesson plans that consider children's developmental needs, interests, creativity, and playfulness. You also may gain a wealth of ideas from the children!

Appendix A (Glossary) answers questions about definitions relating to motor development, movement concepts, and literacy concepts. These words are in bold font throughout each lesson plan, cueing you that a definition is available. This list of terms, although not inclusive, will give you a good start in understanding the activities included, and in easy planning of suggested lessons.

Appendix B (Resources) includes a wide variety of resources that will assist you in moving beyond the ideas and activities in this book. Exploring additional avenues for gathering new ideas will add depth to lessons and make extending them simple.

Appendix C (Materials) was our favorite list to compile. In addition to describing some of the equipment used in the lesson plans, we included additional equipment and materials that we have found invaluable in providing movement opportunities to young children.

Finally, we have included an alphabetical Title Index, Author Index, and Recorded Music Index. You will find that certain authors write children's books with active learning in mind, and we wanted to help you find books by these authors.

Our goal is to support early childhood educators by enhancing literacy skills that make story time exciting, as well as to encourage active, healthy lifestyles in young children. It is our sincere hope that, through the ideas presented in this book, you will find your own "literature in motion" to continue to create engaging lessons throughout your career. Ready? Let's get moving!

References

Block, B.A. 2001. Literacy through movement: An organizational approach. *Journal of Physical Education, Recreation, and Dance,* 72(1), 39-48.

Carmona, R. 2005. The value and promise of every child. United States Department of Health & Human Services. Available online at: www.surgeongeneral.gov/news/speeches/02072005.html.

Carmona, R. 2005. United States Department of Human Health Services. General's Call to Action. Available online at: www.surgeongeneral.gov/topics/obesity/calltoaction/fact_adolescents.htm.

Elkind, D. 2000-01. Cosmopolitan school. *Educational Leadership,* 58(4), 12-17.

Elliott, E. & Sanders, S. 2004. The issues: Children and physical activity. *PBS Teacher Source.* Available online at: www.okwoolard.com/commentary/keep_children_moving.html.

Gopher Sport, Active and Healthy Schools, 2004. Available online at: www.activeandhealthyschools.com.

Medical News Today. May 4, 2005. "Bill Clinton in drive to tackle childhood obesity." Available online at: www.medicalnewstoday.com/medicalnews.php?newsid=23813.

National Association of Sport and Physical Education (NASPE). 2002. *Active start: A statement of physical activity guidelines for children birth to five years.* AAHPERD Publications.

National Association of Sport and Physical Education (NASPE). 2004. *Physical activity for children: A statement of guidelines for children ages 5-12. Second Edition.* AAHPERD Publications.

Nestle, M. 2006. Food marketing and childhood obesity—A matter of policy. *New England Journal of Medicine:* 354:2527-2529 June 15, 2006 Available online at: http://foodpolitics.com/pdf/foodmktg.pdf

Connecting Literacy and Movement

Part One

The Early Literacy Framework

Literacy is the ability to listen, speak, read, and write in a particular language. Infants begin to acquire information about literacy from the moment of birth. When nurturing parents and caregivers talk to babies about their surroundings, they provide literacy nourishment for the foundation of developmental **listening, speaking, reading,** and **writing** skills. An adult's responsiveness to a child's early language often takes the form of asking questions, supplying words that describe objects and actions, and extending a child's sentence, which set up language turn-taking interactions we call conversation. Conversations provide a child with language structure, the use of **voice inflection** in speaking, and of course, an ever-growing vocabulary bank.

Children enter early childhood environments with a wide range of language, reading, and writing experiences. In early childhood classrooms, there are children with different levels of **literacy** development. Best practices in early childhood education support the importance of meeting each child where he or she is on the **literacy continuum** and the goal of providing experiences that are responsive to individual developmental

Note: All terms in bold are explained in greater detail in the Glossary on Appendix pages 188-199.

25

needs. Individualized learning opportunities take into account a child's prior experiences, strengths, needs, and interests. As teachers, we are well on our way to promoting literacy development if we tap into what children do well and what interests them.

Speaking

Simply stated, speaking is the oral expression of language in order to communicate. At a very early age, children learn that the sounds they make elicit a response from adults. Babies learn that using language will help get their needs met. They also learn that talking is a pleasant activity and plays a large role in their culture. As children get older, speaking opportunities allow them to develop conversation skills, the ability to ask and answer questions, and the ability to develop and use increasingly complex sentence structure and vocabulary. Opportunities to use oral language also give children a means to demonstrate their level of understanding of language, including word meaning, grammar, and intent (Strickland, 2006).

Listening

Listening is the ability to hear and receive information for understanding. An environment rich in oral language affords children an opportunity to build sensitivity to the sound system of their language, and to develop *phonological awareness* (the awareness of the sound structure of language in general) and *phonemic awareness* (the ability to recognize spoken words as a sequence of sounds). The smallest sounds in words are referred to as **phonemes** (Yopp & Yopp, 2000). As children develop, the awareness of the sound system of their language and the ability to hear specific sounds in words set the stage for **reading.**

Speaking and listening are both separate and interrelated skills. You can foster development of these skills by engaging children in books that include **rhythm** and **rhyme, predictable text,** and poems. Additional language activities include singing and reciting fingerplays, songs, and chants; clapping syllables in words; using **alliteration;** and exploring **onomatopoeia**.

Reading

Reading is the ability to understand signs, symbols, and printed matter in order to gain information. The process of reading begins early in life. Often, the first step is "reading" **environmental print**. Just think about the number of times you have witnessed children identifying a place such as McDonald's™ or Toys 'R Us™ when they see its symbol, logo, or name. Children's everyday experiences with print greatly influence their ability to understand what is read to them and what they read on their own. The more limited a child's experiences prior to school, the more likely he or she will have difficulty with reading development (Snow, Burns, & Griffin, 1998). Children with limited experiences will require extra time and attention to catch up to their peers. Immersing them in a **literacy-rich environment** is a good first step in helping the children experience success in literacy.

Concepts of print include:
- ▶ book concepts (titles, **authors,** and **illustrators)**
- ▶ print conveys meaning (carries a message)
- ▶ illustrations, signs, and symbols carry meaning
- ▶ directionality (print is read from left to right, top to bottom)
- ▶ concept of word (words match speech, words are composed of letters and have spaces between them)
- ▶ letter knowledge (letters in words can be named)
- ▶ **phonemic awareness** (sounds in words are represented by letters or combinations of letters)

You can help children increase their knowledge of print by creating a print-rich environment and planning for reading engagement opportunities throughout the day. Reading aloud to children (at home and at school) remains the single most important factor in developing successful readers.

Writing

Although writing is often separated from the reading process, the process of reading and writing can give children a sense of power and a feeling of control over their ability to gain knowledge and to communicate their ideas. Young children often write before they read (Routman, 2003). Using symbols, drawings, and invented spelling are developmentally appropriate strategies for young children and should be encouraged. Offering positive support will ensure that children will continue exploring the writing process.

Through frequent, thoughtful, and non-intrusive observation of children, you can begin to form a picture of each child as a language user and a reader and writer. Armed with this information, you can plan exciting learning opportunities for unstructured and unscripted use of language and exploration of reading and writing. Encourage playing with literacy and taking risks. For example, use positive reinforcement when children recite a story from memorization (instead of reading each printed word). Accepting "scribble writing" (young children "scribble write" before they are able to write conventionally) promotes the idea that being able to write thoughts and spoken words is important. This is particularly important for English language learners or children with underdeveloped language. These children may be timid or unsure of their abilities. Risk-taking is not likely to happen if children are afraid to make mistakes. All children flourish if they perceive themselves as confident and competent learners.

In addition to child-directed experiences, daily opportunities should include plans for intentional teaching. Using what you know about each child, you can design whole class, small group, and individual activities that will help you meet the diverse levels of development in your group of children. With guidance and encouragement, children will explore the activities you have planned independently. The key for developing independent learners is flexibility. Young children want and need to be in charge of their learning. Offer positive support for children who wish to change your ideas and come up with their own. Be patient! Creating a classroom environment where children's prior knowledge, thoughts, and ideas are respected will take time and continuous attentiveness.

The Movement Framework

Recent brain research indicates that **cognition** (the process of learning and knowing) and movement are very closely linked. When children are active, neural connections (the axon/dendrite pathways that allow us to process information) are made in the brain that provide the framework for cognition and promote more advanced brain development.

Our senses give us information about the physical conditions of our body and the environment around us. The brain must organize all of these sensations by locating, sorting, and ordering them. When an infant uses his or her senses to interact with the environment, novelty and curiosity are the means through which the infant brain grows and learns. Novelty and curiosity encourage movement, which is critical for complete sensory and motor integration. Infants thrive on experiences that are stimulating, nurturing, and positive. This rich sensory diet includes interesting sounds, positive songs and language, lots of touch (**tactile** input) from loving family members, varied visual stimulation such as color and motion, and a variety of smells and taste experiences. These interactions lay the foundation for the development of motor and language skills, along with social and emotional growth.

Even before birth everyone participates in this growth process to one degree or another. For ease of understanding, this process has been divided into four parts on a movement continuum.

The Movement Continuum

There are four foundation levels of sensory input that demonstrate sensory and motor integration along the movement continuum that are crucial to an individual's ability to learn.

▶ The first level is generally in place within the first two months of life. At this level, the infant is taking in all kinds of information from hearing, seeing, and a variety of touch sensations. Also, the way the infant is held, picked up, and put down changes the infant's head position, which affects how the infant learns to respond to changes in order to sort and organize those sensations for further use. This level is called the *primary sensory system* foundation, which is generally in place by two months and includes the development of the following:

> **Visual, olfactory, and auditory senses** (sight, smell, and sound),
> **Proprioception** (sense of body and head position with response from the joint/skin/muscles),
> **Vestibular** (body response to changes in the head position), and
> **Tactile** (sense of touch).

▶ The second level is the *perceptual motor systems* foundation, which should be in place by one year of age. At this level, the baby is beginning to be aware of his or her body parts, such as hands, feet, tummy, mouth, eyes, nose, and ears. From this awareness and a developing mental body image, the infant begins to purposefully change his or her head position and body position, and begins to push himself or herself up, developing the following:

> **Cross lateralization** (crossing the **midline** such as reaching across the midline, crawling, and so on),
> **Motor planning** (such as rolling over, creeping, crawling, standing, walking),

All terms in bold are defined in the Glossary on pages 188-199.

Lateralization (hand preference),
Bilateral coordination (use of two hands, two feet together), and
Body perception (body part awareness).

▶ The third level is the *perceptual motor skills* foundation that should be in place by around three years. This level includes the following:
Purposeful play activities,
Visual/motor integration,
Eye-hand coordination,
Visual perception, and **auditory perception**.

▶ Finally, the fourth level is the foundation for **cognitive** applications that support academic readiness. This foundation is generally in place by six years of age and includes integration and specialization of the body and areas of the brain such as:
Visualization, hand preference, and the abilities to access working memory, **recall**, and comprehend past, present, and future events.
Also included is the ability to regulate behavior and focus attention, the ability to sit and attend to detail, the ability to coordinate complex motor skills, and the ability to learn academic skills, including abstract thought and reasoning.

As children proceed along the **movement continuum** in their sequence of development, they use abilities from each level to develop building blocks that become the basis for more complex and more mature development. The movement continuum eventually allows for development of more efficient movement patterns that help to "grow" the brain, and lead to more efficient processing of information and greater capacity for learning (Jensen, 2000). For this reason, the power that play contributes to the physical, emotional, social, and mental development of the child is critical.

Learning takes many routes. Almost all children are, at any one time, **visual learners, auditory learners, tactile learners,** and **kinesthetic learners.** They are multi-modal learners, meaning that they learn using one or more senses to receive information before responding to it. While most children have preferred senses or modalities for learning, it is interesting to note that for some activities, a child may seem to receive information better using one or two modalities (for example, both visual and auditory) and with other activities they use other senses (for example, tactile and olfactory). This highlights the importance of creating learning engagements

that provide a variety of opportunities for children to receive input and make sense of that information.

During the rapid brain growth of childhood, the brain is receiving and organizing messages and information. When a child practices an activity repeatedly, a strong neural response is developed with many thousands of neurons linking together to make a particular neuromuscular response.

Children move for the joy of it, but while they are learning to walk, run, jump, gallop, hop, skip, slide-step, and leap, they are also developing higher areas of the sensory and motor cortexes. In that way, a child masters a particular sensory motor element, and it becomes integrated into the system.

Developmentally, it is important to provide as many movement opportunities as possible during the child's day. Conversely, a lack of physical activity can lead to unhealthy conditions of overweight and obesity in young children, which can lead to Type II diabetes and heart conditions. Recent research on the emotional and social effects of obesity in children indicates that physical activity can have a tremendous positive impact. Research by the NIHCM (National Institute for Health Care Management) Foundation notes that if kindergartners were provided one hour of physical education per day, the children at risk for being overweight could be reduced by 60%.

The movement lesson plans and ideas offered in this book provide a variety of fun activities that will get children up and moving as you read to them and engage them in enjoyable experiences that will help them move and learn.

Connecting the Frameworks

How often have you found yourself reading to a group of children and had the sense that they were not engaged in the read-aloud? Some children appear to be daydreaming; others are itching to move. For all children, *active engagement* in Story Time is vital for learning. Active engagement describes children's cognitive state while listening to the story, which enables them to connect to the story. However, for all children, and particularly children who need "wiggle time," becoming physically engaged in the story enhances literacy learning and motor skills. Children's enjoyment of Story Time is enhanced when they are emotionally and physically engaged in the story. This in turn leads to greater understanding because the child's brain and body are prepared for learning.

How are literacy skills and motor skills connected? What is the benefit of integrating movement during Story Time? How will children respond to an active story time? Teachers are always looking for ways to present story time lessons that meet the academic needs of our children.

▶ Children will have a better understanding of concepts such as *over, under, around, through, beside,* and *between* if they have an opportunity to explore actively these concepts.

▶ Combining literacy and movement by asking children to move in a way that reflects the meaning of a word increases their comprehension and helps them have improved memory and recall.

▶ For children who have difficulty sitting still during Story Time, creating active lessons recognizes and supports, in a very positive way, their need to move.

▶ If children have joyful reading experiences, they are more likely to look at or read books even when adults are not able to join them.

▶ Children who remember the sense of self-confidence they had when they were actively engaged in stories are more inclined to engage in play that is more physical.

When you present the lesson plans in this book, you and your children will experience the joy of story time in a fundamentally different way. You will address the increasingly critical need to get children up and moving, as well as meet academic goals for literacy development.

Selecting the Literature

One of the great joys of teaching is selecting literature to share with children. The children's books that we selected for *Read! Move! Learn!* encourage children to be involved actively during story time, integrating literacy learning with physical movement. Each book and its accompanying lesson plans have been explored by countless children ages 3–7 and have been given the "kid stamp" of approval!

As you get to know the children in your group, note their interests and passions and use this information to help you select books for active story times. Consider inviting the children to be a part of choosing the stories. Some teachers select literature to support thematic instruction or units of study. The children's books featured in *Read! Move! Learn!* are ones that are popular with children, readily available, lend themselves to physical movement, and support thematic instruction or units of study.

Creating a Movement Environment

The lesson plans created for each featured book are open-ended and are designed to allow for modifications based on the space you have available. Many of you have space for active Story Times, and some of you will have to modify the ideas in this book because you have small Circle/Story Time areas. If you have a small area, consider using the hallway or the outdoor area. If you are lucky enough to have access to a gym or multi-purpose room, use this space for some of the activities in this book. As with all learning experiences, safety is the first consideration.

Rounding Up the Materials

Many of the activities and games in this book do not require any materials. Most of the materials can be found in teacher supply catalogs, local variety stores, or by scouring thrift stores. You can even make some of the materials, such as yarn balls, scarves, and beanbags (see Appendix C on pages 207-212).

It is a good idea to have all of the small materials, such as foam balls and musical instruments, in a container near your circle time area. Baskets with lids work well as storage containers. Everything is at your fingertips, but the items are not a distraction to the children. If you are using music for your lesson, be sure to run through the selections before the children arrive.

Carrying Out the Lesson

Each featured book has a lesson plan that consists of:

▶ Theme Connections
▶ What's the Book About?—a brief description of the book
▶ Lesson Objectives—based on the content of the book
▶ Action Vocabulary—movement vocabulary found in the book
▶ Concepts Explored—concepts related to the book
▶ Developing Literacy Skills—an active Story Time highlighting literacy skills
▶ Moving to the Story—active learning related to the story
▶ Developing Motor Skills—active experiences and activities related to the book
▶ Safety Tip—tips to consider to ensure children's success with the activity and overall safety
▶ More Books to Share—more books related to the theme
▶ Music Suggestions—music to accompany or expand the lesson

You will find words in bold throughout the book. The definitions for these words are in the Glossary on pages 188-199.

As you review each featured book, you will notice that some directions, suggestions, and ideas are repeated. Each of the featured books is an opportunity for literacy and movement skill development; therefore, we included common teaching strategies in every lesson, even though it might appear to be redundant.

Depending on the space you have available, you may want your whole class to participate in the action lesson plans at one time. To accomplish this, it may be as simple as pushing back some of the furniture surrounding your circle time area. When it is not possible for the whole group to participate, work with smaller groups of children. This can be accomplished in several ways. If the story and physical activities lend themselves to dividing parts of the story and movements, assign specific sections of the lesson to a few children and each small group takes a turn participating. Another way is to have small groups step into the center of the circle and move to the story. Most children enjoy being the "audience" as they wait their turn. Remind the audience about their responsibilities— quiet, attentive listening—to help them wait respectfully.

As you explore the featured books and lesson activities, be prepared for the children to respond in different ways. If your story time has had a focus on literacy and not movement, some children will be delighted at the opportunity to get up and move. They may be boisterous or a bit silly. Other children may be timid and somewhat reluctant to jump in. Gentle reminders about appropriate behavior and positive encouragement are the best guidance to ensure fun, safe, and productive learning experiences.

References

Jensen, E. 2000. *Learning with the body in mind.* San Diego, CA: The Brain Store.

Kranowitz, C. 1998. *The out-of-sync child: Recognizing and coping with sensory integration dysfunction.* New York, NY: The Berkley Publishing Group.

National Institute for Health Care Management (NIHCM) Foundation. August, 2004. "New Research Shows More Physical Education Time Sharply Reduces Overweight in Children. Being Overweight Also Has Implications for Behavior and Academic Performance." [Online]. Available: ww.nihcm.org/OYCpress.html.

Routman, R. 2003. *Reading essentials: The specifics you need to teach reading well.* Portsmouth, NH: Heinemann.

Snow, C., Burns, M.S., & Griffin, M. 1998. *Preventing reading difficulties in young children.* Washington, DC: National Academies Press.

Strickland, D. S. 2006. "Language and Literacy in Kindergarten." *K Today: Teaching and Learning in the Kindergarten.* Washington, DC: National Association for the Education of Young Children, 73-84.

Yopp, H., & Yopp, R. 2000, October. "Supporting Phonemic Awareness Development in the Classroom." *The Reading Teacher,* 54(2), 130-143.

Read, Move, and Learn with Books

All terms in bold are explained in greater detail in the Glossary on Appendix pages 188-199.

And Everyone Shouted, "Pull!" A First Look at Forces and Motion

by Claire Llewellyn, illustrated by Simone Abel

What's the Book About?

This book will energize even the quietest children as they join farmyard animals who are working hard to figure out how to take a heavy load of produce to market. The scientific concept of motion—push and pull—is explained in understandable language and colorful illustrations, which is perfect for young children.

Theme Connections

Animals
Cooperation
Opposites

Lesson Objectives

Children will:
1. Build action vocabulary.
2. Build conceptual understanding.
3. Explore the concepts of force and motion.

Action Vocabulary

Carry
Pull
Push
Roll
Turn

Concepts Explored

Downhill
Force
Heavy
Light
Motion
Uphill

Developing Literacy Skills

▶ Read the title of the book and then ask the children what the cover illustration tells them about the storyline.
▶ Ask the children to share what they know about pushing, pulling, and carrying things.
▶ *And Everyone Shouted, "Pull!"* integrates literacy skills with science concepts. The story format and illustrations allow the children to create a mental image of new vocabulary.
▶ As you read the story, emphasize vocabulary and concept words. Talk with the children about the animals' conversations in the white conversation bubbles.
▶ Use the glossary at the end of the book as a way to check the children's comprehension.
▶ Older children will enjoy discussing the list of Fun Facts in the book. This is a great way to develop differentiated learning opportunities.

Moving to the Story

▶ Read the story to the children again. As you read, invite the children to interpret the story by moving their bodies to show how they might move something uphill as compared to downhill, move a heavy load compared to a light load, and how moving through soft, muddy ground might look.
▶ Encourage the children to use sound effects as they move.

Developing Motor Skills

Push and Carry

Materials: Box • Beanbags

▶ Divide the children into several teams of even numbers of children. Split each team so each half of the team is facing one another from opposite ends of the space.

Choose a space that allows children to move. Consider using a hallway if you do not have access to a gym or multipurpose room.

▶ Place a box full of beanbags in front of the team members lined up at one end of the space. When you say "Go!" the child in front of the box picks it up and carries the box to his or her team across the room and then goes to the end of that line.

▶ The receiving teammate places the box on the floor, pushes it back across the room and moves to the end of that line. Switching to the opposite line allows the children to experience both pushing and carrying.

▶ Be sure to allow enough time for each child to have at least one opportunity to experience pushing and carrying.

Safety Tip: It is important to first show children how to pick up items that are heavy: Squat low, keeping your back straight. Get as close to the heavy object as possible and lower your body by bending at the hips and knees to pick up the item. Keep your head up so you do not use your back to lift. Use the big muscles in the legs to pick up a heavy object so your back won't get hurt.

Everybody Pull!
Materials: Chalk or tape • Rope • Small flags or pieces of cloth
Note: This activity will be most successful for 5−7-year-olds. You may want to invite younger children to play a variation of Tug-of-War by attempting to pull you or another teacher across the middle line with a long rope.

▶ Draw a line down the middle of the activity space, or create a line with tape.

▶ Help the children find partners of similar size and strength.

▶ One partner stands on one side of the line, and the other partner stands on the other side of the line.

▶ Give each pair of children a rope and have the children stand so the middle of the rope is centered over the line.

▶ When you say, "Pull!" each child attempts to pull the other over the line.

▶ Invite the children to explore different ways of pulling by facing toward their opponent and away from their partner. Explore other possibilities. Have the children switch partners after a couple of tries.

▶ Divide the children into two equal teams of approximately the same height and weight. Provide a long, thick rope with a flag tied onto the middle, and two additional flags on each side, several feet from the center flag. This is where the first child will hold onto one side of the rope. The goal is for one team to pull the other team's flag across the middle line. Ask the children to share their suggestions about how to work cooperatively to accomplish their goal.

More Books to Share
Push and Pull by Patricia J. Murphy
Push and Pull by Hollie J. Endres
Pushing and Pulling by Peter Riley

Music Suggestions
Heel Toe Away We Go by Kimbo Educational. Song: Sailor's Hornpipe
Perceptual Motor Rhythm Games by Jack Capon and Rosemary Hallum. Song: Shoemaker's Dance

Around and Around
by Patricia J. Murphy

What's the Book About?

This book describes circular movement, force, and gravity using language that preschoolers and kindergartners can understand. The colorful photos show children in a world where many things go around and around.

Theme Connections

Cooperation
Spatial concepts
Things in motion

Lesson Objectives

Children will:
1. Build action vocabulary.
2. Build conceptual understanding.
3. Explore circular motion.
4. Explore gravity.

Action Vocabulary

Pull
Push
Somersaults
Spin
Start
Stir
Stop
Travel
Turn

Concepts Explored

Around
Centrifugal force
Circle
Force
Gravity

Developing Literacy Skills

▶ Show the children the cover of the book. Invite the children to predict the storyline based on the cover.

▶ Because some children may want to share their experiences of playing on a merry-go-round, be sure to allow enough time for conversation.

▶ This book introduces the concepts of gravity and centrifugal force. As you read the story, ask the children to talk about the similarities and differences in each picture. For example, how is a Ferris wheel similar to a merry-go-round? How are they different?

▶ As the children talk, encourage them to explain their thinking. Comparing and contrasting is an excellent way to develop comprehension skills, as well as the ability to analyze what is read.

▶ At the end of the story, ask the children to think of additional objects that can be moved around and around. This will allow them to extend their knowledge of ideas and concepts.

Moving to the Story

Materials: Small parachute or round tablecloth • Carousel music

▶ A colorful carousel is pictured in the book. Create your own carousel using a small parachute (or tablecloth).

▶ The children space themselves around the parachute and hold on with their right hand.

▶ Play carousel music as the children walk around in a circle, moving up and down like the ponies on a carousel.

▶ Play the music a second time. The children reverse the direction by holding the parachute with their left hands.

Developing Motor Skills

Spinning and Turning Objects

Materials: Objects for spinning

▶ Children enjoy experimenting with spinning objects. Invite them to gather several objects from the classroom and, working independently or with a partner, explore a variety of ways to spin and turn their items. Things that are fun to spin include:
  ▶ Pinwheels, purchased or made by the children
  ▶ Yo-yos
  ▶ Tops and dreidels

- A button wound up on a string
- Hoops
- Balls

Safety Tips: Remind the children to be careful of others when spinning and turning objects or themselves. Be sure to allow enough space for the activities.

Spinning and Turning

Materials: Mats or other soft surfaces

- Ask the children to **recall** how the people in the book moved around and around. Two examples are the ballerinas dancing around in circles and the little boy doing a somersault.
- Invite the children to explore a variety of ways to move their bodies or a part of their bodies around and around. Children will be most successful moving on a smooth surface with only socks on their feet. Suggestions include:
  - dancing around in circles;
  - spinning on one foot;
  - spinning on bottoms, knees, tummy, or back;
  - turning both arms around and around; and
  - turning a leg, the head, and even the tongue around and around.
- Through exploration, the children will discover that a smaller mass (staying tucked in a ball) will spin faster than a larger mass (spreading arms and legs wide). Encourage the children to change and alternate directions as they explore these activities.
- Children also enjoy rolling. If you have a soft surface such as a carpet or a tumbling mat, show the children how to do sideways rolls (**log rolls**) and **egg rolls** (see Glossary page 196).

More Books to Share

Everyday Science Experiments at the Playground by John Daniel Hartzog
I Fall Down by Vicki Cobb
Spin Around by Dana Meachen Rau
What Is Gravity? by Lisa Trumbauer

Music Suggestions

Here We Go Loopty Loo and Songs to Make You Move by The Learning Station. Song: Here We Go Loopty Loo
It's Toddler Time by Kimbo Educational. Songs: Teddy Bear; Spinning Tops; 'Round and 'Round We Go
Movin' & Shakin' by Russ InVision. Songs: Ring Around a Rosy; Here We Go Loopty Loo; Sit Down, Turn Around
Smart Moves 2 Preschool thru 1st by Russ InVision. Songs: Take That Rope; We Are Rolling; Go 'Round the Village; Hot Potato

Back and Forth

by Patricia J. Murphy

What's the Book About?

Colorful photos show children back and forth motions, and simple text encourages emergent readers to read on their own or to a friend. Movement examples include those on a playground, at home, or at school.

Theme Connections

Things in motion
Spatial concepts

Lesson Objectives

Children will:

1. Build action vocabulary.
2. Build conceptual understanding.
3. Explore back-and-forth motion.
4. Explore the meaning of a pendulum.

Action Vocabulary

Pull
Push
Rock
Rub
Spread
Sway
Swing
Swish
Wag
Wave

Concepts Explored

Back and forth
Backward
Forward
Motion
Pendulum

Developing Literacy Skills

▶ Begin by showing the book's front cover to the children. Ask the children to predict the storyline.

▶ Invite the children to talk about their experiences with swinging. Allow enough time to hear from everyone who wants to share a story about swinging.

▶ When you read the first page, ask the children to place two fingers from one hand on their knee. Show them how to move their fingers backward and then forward, in a sweeping motion.

▶ Read the second page and ask the children, "Do you know how many things move back and forth?" After the children have shared their ideas, continue reading the story. The concepts that motion starts with a push or a pull and that a pendulum swings back and forth may be difficult for some children to comprehend but the pictures will help.

▶ Several of the concepts can be supported by using the pictures at the end of the story. When you are finished with the book, ask the children if the ideas of back-and-forth motion in the story helped them to think of other things that move this way. The following activities will help to reinforce these concepts.

Moving to the Story

▶ Reread the story and invite the children to get up and move the same ways the **characters** and objects in the story are moving.

▶ Encourage the children to explore all movement possibilities. There is no right or wrong way to move.

Developing Motor Skills

Hand Tossing

Materials: Beanbags or yarn balls (see Glossary pages 211-212 for directions)

▶ This is an independent activity.

▶ Give each child a beanbag or yarn ball. The children toss the beanbag or ball back and forth, from hand to hand several times.

▶ This activity is great for **eye-hand coordination**.

Rolling a Ball

Materials: Balls

▶ Divide the children into pairs. Instruct each pair to sit in a straddle with the legs spread wide apart with their partner sitting opposite them.

▶ Give each pair a ball. As they gently roll the ball between the two of them, each child stops the ball with both hands and then rolls it back, while saying, "Back and forth." Repeat for a few minutes.

▶ Ask the children to stand up and with the inside edge of the foot, gently kick the ball to their partner who will trap the ball with a foot and then gently kick it back. Challenge the children to successfully kick and trap the ball several times in a row.

▶ The children switch partners and continue the activity.

Pendulum Swing

Materials: Scarves

▶ If possible, give each child two scarves, one for each hand. Give the children a moment to explore swinging the scarves back and forth.

▶ Ask the children to **recall** the objects in the book that moved as a pendulum. Tell the children that their shoulders will be the top of the pendulum.

▶ Play marching music and have the children march around the room swinging each scarf back and forth, up and down, or side to side as they travel. Encourage the children to say the words "back and forth" as they swing the scarves.

▶ For an additional challenge, ask each child to hold just one scarf and to find a partner. The pair stand and face each other, with each holding their scarf in their right hand. Each child will reach for the corner of their partner's scarf with the left hand. (This may become a problem-solving activity). The children will keep their arms very straight and swing them back and forth in unison as a pendulum.

More Books to Share

Back and Forth by Lola M. Schaefer
Bing: Swing by Ted Dewan
Pig on a Swing by Jenny Nimmo
Swing Otto Swing by David Milgrim

Music Suggestions

Get a Good Start by Kimbo Educational. Song: Warm-Up Time

The instrumental songs on this CD may be used for improvisation to explore the various body parts that will swing back and forth or side to side, such as arms, legs, and the head.

Barn Dance!

by Bill Martin Jr. and John Archambault, illustrated by Ted Rand

What's the Book About?

On a sleepless night, a young boy follows rhythmic sounds to the barn and finds a scarecrow warming up his fiddle. The barnyard animals come from far and near, a wild hoedown begins, and the young boy joins in the fun. The beautiful illustrations will have young readers believing they are actually there in the middle of the night, tapping their toes and clapping their hands.

Theme Connections

Animals
Imagination
Nighttime

Lesson Objectives

Children will:

1. Explore new vocabulary.
2. Explore rhyming text.
3. Explore early American dance culture.
4. Experience square dance steps.

Action Vocabulary

Blink	Flop	Stretch
Dance	Hide	Tiptoe
Fall	Leap	Whirl
Fiddle	Plink	

Concepts Explored (Square Dance)

Bow	Right-hand-round
Curtsey	Rocket to the moon
Do-si-do	Round n' Round
Hurry home	Spin
Left-hand-round	Wagon-wheel
Partner	

Developing Literacy Skills

▶ Introduce the book's authors and illustrator to the children. Show the children the front and back book covers and invite the children to predict the storyline.

▶ Read the title and ask the children to share any experiences they have had with square dancing. This discussion will set the stage for reading the story.

▶ This story's text and illustrations are so rich that you will want to read the story to the children twice. During the first reading, ask the children to listen to the rhyming text. Use your voice to emphasize the **rhyme**.

▶ Turn the pages slowly so you can point out the central focus in the illustrations. After you finish reading the book, ask the children to share their impressions of the story. Note their thoughts.

▶ Read the story a second time. Ask the children questions that prompt them to explore the ideas and concepts in the book. Depending on the attention spans of the young learners in your class, ask only one or two questions for each page. Your questions will encourage the children to generalize their knowledge to new situations. Building conceptual understanding with guided questioning strategies increases children's comprehension.

▶ When you are finished with the story, the children will be ready for some dance action!

Moving to the Story

Materials: Kerchiefs or straw hats, optional

▶ As you reread the book to the children, invite them to act out the storyline. You may want to provide kerchiefs or straw hats for this activity.

▶ Remind the children that square dancing always has a "caller" who uses rhymes to tell everyone what to do. Invite the children to design their own calls and moves using rhyming phrases.

Developing Motor Skills

Learning to Square Dance

Materials: CD player and appropriate music

▶ Explain to the children that they will be learning square dancing, which is an American folk dance. Teach them the square dance steps from the book.

- ▶ Ask the children to find a partner.
- ▶ Begin by introducing one or two of the following steps without the music.

  Bow: Place one hand on the stomach and one hand on the back. Bow forward, bending at the waist.

  Curtsey: Greet partner by bending at the knees, placing one foot behind, and lowering the body.

  Right-hand-round: Grasp your partner's right hand and circle around one another.

  Left-hand-round: Grasp your partner's left hand and circle around one another.

  Round n' round (both hands 'round): Partners hold both hands and circle around one another.

  Promenade ('hurry home'): Partners stand side-by-side, holding hands, and move around the room in a circle.

  Do-si-do: Partners move forward, passing right shoulder to right shoulder, with arms folded across the chest. Without turning, they step around one another back-to-back and return to face one another.

  Spin: Partners hook right or left elbows and spin around.

  Wagon-wheel: Partners stretch out right arms, very tight and straight, placing one hand on top of the other, and move the "wheel" around. Reverse the move by using left arms.

  Rocket to the moon: Partners grasp opposite hands (right to left). Arms are lifted and one partner dips under the arch, points the free hand "to the moon" and steps back. The other partner repeats the step.

- ▶ After practicing one or two steps, add instrumental music and call out the dance steps. Don't worry if some pairs need extra time to complete the dance steps. The other children can just repeat the step.
- ▶ Teach the children additional steps after they have mastered the first ones.

Safety Tips: Remind the children that appropriate behavior allows everyone to stay safe and have fun. Review the concepts of moving in general space and with a partner. Be sure that the space is large enough to accommodate dancing without the children bumping into chairs, tables, or other objects.

More Books to Share

Cindy Ellen: A Wild Western Cinderella by Susan Lowell

Hootenanny Night by Constance Andrea Keremes

Mama Don't Allow by Thacher Hurd

Pigs in the Corner: Fun with Math and Dance by Amy Axelrod

Music Suggestions

All-Time Favorite Dances by Kimbo Educational. Songs: Virginia Reel; Cotton-Eyed Joe

Get Ready to Square Dance by Kimbo Educational. Songs: Cotton-Eyed Joe; Oh Belinda; Shoo Fly; Turkey in the Straw, with instruction guide

Heel Toe Away We Go by Kimbo Educational. Songs: Little Brown Jug (both vocal and instrumental); Shortnin' Bread (use vocal for three- and four-year-olds)

Shake, Rattle & Rock by Greg and Steve. Song: Barnyard Boogie

Square Dancing Made Easy by Jack Capon and Rosemary Hallum. Songs: Any or All

We All Live Together, Volume 5 by Greg and Steve. Song: Old Brass Wagon

Bug Dance
by Stuart J. Murphy

What's the Book About?

Coach Caterpillar is teaching the bugs a new dance in gym class. Sound easy? Not if you are a centipede! Centipede has a hard time getting all his legs to move in the same direction at the same time. The book includes "The Bug Dance" instructions, complete with arrows so children can utilize visual cues when they learn the dance.

Theme Connections

Feelings
Humor
Insects and bugs
Opposites
Spatial concepts

Lesson Objectives

Children will:
1. Explore rhyming text.
2. Explore directionality.
3. Experience following verbal directions.
4. Experience simple rhythmic steps.

Action Vocabulary

Dance	Plop
Dodge	Spin
Flop	Tag
Hop	Trip
Jig	Turn
Jump	Wiggle
Jumping Jacks	

Concepts Explored

Backward	High
Forward	Left
Graceful	Right

Developing Literacy Skills

▶ Introduce the book's author and illustrator. Read the title and show the children the front cover. Ask them to predict the storyline. Many children are interested in bugs, so this book will capture their attention.

▶ Ask the children if they know how many legs most bugs have. Insects have six. Draw the children's attention to the centipede. Explain that it is an arthropod, so it has many legs. Will Centipede's many feet make it easier or harder to dance?

▶ Begin story time by showing the children the page spread that outlines "The Bug Dance" with easy-to-follow sketches, along with the words to the song.

▶ Ask the children to use one finger from each hand to do "The Bug Dance" on the floor in front of them as you read the directions.

▶ There will be opportunities throughout the story for the children to follow along with their "dancing fingers." This will help the children integrate the directional words of forward, backward, right, and left with corresponding body movements.

▶ At the end of the story, ask the children to sing the song (found at the back of the book) as they move their fingers.

▶ As you read the story, allow enough time for the children to focus on the illustrations. They will find that each bug has his or her own endearing qualities, except for Inchworm!

▶ After Story Time, engage the children in a discussion about the value of hard work and a positive attitude when tackling difficult tasks.

Moving to the Story

▶ There are 13 action vocabulary words in *Bug Dance*. After reading the story, invite the children to do each of the activities that the bugs in the story did.

▶ Encourage the children to invent their own games using some of the action words.

Developing Motor Skills

Bug Dance

Materials: 4 sheets of construction paper, numbered from 1–4 • Tape • CD for playing music (see suggestions on the right)

If the space is too small to accommodate all children at one time, divide the class into small groups that suit the space you have.

▶ The book provides a detailed description and illustration of the line dance "The Bug Dance" that the children can do after the story has been read. Clarify or simplify any movements that are confusing or too difficult for the children.

▶ Consecutively, number the walls in order from 1–4 and tape the corresponding piece of numbered construction paper on each wall.

▶ Have the children stand in four or five lines, depending upon how many children are in the classroom or in the group. All should face you and wall number one.

▶ Demonstrate jumping a quarter turn around to face wall number two, then another quarter turn to face wall number three, then wall number four and the fourth jump turn will bring them right back where they started at wall number one.

▶ See if the children can first perform single jump turns when you call out the number of the wall to turn to.

▶ Now you are ready to instruct the children to step two times to the left, then immediately step to the right on the right foot, followed by the left, right, and left.

▶ With the weight now on the balls of both feet, instruct the children to jump forward, jump backward, and jump one-quarter turn to the right, and begin again.

▶ For younger children, you may have to place a piece of colored tape on the right shoe or sock. By doing this, you accomplish two things: you give them a visual cue of the direction they will be turning, and you will also give them a visual of which foot not to stand on after the second step to the left.

▶ A great complementary music selection is "The Boogie Walk" on *We All Live Together, Volume 2*. The steps are very similar and the music is great.

Safety Tips: Make sure that all children are wearing appropriate footwear. You may want to have a child remove his or her shoes if there is a safety concern, such as shoes with heels or backless shoes.

More Books to Share

¿Comos nos orientamous?/We Need Directions! by Sarah E. De Capua

How Many, How Much? by Rosemary Wells

Left Hand, Right Hand: A Hands-on Book About Left and Right by Janet Allison Brown

Sock Monkeys Do the Monkey Monkey! by William B. Winburn

Music Suggestions

Bugsters Tunes and Tales by Russ Invision. Songs: All are fun

Get a Good Start by Kimbo Educational. Song: Jumping Jacks

Kids in Action by Greg and Steve. Song: Conga Line

My Bear Gruff by Charlotte Diamond. Song: Wee Kirkcubdright Centipede

"So Big" Activity Songs for Little Ones by Hap Palmer. Songs: Ten Wiggle Worms (Part I); Ten Wiggle Worms (Part II)

Tony Chestnut and Fun Time Action Songs by The Learning Station. Song: Shiny Clean Dance

We All Live Together, Volume 2 by Greg and Steve. Song: The Boogie Walk

Cha-Cha Chimps

by Julia Durango, illustrated by Eleanor Taylor

What's the Book About?

Mama Chimp has just put her 10 young chimps to bed for the night, but they sneak out to Mambo Jamba's to dance with the animals. When Mama finds the chimps she sends them home, but the story has a surprise at the end. Your class will thoroughly enjoy making the monkey sounds in the story and trying the dances mentioned in the book.

Theme Connections

Animals
Counting
Exercise

Lesson Objectives

Children will:
1. Count backwards from 10.
2. Experience **predictable text**.
3. Explore a variety of dances.
4. Explore rhyming text.

Action Vocabulary

Hustle	Stomp
Shake	Strut
Skitter	Sway
Slither	Tumble
Sneak	

Concepts Explored (Dances)

Belly dance	Jitterbug
Cha-cha-cha	Limbo
Clog	Polka
Conga line	Samba
Hokey Pokey	Tango
Jig	

Developing Literacy Skills

▶ Introduce the book's author and illustrator. The delightful front cover will help the children predict that the book is about chimps. Invite the children to share with you everything they know about chimps.

▶ Read the title to the children and explain what that "cha-cha" is a dance. Tell them that the 10 little chimps will learn many new dances.

▶ *Cha-Cha Chimps* is written in rhyme and uses a repeated phrase. This repetition helps children predict the text and interact with the story.

▶ Begin story time by introducing the repeated phrase to the children. Point out that on each page, the numeral will change. Prompt the children to "read" this part with you by pointing to the phrase. If they are interested, ask the children to guess what the number will be.

▶ Mama Chimp appears at the end of the story. This provides another opportunity for the children to predict the storyline and the story ending. Ask, "How will Mama Chimp react when she finds out the little chimps snuck out for the night?"

▶ Sharing thoughts and ideas with the class will enhance their vocabulary. It will also give you an opportunity to note where children are in their literacy development.

▶ Invite the children to explore alternative endings to the story. This oral exercise builds children's confidence as they develop writing skills for their own stories.

Moving to the Story

Materials: CD player and any suggested CD, or your own favorite

▶ Allow the children time to make up their own dances and either play your own music, such as "The Freeze" from *Kids in Motion,* or invite them to bring music from home, and watch to see what they have come up with.

▶ Use maracas, castanets, tambourines, or others items as accompanying instruments.

Developing Motor Skills

Let's Dance

Materials: Parachute or king-size sheet (optional) • Music appropriate for each dance • A stick for the limbo • Maracas, castanets, and tambourines as accompanying instruments

▶ After reading the story, ask the children which dances they know how to do. Most will probably say the "Hokey Pokey," which is a great dance for young children, and most children know this music with the accompanying actions.

▶ For additional fun and excitement, add a parachute or king-size sheet as a prop for doing the "Hokey Pokey." As you call out each body part (hands, elbows, head), demonstrate how to place each body part over the topside of the parachute, toward the parachute (hips and backside), or under the parachute (feet and whole self). When the children turn around, instruct them to release the parachute with one hand, reach around behind with the second hand as they turn, and then regrasp the parachute with the first hand following. Again, you will need to demonstrate this. When the children hear the words, "Do the Hokey Pokey" instruct them to shake the parachute up and down.

▶ Before doing the Hokey Pokey, have the children practice lifting the parachute up. Remind them to hold on (don't let go) as they step under for the "whole self in and shake it all about" part.

▶ Children who are five or older are ready to try the cha-cha. Have them arrange themselves in two lines facing you. Begin by instructing them to do three quick small steps in place, and say, "1, 2, 3" as they move their feet up and down. After they can count and step, tell them to say "cha-cha-cha" as they do the three steps. Then instruct them to step back quickly on one foot and then repeat the three "cha-cha-cha" steps. Then ask them to step forward quickly on the other foot and then repeat the "cha-cha-cha" steps. If appropriate, put on some Cha-Cha music for the children to listen to as they dance.

▶ Explore other dances and musical rhythms. Encourage the children to find the similarities and differences in the music and, if appropriate, the steps.

Safety Tips: Remove all furniture and any rugs or mats from the movement area. Remind the children to stay within their own personal space and be aware of other movers.

More Books to Share

Caps for Sale by Esphyr Slobodkina
Curious George by H. A. Rey
Little Monkey Says Goodnight by Ann Whitford Paul
Sock Monkey Boogie-Woogie by Cece Bell

Music Suggestions

All-Time Favorite Dances by Kimbo Educational. Songs: All are fun to try; Conga Line; The Twist; The Hokey Pokey; The Chicken
Jump Start Action Songs with Ronno by Kimbo Educational. Songs: Twist! Top! Hop!; The Pelican Polka
Kids in Action by Greg and Steve. Songs: Conga Line; Get Ready, Get Set, Let's Dance
Kids in Motion by Greg and Steve. Song: The Freeze
Shake, Rattle & Rock by Greg and Steve. Song: Limbo Rock

Clap Your Hands
by Lorinda Bryan Cauley

What's the Book About?

This classic book is a boisterous movement adventure starring a joyful cast of children and costumed animals. The rhyming text invites listeners to get up and join the fun, clapping, stomping, shaking, wiggling, and even making silly faces. This high-energy book will be a classroom favorite.

Theme Connections

Humor
Imagination
Parts of the body

Lesson Objectives

Children will:
1. Explore body part identification and movement.
2. Explore following directions.
3. Explore interpretive movement.
4. Explore rhyming text.

Action Vocabulary

Balance	Rub
Clap	Shake
Close	Slap
Count	Somersault
Crawl	Spin
Flap	Spread
Fly	Stand
Hop	Stomp
Jump	Wave
Pat	Wiggle
Reach	

Concepts Explored

Parts of the body

Developing Literacy Skills

▶ Introduce the children to the author and illustrator, Lorinda Bryan Cauley. Read the book title and tell the children that the **characters** in the book will invite them to move many parts of their bodies, not just their hands.

▶ Tell the children that as you read the book, the text will invite them to make animal sounds, find things, and act rather silly!

▶ Begin Story Time by asking the children to stand in their **personal space**.

▶ Encourage the children to act out the story as you read it. As you read the book, be sure all of the children have an opportunity to see the book's illustrations.

▶ Depending on the size of your area, you may want to adapt several of the book's action ideas. For example, "Find something yellow…" can be simplified by asking the children to point to something yellow. This will encourage the children to stay in their personal space as you read the story.

▶ The book's simple rhyming text gives children an opportunity to explore words that rhyme. You may want to read each verse, pause before reading the last word, and wait for the children to complete the rhyme. Be sure to prompt the children about your expectation to have them join you in reading.

▶ Note which children are able to find the correct rhyming words. When you revisit this book later, expect to see development in this literacy skill.

Moving to the Story

▶ This is such a fun story to act out as the story is being read. The children begin to anticipate what comes next.

▶ Ask the children to look at the pictures before you read the words to them so they will see the story.

▶ You may find it necessary to change some of the wording in the book. For example, when you reach the page about telling a secret, you may ask the children tell one another a secret, and get a secret back. In other words, try to have all of the action going on between the children rather than with you.

Developing Motor Skills

Bunny Hops, Frog Jumps, and More!
Material: CD with suggested music (see list on the right)

▶ Before reading the story again, you might want to review a few actions such as a bunny jump or frog jump.

▶ Give the children time to copy the animal actions correctly. These are important sensory motor activities that aid in sensory integration and brain organization.

▶ Read the book and encourage the children to move the same way the animals and children are moving.

More Books to Share
Clap Your Hands: An Action Book by David Ellwand
If You're Happy and You Know It, Clap Your Hands! by David A. Carter

Music Suggestions
It's Toddler Time by Kimbo Educational. Song: If You're Happy and You Know It (instrumental)

Safety Tips: Make sure the space is free of all chairs, tables, or other things the children might bump into as they move about to the words of the story. Remind the children to look before they move in a given direction to avoid colliding with another person. You might ask them to look at the characters' feet in the story. Are their shoes on or off? Ask them why they think all shoes are off. Do they think that it is for safety, so no one accidentally kicks another?

Color Dance
by Ann Jonas

What's the Book About?

Color Dance features four children engaged in a free-flowing dance with colorful scarves. Each of the three girls represents the primary colors: red, yellow, and blue. The boy is dressed in black and white. The dance brings the children and their colored scarves together to create a rainbow of colors. The illustrations bring to life the light, airy quality of the scarves billowing over the children as they bend, leap, reach, and twirl.

Theme Connections

Colors
Imagination

Lesson Objectives

Children will:
1. Explore primary colors.
2. Create secondary and complementary colors.
3. Experience creative dance using scarves.
4. Explore creative movement to music.

Action Vocabulary

Dance
Mix

Concepts Explored

Primary colors (red, blue, yellow)
Secondary colors (green, purple, orange)

Developing Literacy Skills

Materials: Small squares of cellophane in red, blue, and yellow

▶ Introduce the children to the author and illustrator, Ann Jonas. Read the title to the children and ask them to predict the storyline. If the children look carefully at the front and back cover illustrations, they may be able to figure out that the dancers will create new colors by putting their scarves together. You may want to point out the overlapping colors if the children do not make this observation.

▶ Before reading the story, give each child three small squares of cellophane, one red, one blue, and one yellow. Tell the children that they may play with the colored squares as you read *Color Dance*.

▶ Take your time reading this short story to the children. The illustrations of the colorful, billowing scarves will give the children ideas for how to move.

▶ Invite the children to experiment with their colored squares as you read the story.

▶ Ask the children if they have other words for the colors created in the story. For example, a child might use lavender instead of purple. The new vocabulary will be interesting to many children. Ask the children to look around the room and identify things that are the same colors as shown in the story.

Moving to the Story

Materials: Lightweight scarves in primary colors (red, blue, and yellow)

▶ If you have the kind of scarves shown in the story, encourage the children to make up their own color dance.

▶ If appropriate, help the children prepare this dance for a parent's night or a school event. This gives the children performance opportunities.

Developing Motor Skills

Air Drawing with Streamers or Scarves

Materials: Scarves or streamers in primary colors (red, blue, and yellow) • Tape or CD of music and tape or CD player

▶ Many streamers and scarves come in primary colors.

▶ Give each child a scarf or streamer.

▶ Play one of the music suggestions (see the following page) or choose your own music.

- Model the following for the children as you ask them to move with you:
    - forward arm circles
    - backward arm circles
    - helicopter circles overhead
    - up and down arm movements with marching
    - circles in front of the body
    - rainbow curves overhead and side to side
    - combined arm movements made into a dance with streamers or scarves

Color Mix Up

Materials: Colored cellophane paper in primary colors • Tape or CD of music and tape or CD player • Scarves or streamers

- After reading the story, talk about primary colors and how they make secondary colors when mixed together in specific combinations. Take out large squares of primary colored cellophane.
- Give each child one large square.
- Have the children partner with someone who has a different primary color. Encourage them to place the pieces of cellophane one on top of the other. Ask the children who made the color orange, the color purple, or the color green. They may already have practiced this in the beginning activity.
- Call out a locomotor skill and have the children walk, jump, skip, hop, or gallop around the room until you call out "Color Mix Up." The children must then quickly freeze and put their color together with someone near them. They may end up with a primary color such as yellow on yellow, or they may freeze with a secondary color such as red on blue (purple).
- Each pair calls out the color with which they "froze." If a child ends without a partner to mix up with, encourage him or her to come to a special "mixing spot" where you will provide a second color with which to "mix up."
- Put on some instrumental music with a moderate beat. Classical music is nice.
- Give each child a colored scarf.
- Ask the children to toss a scarf up in the air and let it land on their head, arm, back, face, or other body part.
- Tell the children that when you stop the music and say "freeze," they are to stand beside someone with a different color, hold the scarves up in the air together, and call out the secondary color formed by combining the two colors together.

More Books to Share

A Color of His Own by Leo Lionni
Little Blue and Little Yellow by Leo Lionni
Mouse Paint by Ellen Stoll Walsh
Planting a Rainbow by Lois Ehlert

Music Suggestions

Can a Cherry Pie Wave Goodbye? by Hap Palmer Music, Inc. Songs: Put a Little Color on You; Parade of Colors
Can Cockatoos Count by Twos? by Hap Palmer Music Inc. Song: Colors in Motion
Get Funky and Musical Fun by The Learning Station. Song: If You're Wearing Colors
Movin' & Shakin' for Youngsters by Russ InVision. Song: The Bingo Rainbow
Smart Moves 1 Tots thru Pre-K by Russ InVision. Song: Can You Find the Color?
Start Each Day with a Song by Music With Mar. Inc. Song: Primary Colors
We All Live Together Vol. 5 by Greg and Steve. Song: Rainbow of Colors

Safety Tip: Remind the children not to be "space invaders" and to stay within their own personal space as they move around the room.

Dinosaur Dinosaur
by Kevin Lewis, illustrated by Daniel Kirk

What's the Book About?

Dinosaur's day begins with a roar! He spends the rest of the day with dinosaur friends playing soccer, jumping rope, and running free. At the end of a long day, Mom collects Dinosaur, takes him home, feeds him, and helps him get ready for bed. The book is written in rhyme and is full of action words. Dinosaur lovers will be delighted by the illustrations. This is a great book to encourage outdoor play.

Theme Connections

Dinosaurs
Families
Imagination

Lesson Objectives

Children will:

1. Explore interpretive movement.
2. Explore nonsense words.
3. Explore rhyming text.
4. Experience motor skills

Action Vocabulary

Bounce	Run
Hop	Stomp
Jump	Stumble
Pounce	

Concepts Explored

Busy	Peek-a-boo
Grumpy	Pout
Happy	Sleepy

Developing Literacy Skills

Materials: Dinosaur puppets, stuffed dinosaurs, or plastic dinosaurs

► Before reading the book, give each child a dinosaur puppet, plush dinosaur, or plastic dinosaur. If there are not enough to go around, the children can share.

► Begin story time by introducing the children to the book's author, Kevin Lewis, and illustrator, Daniel Kirk.

► Talk about what the front and back covers say about the storyline. Invite conversation about the activities in which the dinosaurs are participating.

► As you read the book, invite the children to act out the story with their dinosaurs. This creates a lively story time so be prepared to keep the children engaged with the story.

► Draw the children's attention to the details on each page spread. The story ends quietly with Dinosaur in bed and sound asleep.

The text has many pairs of rhyming words. For older children, explain that each pair of words rhymes with either a real word (yummy-tummy), a nonsense word (bubbly-wubbly), or the same-word pairings (looky-looky). The print is large enough for children to see and help you read the words. Experiences with this kind of word play will help to increase children's **phonemic awareness**, an important literacy skill.

Moving to the Story

▶ As you read the story a second time, suggest that the children act out various rhyming parts on each page. Give them a certain amount of time to act out the page that you read, and then ring a chime (or another item) to bring the children all back together and listen quietly for the next part.

▶ Allow enough time for the children to engage their imaginations, but provide boundaries so they are careful of the environment and one another and do not act silly or too rambunctious.

▶ The story ends quietly with Dinosaur in bed and sound asleep. This is a good way to transition to another activity.

Developing Motor Skills

Move like the Word
Materials: CD player and music (see suggestions on the right)

▶ Read each action vocabulary word to the children. Explain that you want the children to think carefully about each word and what it would look like if they were to do it.

▶ Now read each word one at a time, and provide a minute or so for the children to explore each vocabulary word. For example, as the children begin to explore how to stomp, ask them:
  ▶ Do you use your entire foot to stomp?
  ▶ Can you stomp on just the balls of your feet? How?
  ▶ What would that look like?
  ▶ Is stomping a heavy action or light action?

▶ Consider asking the children to change the direction of the movement, such as forward, backward, sideways. Consider levels, such as stomping or jumping at a high level, crouched, or very low. Consider pathway changes such as bounce in a zigzag pattern, a circle, or a straight line.
  Note: Provide a space that is large enough for the children to move from one side of the room to the other.

More Books to Share
Busy Dinah Dinosaur by B.G. Hennessy
How Do Dinosaurs Eat Their Food? by Jane Yolen
How High Can a Dinosaur Count? and Other Math Mysteries by Valorie Fisher
Little Dinosaur by Mike Thaler

Music Suggestions
The instrumental selection of "Five Huge Dinosaurs" on the Rockin' Reading Readiness CD is lots of fun to create a mood for dinosaur movements. Try any or all of the music selections, if available. Many CDs can be found in libraries.

Rockin' Reading Readiness by Kimbo Educational. Song: Five Huge Dinosaurs
Tunes for Tiny Tots by Mar. Song: Will You Ever See a Dinosaur?
Late Last Night by Joe Scruggs. Song: Please Don't Ever Bring a Tyrannosaurus Rex to Show and Tell

Dinosaur Roar!
by Paul and Henrietta Stickland

What's the Book About?

Dinosaur Roar! combines large, colorful illustrations with playful rhymes that introduce opposites to young audiences. Children will enjoy imitating the dinosaurs as they explore actions and concepts such as fast, slow, above, and below. The story ends with the dinosaurs gathering for lunch, making this the perfect story to read before snack or lunch!

Theme Connections

Dinosaurs
Opposites
Spatial concepts

Lesson Objectives

Children will:
1. Explore the concept of opposites.
2. Explore letter sounds.
3. Explore rhyming text.
4. Explore interpretive movement.

Action Vocabulary

Gobble
Munch
Nibble
Scrunch

Concepts Explored (Opposites)

Above/below	Roar/squeak
Clean/slimy	Short/long
Fast/slow	Spiky/lumpy
Fat/tiny	Sweet/grumpy
Fierce/meek	Weak/strong

Developing Literacy Skills

▶ Introduce the children to the book's authors and illustrators, Paul and Henrietta Stickland.

▶ Ask the children to read the title of the book with you. The book cover illustration will support even the youngest child's emerging literacy skills. This quick introduction is all you will need to set the stage for story time.

▶ Hold the book so the children can see the full-page spread each time you turn the page. This will allow them to see the opposites clearly. The illustrations are fun and captivating.

▶ Invite the children to help you read the book. Tell them that the words on each opposite page have opposite meanings. This concept will become clear to the children as you read the book.

▶ Read the left-hand page and pause just long enough for the children to suggest an opposite word to complete the right-hand page. Emergent readers might offer a word that is an opposite, but not the word in the text. Provide support to the child by pointing to the word in the text and prompt the child to use his or her letter-sound knowledge to sound out the word. Taking risks in reading is important to the child's reading journey and should be encouraged and supported.

Moving to the Story

▶ Read the story through a second time so the children can focus on acting out each of the concept words.

▶ Ask each child to choose a partner. Let the pairs decide who will act out the concept on the left side of the page spread and who will act out the concept on the right side.

▶ As you say the word on the left side of the page spread, give those children an opportunity to act out that word. See if anyone can remember the word on the right side of the page spread before the partner acts out that word.

Developing Motor Skills

Concept Identification

Materials: CD player and music (see selection listed on the right)

▶ This book is full of concepts for children to identify or show. In addition to the literacy skills to identify when using these words, you may also want to set up the learning environment by arranging some items around the room that allow the children to demonstrate their understanding of the opposite concepts, such as *above* and *below*.

▶ After you read each page, stop reading and then ask the children to look around them and point to something that they identify with the particular word.

▶ When you reread the story, choose several children to move to an example of what they see. For example, they might see something clean, something slimy, something short, something sweet, or something tiny. Also encourage the children to show emotional concepts such as *fierce, meek,* and *grumpy*.

▶ If you have any music selections for opposites, invite the children to move to the music and act out the opposites.
Note: A small movement space is okay unless the children are going to be moving to the music selections.

Safety Tip: Remind the children to stay in their own personal space when moving around the room.

More Books to Share

The Foot Book: Dr. Seuss's Wacky Book About Opposites by Dr. Seuss

Kids Do, Animals Too: A Playground Book of Opposites by Debora Pearson

Opposites by Monique Felix

Sam's Opposites by Yves Got

Music Suggestions

Fun and Games: Learning to Play— Playing to Learn by Greg and Steve. Song: Opposites

Late Last Night by Joe Scruggs. Song: Please Don't Ever Bring Tyrannosaurus Rex to Show and Tell

Rock N' Roll Songs That Teach by The Learning Station. Song: Opposites

Tunes for Tiny Tots by Mar. Song: Will You Ever See a Dinosaur?

Dinosaurumpus!
by Tony Mitton, illustrated by Guy Parker-Rees

What's the Book About?

Children will be eager to join the dinosaurs as they head down to the sludgy old swamp to hold an earth-shaking "dinosaurumpus." This book is written in tongue-twisting rhyme and is full of **onomatopoeia**. The illustrations are wildly colorful and add to the festive feel that this story is sure to create in your classroom.

Theme Connections

Dinosaurs
Exercise

Lesson Objectives

Children will:
1. Explore rhyming text.
2. Explore onomatopoeic words.
3. Experience motor skills.
4. Explore interpretive movement.

Action Vocabulary

Dive	Shake	Swirl
Hop	Shiver	Swoop
Jiggle	Shudder	Tumble
Jump	Spin	Wave
Romp	Stomp	
Run	Swing	

Concepts Explored (Onomatopoeic Words)

Bomp	Snip
Clatter	Thwack
Donk	Wallop
Sizzle	Zing
Snap	Zoom

Developing Literacy Skills

▶ Unless you are familiar with dinosaur names, spend a few minutes learning the names before you read the book to the children.

▶ Introduce the book's author, Tony Mitton, and illustrator, Guy Parker-Rees. Read the title of the book and ask the children to predict the storyline. The front cover illustration might lead the children to guess what the book is about but the title might not lead them to the same conclusion. It is not until the end of the story that "dinosaurumpus" is defined. Tell the children to listen carefully to the story so they can guess the meaning of "dinosaurumpus."

▶ As you read the book, there are many concepts to focus on, including rhyme and repeated phrases. Teach the children the phrase about the swamp that is repeated throughout the book. Invite the children to say this part with you. Use inflection to emphasize the rhyming and onomatopoeic words, saying them in a deep voice and with a staccato-like delivery.

▶ Linger on each page for the children to absorb the many details of each of the pages.

▶ At the end of the story, ask the children to **recall** words they found interesting or unusual. This will help to develop the children's vocabulary and comprehension skills. You may want to read the action vocabulary and onomatopoeic words with the children. Note the children's progress in developing literacy skills.

Moving to the Story

▶ The names of the various different dinosaurs are not easy to pronounce; however, most children seem to know them all. As you read the story for the first, second, or third time, ask the children to help you say the dinosaur names. They will be very proud to help you.

▶ Begin with the children standing outside the circle area. Let the children choose which dinosaur that they want to imitate. As you read the story, invite each child to step forward to act out his or her chosen dinosaur.

▶ Encourage the children to act out the repeating phrase in the book.

Developing Motor Skills

Onomatopoeic Actions

Materials: CD player with "Five Huge Dinosaurs" on *Rockin' Reading Readiness,* optional

▶ As you say each of the 10 onomatopoeic words invite the children to demonstrate the action of the sound of each word.

▶ Next, invite the children to demonstrate each of the sixteen action vocabulary words as you say each one. Focus on action words such as "jumping (up and down)," "twisting (spinning)," and "shaking."

▶ Ask the children to name the body part to use for each motion. For example, when you say "swirl," ask the children which body parts "swirl."

▶ Running is something that can be done in place, unless you go to a larger room or outside. Tell the children to place their hands at the height that their leg bends at the hip and to see if they can run in place lifting their knees up to their hands each time.

▶ When you read the story, remember to encourage the children to say the repeating chant along with you.

▶ "Five Huge Dinosaurs" on *Rockin' Reading Readiness* is a great piece of accompanying music. Use the selection with words or without.

Safety Tips: Be sure there is enough room for the children to move about without bumping into one another. Remind the children to find their own place in space and to share the general space.

More Books to Share

Dancing Dinos by Sally Lucas
Dinosaurs Dance by Larry Dane Brimner
Dinosaurs Dancing by Luella Connelly
Drumheller Dinosaur Dance by Robert Heidbreder

Music Suggestions

Late Last Night by Joe Scruggs. Song: Please Don't Ever Bring a Tyrannosaurus Rex to Show and Tell
Rockin' Reading Readiness by Kimbo Educational. Song: Five Huge Dinosaurs
Tunes for Tiny Tots by Mar. Song: Will You Ever See a Dinosaur?

Do Donkeys Dance?

by Melanie Walsh

What's the Book About?

Children will giggle with delight as you read the story's silly questions, which are met with appropriate answers, but the guessing is still fun. The illustrations are quite colorful and are sure to hold the attention of young children.

Theme Connections

Animals
Exercise
Humor

Lesson Objectives

Children will:

1. Explore motor skills.
2. Explore movement concepts.
3. Explore voice inflection when asking questions.
4. Respond to questions.

Action Vocabulary

Buzz
Fly
Hang
Hop
Leap
Stork/Flamingo Stand
Swim

Concepts Explored

Around
High
Up
Upside down

Developing Literacy Skills

▶ Begin by introducing the book's author and illustrator, Melanie Walsh. Show the book's front and back covers to the children.

▶ The answer to the question posed by the title of the book, *Do Donkeys Dance?* is answered with an illustration of a ballerina and no text on the title page. This sets the stage for the remainder of the book.

▶ The colorful illustrations of the simple questions appeal to young children. The children will laugh at the absurdity of the questions posed.

▶ Allow lots of time for young learners to offer answers to the questions. The type on each page is large enough for the children to help you read the words.

▶ Point out the question marks and explain to the children that this punctuation mark means the reader must change his or her voice. Model for the children how you use **voice inflection** to distinguish between a statement and a question.

Moving to the Story

Materials: Index cards • Markers

▶ Make index cards with a word and a picture demonstrating each animal and action. For example, bees buzzing, kangaroos leaping, and bats hanging upside down.

▶ While the children are still seated, ask them to find a partner and then sit next to that partner.

▶ Each pair chooses an index card and decides how they will act out the animal and the action on the card.

▶ One pair at a time acts out the animal and action and the rest of the children guess the animal and the action. If you have duplicates of an animal and action, two or more partners can act it out differently. Remind the children to be courteous to one another while they are waiting their turn to act out a part.

Developing Motor Skills

Seven Moves

Materials: CD player with "7 Jumps" on *Perceptual Motor Rhythm Games* or other instrumental music
Note: "7 Jumps" was originally wordless folk music and lends itself to many

locomotor skills and other movement activities. If you do not have this particular piece of music, you can improvise using any lively instrumental piece. At the appropriate time, stop the music and provide the beats using a drum, triangle, or other instrument.

▶ While listening to the music, do the following seven actions with the children, followed by the balances listed below from the book: dance like a ballerina, buzz like a bee, leap like a kangaroo, hang like a bat, hop like a flea, swim like a fish, and stand on one leg like a flamingo.

▶ There are seven pauses in the music in which balancing movements are done after each horn beep. For example, the children dance like a ballerina and when the music stops, on the first beat of a drum, blow of a horn, or sound of another instrument, the children balance on one foot.

One beat: Balance on one foot until the music begins again. When it begins, the children buzz like a bee until the music stops again.

Two beats: Balance on one foot and then the other foot. When the music begins again, change the movement to leap like a kangaroo until the music stops.

Three beats: Balance on one foot, then the other foot, down on one knee, then hang like a bat until the music stops. (To "hang like a bat," suggest that the children lie on their backs and put their feet together up in the air.)

Four beats: Balance on one foot, then the other foot, down on one knee, down on two knees, and then hop like a flea until the music stops.

Five beats: Balance on one foot, then the other foot, down on one knee, down on two knees and one elbow, and then swim like a fish.

Six beats: Balance…two knees, one elbow, two elbows, and then stand on one leg like a flamingo.

Seven beats: Balance each sequential balance on each successive beat until at last everything is down with the head to go down last and change the movement one last time to any movement that was a favorite.

▶ You will need to do each of the activities with the children (if possible) so they have a visual model to copy. After modeling the activities of the first dance for them, you may want to ask the children to come up with their own actions.

More Books to Share
And the Dish Ran Away with the Spoon by Janet Stevens
What Are You So Grumpy About? by Tom Lichtenheld
Why Should I Eat Well? by Clarie Llewellyn
Word Bird Asks: What? What? What? by Jane Belk Moncure

Music Suggestions
Can a Cherry Pie Wave Goodbye? by Hap Palmer. Songs: Can a Cherry Pie Wave Goodbye?; Animal Quiz Part One; Animal Quiz Part Two
Perceptual Motor Rhythm Games by Jack Capon and Rosemary Hallum. Song: 7 Jumps

Down by the Cool of the Pool

by Tony Mitton, illustrated by Guy Parker-Rees

What's the Book About?

This story will have children on their feet as they join in the dance with a variety of silly farmyard animals. The animals join Frog in a dance, each in their own unique way. The book is written in rhyme with **predictable text** on each page. The zany animals are vibrantly colored and their movements are so well depicted that children will not be able to sit still.

Theme Connections

Animals
Colors
Habitats
Humor

Lesson Objectives

Children will:
1. Explore rhyming text.
2. Experience repetition in text.
3. Explore a variety of motor skills.
4. Explore the concept of uniqueness.

Action Vocabulary

Bound	Prance
Bump	Stamp
Crash	Skip
Dance	Slip
Drum	Splash
Flap	Topple
Flop	Trip
Frisk	Wiggle
Hop	

Concepts Explored

Creative dance
Uniqueness

Developing Literacy Skills

▶ Introduce the children to the book's author, Tony Mitton, and illustrator, Guy Parker-Rees. Draw the children's attention to the front book cover. Read the title of the book and ask the children for predictions about the storyline. The concept of "uniqueness" in movement is rather subtle for young children so you may want to suggest that the children listen and watch for the different ways the 10 animal **characters** move in the story.

▶ As you read the story, emphasize the rhyme. This will make it easy for the children to join you in saying the repeated phrases. Words that are set to a chant are easier to remember than phrases without a "sing-song" quality to them.

▶ This is a cumulative story, with the actions made by each animal added on as each character is introduced. When reading the text, point to the animal and pause for a moment so the children can name the animal. Continue reading the text and, once again, pause just before you read the action that the animal performs or the sound it makes. You will find that the children will likely remember the animals and action words more easily than the rest of the text.

▶ After the story, ask the children which animal character was their favorite and why. You may want to engage the children in a discussion about each animal's unique way of dancing and the fact that they all seem to enjoy themselves, no matter how they danced.

▶ Challenge the children to **recall** each animal in the story. Name the animal and wait for the children to call out the action words associated with that character. This simple activity helps develop recall and retelling skills.

Moving to the Story

▶ In addition to reading the story a second time and suggesting that the children act out each of the 17 movements that the animals do, you may want to include some background music to accompany the dance as you read the story.

▶ Any instrumental music with a moderate tempo will work, as long as it has an easy beat to chant to.

Developing Motor Skills

Moving like Animals

Material: CD player with music (see suggestions on the right)

▶ Ask the children to find space in the room to try out each of the action words in the book. Some words are free exploration and impromptu such as "frisking" like a dog or prancing like a pony. Others have specific patterns and movement qualities such as "prance" like a pony or "flap" like a duck.

▶ You or a child may need to demonstrate the actions *hop, flap, prance,* and *skip.* The other movements can be left to the imaginations of the children.

If your space is not large enough to accommodate all of the children moving at the same time, divide the class into smaller groups.

▶ Read the story again later that day or at a different time, and invite the children to stand and be ready to move along with the animals.

Safety Tip: As always, remind the children to maintain their own place in space and to be aware of others around them.

More Books to Share
Angelina Ballerina by Katharine Holabird
Baby Can't Sleep by Lisa Schroeder
The Dancing Tiger by Malachy Doyle
Piggies by Audrey Wood

Music Suggestions
Kids in Action by Greg and Steve. Song: Bop 'Til You Drop
Shake, Rattle and Rock by Greg and Steve. Songs: Barnyard Boogie; Stop and Go

The Emperor's Egg

by Martin Jenkins, illustrated by Jane Chapman

What's the Book About?

Imagine living in Antarctica in the middle of winter with an egg on your feet and nothing to eat for two months! That is the life of the male Emperor penguin. This outstanding science book is written in story form. The habits and behaviors of male and female Emperor penguins will fascinate the children, including the fact that "papa penguin" is in charge of the egg and the chick's first few weeks of life.

Theme Connections

Animals
Cooperation
Families
Winter

Lesson Objectives

Children will:
1. Create a plan for learning.
2. Experience various motor skills.
3. Explore interpretive movement.
4. Explore non-fiction text.

Action Vocabulary

Bump
Egg roll
Huddle
Push
Shuffle
Slide
Tuck
Trundle
Waddle

Concepts Explored

Snuggle

Developing Literacy Skills

▶ Introduce the book's author, Martin Jenkins, and illustrator, Jane Chapman. Read the title to the children and ask them to predict the storyline. Many children are fascinated with penguins and will want to share what they know.

▶ Before reading the story, you may want to create a **KWL chart** (What Do We **K**now?; What Do We **W**ant to Know?; and What Did We **L**earn?). Make a list of the information the children know and a list of things they want to know. Tell them they will find the answers to many of their questions in the story.

▶ Prior to reading the book, give each child a piece of recycled paper to wad up into a ball. Tell them that this represents the Emperor penguin's egg. Tell the children to imagine that their fingers are a penguin and that the children are to keep their egg safe.

▶ Moving an object (using their fingers to move the paper egg) while hearing and saying a word will help the children learn and understand the meaning of the word.

▶ When you are finished reading the book, refer to the KWL chart. Begin by reviewing the first column—What Do We Know? Talk with the children about the information in this column based on what they now know after hearing the book. Read the second column and ask the group if they found the answers to their questions. Invite the children to complete the "What Did We Learn?" column with their newly acquired knowledge.

▶ Post the chart in the classroom so you and the children can revisit this lesson. The children are now ready to move like penguins!

Moving to the Story

Materials: An "egg" (wadded-up papers, beanbag, or yarn ball)

▶ This story is a lot of fun for the children to act out as you read aloud. Be sure to remind the children to be gentle with their "egg."

▶ Ask the children how long they think they can waddle around as you read the story. Ask how the children might form a huddle and move all together in one direction. Remind them to control their egg.

▶ Afterward, engage the children in a discussion how the children decided which direction the group moved in. This can turn into a cooperative activity. Allow the children some time to plan how they will trundle very slowly with their egg in their huddle. You may want to practice whistling and trumpeting for extra fun.

Developing Motor Skills

Pass the Egg

Materials: An "egg" (wadded up paper, beanbag, or yarn ball) • An incline mat, optional • Parachute, optional

▶ Words such as *huddle, shuffle,* and *waddle* may be new to some children.

▶ Encourage the children to waddle and shuffle about the entire room with an "egg" tucked between their ankles after reading the story.

▶ Ask the children to find a partner. One child will have the "egg" between his or her feet. As with the real Emperor penguins, the object is to see if the children can pass an "egg" from one partner to the other. Can they do it without the "egg" falling to the floor or rolling away from them?

▶ Suggest that the children pretend to be the "egg." They lie down, tuck their legs and arms together into a ball, and roll sideways. This is called an **egg roll**.

▶ If possible, give the children an opportunity to slide like the penguins do on ice. Set up an incline mat, if available. Allow the children to start at the high end of the mat, lie down on their stomachs facing forward or backward, and while holding their eggs between their feet, push or pull themselves down to the low end of the mat without losing their "egg."

▶ Ask the children to describe other things to do that penguins do.

More Books to Share

And Tango Makes Three by Justin
    Richardson and Peter Parnell

Penguin ~~~~ Taylor

~~~~ ty Tatham

~~~~ Helen Lester

~~~~ns

~~~~ *mp for Kids* by
~~~~ ng: Penguin
    Waddle

Animal Walks by Kimbo
    Educational. Song: Penguin

~~~~ *Songs, Activity*
~~~~ *k.* Song: Walk

handwritten note: waddle + huddle

handwritten note: ← egg roll

Finklehopper Frog
by Irene Livingston, illustrated by Brian Lies

What's the Book About?

When Finklehopper Frog notices that many of his neighbors are avid joggers, he decides to buy a jazzy jogging suit and join them. The other joggers laugh at Finklehopper's jogging suit and make a point of telling him that his hop is not a jog. One sensible animal (another hopper) meets Finklehopper and convinces him that he just has to be who he is. The story celebrates individuality and tolerance.

Theme Connections

Animals   Friends
Exercise   Self-esteem
Feelings

Lesson Objectives

Children will:
1. Explore rhyming text.
2. Experience rich vocabulary in text.
3. Explore acceptance and tolerance of diversity.
4. Experience motor skills.

Action Vocabulary

Crawl   Leap
Fly   Run
Hop   Trot
Jog

Concepts Explored

Determined   Silly
Happy   Wondering
Heavy

Developing Literacy Skills

▶ The illustrations in the book will capture children's attention. Begin Story Time by introducing the book's author, Irene Livingston, and illustrator, Brian Lies.

▶ Show the children the book's front cover, read the title, and ask them to predict the storyline. Next, draw the children's attention to the inside cover spread. Finklehopper Frog is doing warm-up exercises. This should give the children a clue that Finklehopper will participate in some sort of physical activity.

▶ Emphasize the rhyme in the book by changing your inflection as you read. Pausing a moment before reading the final rhyming word will encourage the children to guess a word that might rhyme with the text. Because guessing the word is difficult with younger children, you may decide to read the text and emphasize the rhyme, but not pause for input from the children.

▶ The text is rich with vocabulary and the illustrations are bright, detailed, and full of action, so encouraging the children to participate in reading might be asking them to attend to too many things.

▶ The main concept in the story is about Finklehopper Frog accepting who he is and feeling good about it. It is also about his friends learning to understand and accept uniqueness in others. As you read the story, let your voice emphasize the feelings and emotions of each of the animals.

▶ After you finish the story, ask the children to share their thoughts about Finklehopper and his friends. Were Finklehopper's friends accepting of him? Encourage and accept all perspectives, as this models acceptance of diverse thoughts and ideas!

Moving to the Story

▶ As you read the story a second time, explain to the children that you are going to pick out some words for them to show facial expressions.

▶ When you come to each of the concepts listed on the previous page, pause after each word, and invite the children to demonstrate what it might look like. You may also invite them to stand and act out each of the words.

Developing Motor Skills

Move like the Animals

Materials: CD player and music (see suggestions on the right)

▶ "I Can Jump Like a Big Green Frog" on *Rowdy Ropes* is fun, with a variety of animal movements that will allow children to explore and imitate the different ways animals move. You may have to demonstrate the movement of each of the animals in the song.

▶ Put on the music and remind the children how each animal walks as you move along with the children. The younger the children, the more they will enjoy having you play with them. Try the other music, too.

Animal Catcher

▶ Do this activity in a gym or an outdoor space, preferably one with grass. One child—the catcher—stands in the center of the open space. The other children stand on one end of the open space. The child in the center says the name of an animal.

▶ All the children move like that animal from one end of the open space to the other end before the child in the middle catches them. When children are caught, they join the child in the middle.

▶ The children in the middle move like the same animal. For example, if the child in the middle calls out "frog," all the children try to move to the opposite side of the room or outdoor space doing frog jumps all the way across, including the child who is trying to catch the frogs by tagging them. If the children can move to the opposite side of the room, they are safe from being caught that time.

▶ Other animal possibilities are ostrich, rabbit, horse, monkey, crab, and kangaroo. Look in the Glossary (pages 192-194) for animal movement descriptions.

Safety Tip: Remind the children to use a two-finger tag touch when playing animal catcher.

Follow the Leader

▶ This is a good activity to do after the children have learned a variety of animal movements.

▶ Ask each child to find a partner. Each will take turns being the leader.

▶ The first child chooses an animal to imitate and moves the way that animal moves. The partner follows by copying the movement. You may want to put on some music such as "Stop and Go" (see list on right).

More Books to Share

Amy's Big Race: The Sound of Long A by Cecilia Minden and Joanne D. Meier
Frog Know Best by Gina Glegg Erickson and Kelli C. Foster
Jog, Frog, Jog by Barbara Gregorich
Marco's Run by Wesley Cartier

Music Suggestions

Kids in Action by Greg and Steve. Song: Can You Leap Like a Frog?
Kids in Motion by Greg and Steve. Song: Animal Action II
Rowdy Ropes by Dinotrax. Song: I Can Jump Like a Big Green Frog
Shake, Rattle, and Rock by Greg and Steve. Song: Stop and Go

Finklehopper Frog Cheers

by Irene Livingston, illustrated by Brian Lies

What's the Book About?

In the story, Finklehopper Frog encourages his friend, Ruby Rabbit, who is worried about losing a race. The story is fast paced, written in rhyme, and full of action words. The story's surprise ending is sure to spark a great conversation among your listeners.

Theme Connections

Animals
Exercise
Feelings
Friendship

Lesson Objectives

Children will:
1. Explore rhyming text.
2. Experience rich vocabulary.
3. Explore motor skills.
4. Discuss the concept of competition.

Action Vocabulary

Frog jump	Rabbit jump
Hop	Race
Kangaroo jump	Run

Concepts Explored

Awesome	Lose
Congratulations	Scared
Excitement	Tense
Good sport	Upset
Grief	Win
Happy	Worry
Hopeful	

Developing Literacy Skills

▶ Begin Story Time by introducing the children to the author, Irene Livingston, and illustrator, Brian Lies. Read the title and ask the children if the front cover and the title give clues about the story.

▶ Share the inside cover spread with the children. The illustrations suggest having a positive attitude, effort, teamwork, and being a good sport. This will help set the stage for reading the story.

▶ The rhythmic text is rich with vocabulary and the illustrations are brightly colored and full of detail. Allow enough time for the children to explore the illustrations. Draw their attention to the facial expressions of the animals.

▶ As you read the story, use your voice to convey the animal's feelings and emotions.

▶ When you are finished reading the story, begin a conversation with the children about competition. Suggest to the children that winning and losing can bring about strong emotions. Listen carefully to what the children have to offer and follow their thoughts and ideas with your own beliefs. It is good to remember that young children are still appropriately egocentric. With supportive experiences and maturation, children will be able to focus on others, as well as their own needs.

Moving to the Story

▶ After exploring various animal walks and movements (check the Glossary on pages 192-194 for descriptions), invite each child to choose the animal walk that he or she would like to use in a race. Help the children set up a racecourse down a hall, outside, or in a gym if possible.

▶ Explain to the children that they are to move as a kangaroo, a rabbit, bear, frog, or the other animal that they have chosen the entire length of the racecourse. In other words, they cannot change animals halfway through the race.

▶ Keep the race course short to maintain more fun. Suggest that the children take turns racing like their animals, and encourage the racers, just as in the story.

Developing Motor Skills

The Race

Materials: Cones or tape for marking the beginning and end of the course

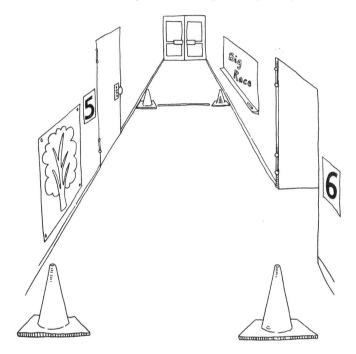

▶ Begin by exploring the emotional concepts and encouraging words from the story. Engage the children in a discussion about their experiences with races, even if it was someone that they watched in a race. Ask them how they felt before and after the race.

▶ If you have a small space, limit the children to race walking, rather than running, or race two children at a time, who are approximately the same size.

▶ When you say, "Go!" the children start racing. They finish when they cross the line on the opposite side of the room, open space, or end of the hall.

▶ If you have a large area, you may want to have a timed race. (Five minutes is a good length of time.) Have all of the children start at the same time. Make certain that the course is well marked with tape or cones, if available, at each corner for the children to go around the outside. The children will have a predetermined amount of time that they are to run or walk for. The children can vote for any given amount from one to five minutes. This can also be used to teach children about time.

More Books to Share

Franklin Plays Hockey by Paulette Bourgeois

The Pumpkin Runner by Marsha Diane Arnold

You're a Good Sport, Miss Malarkey by Judy Finchler

Ziggy's Blue Ribbon-Day by Claudia Mills

Music Suggestions

Kids in Action by Greg and Steve. Song: Can You Leap Like a Frog?

Kids in Motion by Greg and Steve. Song: Animal Action II

Rowdy Ropes by Dinotrax. Song: I Can Jump Like a Big Green Frog

Safety Tip: For any running activity, make certain that the children are well hydrated and have proper footwear.

Five Little Monkeys Jumping on the Bed

by Eileen Christelow

What's the Book About?

Children never tire of this timeless story featuring five very cute, impish monkeys who do not heed their mother's warning about jumping on the bed. The soft pastel illustrations add to the whimsical nature of this gem of a book.

Theme Connections

Animals
Families
Numbers

Lesson Objectives

Children will:

1. Explore rhyming text.
2. Explore repetitive text.
3. Experience counting backwards.
4. Experience motor skills.

Action Vocabulary

Bump
Fell
Jump

Concepts Explored

Repetition in movement

Developing Literacy Skills

▶ Many children will be eager to listen to this familiar story. Introducing the author and illustrator, Eileen Christelow, and telling the children the book title is all you need to do to get the children ready for Story Time.

▶ The book's short prelude describes the five little monkeys getting ready for bed.

▶ Tell the children that they need to get their "monkeys" (five fingers on one hand) ready for the story.

▶ As you read the story, encourage the children to say it with you. The children will quickly learn the rhyme and be able to say it with you. Use the following hand motions to act out the story:

  ▶ Move your fingers up and down as the monkeys jump on the bed.
  ▶ Touch the floor with your fingers as each monkey falls on the floor.
  ▶ Touch your head with your fingers as each monkey bumps his or her head.
  ▶ Hold your thumb to ear and your pinky to your mouth as mama calls the doctor.
  ▶ Shake your finger disapprovingly as you tell the monkeys not to jump on the bed.

▶ After reading the story, draw the children's attention to the last page. Ask them if their mom or dad would jump on the bed like the mama monkey in the story!

Moving to the Story

▶ Play "Five Little Monkeys" (see Music Suggestions on the next page) and see if the children can continue jumping through the entire song. This is a great way of determining their aerobic fitness level.

▶ Ask the children to come up with other activities monkeys could do together. If appropriate, divide your class into groups of five so each group of five can plan their own actions to perform. As each group of five performs, the other children are the audience.

Developing Motor Skills

Follow the Music Man

Materials: CD player and one or more of the music suggestions (see list on the right)

▶ This story is all about jumping for the joy of it, and the music adds to the fun.

▶ After reading the story, invite the children to find their own space and follow the directions in "All the Ways of Jumping Up and Down" on *Walter the Waltzing Worm*.

▶ It is sometimes difficult for young children to understand all of the words to music, especially when it has actions to do; therefore, it is important to model all of the actions so the children hear the music and see the words acted out.

Note: Be sure the children have enough room to jump around and to pretend to fall and land safely.

Although pretend falling is not a true fall, falling safely is an important skill for all ages. Athletes are taught to fall safely by lowering their center of gravity (lowering the body closer to the floor) and turning so they land toward their back side on the padded part of the hip. They are also taught to stretch their arm overhead so their outstretched hands do not stop the fall. This prevents spraining or breaking a wrist.

More Books to Share

Five Little Monkeys Bake a Birthday Cake by Eileen Christelow

Five Little Monkeys Play Hide-and-Seek by Eileen Christelow

Five Little Monkeys Sitting in a Tree by Eileen Christelow

Five Little Monkeys Wash the Car by Eileen Christelow

Five Little Monkeys with Nothing to Do by Eileen Christelow

Music Suggestions

Bugs, Bugs, Bugs! by Schiller Educational Resources. Songs: Five Little Speckled Frogs; Five Little Ladybugs

Literacy in Motion by The Learning Station. Song: Five Little Monkeys

Ready...Set...Move! by Greg and Steve. Songs: Five Little Monkeys; Jump Down, Turn Around

Walter the Waltzing Worm by Hap Palmer. Song: All the Ways of Jumping Up and Down

Five Little Sharks Swimming in the Sea

by Steve Metzger, illustrated by Laura Bryant

What's the Book About?

Five Little Monkeys is the inspiration for this book about mischievous sharks. Young children will be delighted to see how much trouble the little sharks can get into while swimming in the sea. The mother, of course, is right there to phone the doctor with every mishap. The ending message is about wild animals being free.

Theme Connections

Animals
Families
Numbers
Ocean

Lesson Objectives

Children will:
1. Compare and contrast familiar stories.
2. Explore motor skills.
3. Experience **predictable text.**
4. Explore rhyming text.

Action Vocabulary

Ate	Race
Bang	Splash
Bump	Swim
Play	

Concepts Explored

Alone	Hide-and-Seek
Close	Lost
Free	Stuck
Happy	

Developing Literacy Skills

▶ This book has a story that is similar to *Five Little Monkeys* by Eileen Christelow. Begin by reading the title of the book and introducing the author, Steve Metzger, and illustrator, Laura Bryant. Encourage the children to share their ideas about the book. Tell the children the story's ending may be a bit of a surprise!

▶ Invite the children to use the fingers of one hand as the five little sharks. The space in front of them can be their ocean. Encourage them to move their fingers as desired.

▶ Encourage the children to say the repetitive passages with you. Children who are familiar with *Five Little Monkeys* will know when to use the repetitive phrases, but they will need to learn hand motions to go along with the story. Follow the children's lead! Invite them to suggest hand motions and encourage them to be creative.

▶ *Five Little Sharks Swimming in the Sea* offers an opportunity to compare and contrast this book with *Five Little Monkeys Jumping on the Bed.* You may want to list similarities and differences between the two books on large chart paper. This allows you to model writing skills for the children. It also gives the children an opportunity to develop **recall,** comprehension, and analysis skills.

Moving to the Story

Materials: Parachute or large sheet • 3' long strips of crepe paper, optional • Shark puppets or toy sharks, optional • Toy telephone

▶ This is a fun story to act out. Add to the fun by tying a parachute or large sheet over some chairs, or have a few children hold the edges of the parachute. This is the top of the water, so the sharks and other creatures can be under the sea.

▶ Help the children decide who will be the five little sharks, the mama shark, the whale, the manatee, some seaweed. If desired, use green crepe paper as the seaweed. Give three children or two or three pieces of crepe paper that are 3' long. They wave it up and down and back and forth like real seaweed in the ocean.

▶ Give the children shark puppets or toy sharks, or they can pretend to be each of the sea creatures. The children will need a toy telephone.

▶ This is a great time to explore the action vocabulary and concepts explored lists on the previous page. Go over each word with the children and see how they might express or act out each action or concept. Above all, have fun!

▶ Over a period of days, repeat the activity until everyone has a chance to act out a part.

Developing Motor Skills

Help! Shark Nibbled Me!

Materials: 12'–20' parachute or a king size sheet • Scarves for each child

▶ Tell all of the children that they are going to play a game called "Help! Shark Nibbled Me!" This is a game of anticipation. Tell the children, "It's not a matter of if the shark will nibble your toes; it's a matter of when."

▶ The children take off their shoes and arrange themselves in a circle around the parachute, holding onto an edge, shaking out all of the wrinkles, and then sit down with their legs under the parachute extended straight. (This straight-legged position with the feet together is called a "pike position.")

▶ Choose one child to be the first "shark." As the remaining children shake the parachute, the shark goes under the parachute. The shark crawls around under the parachute as the children continue to shake the parachute.

▶ When the shark finds a foot that he likes he gives the toe a gentle squeeze. That child yelps or exclaims, "Help! Shark nibbled me!" and slides down under the parachute to become the new shark. The previous shark comes out and takes the place of the child whose toe he squeezed.

▶ The game will continue until each child has a chance to become the shark. If the children tire of shaking the parachute, urge them to continue until all have had a chance to be the shark.

▶ Another way to play is to begin with two or three sharks under the parachute. Play continues as described above.

More Books to Share

All About Sharks by Jim Arnosky
Sharkabet by Ray Troll
Smiley Shark by Ruth Galloway
Surprising Sharks by Nicola Davies

Music Suggestions

Use any of the music selections and follow the directions in the songs.
Charlotte Diamond's World by Charlotte Diamond. Song: Splishin' and Splashin'
Everyday Activities for Kids by Kimbo Educational. Song: Five Gray Sharks
Musical Scarves & Activities by Kimbo Educational. Song: Under the Sea
Playful Tunes by Alleyoop Music. Song: Swimmin' So Free

Froggy Plays in the Band

by Jonathan London, illustrated by Frank Remkiewicz

What's the Book About?

Froggy forms a marching band to win a prize. Each of his friends grabs an instrument and the group practices for weeks. The big day finally arrives and, true to form for Froggy, things do not go as planned. This story is a good reminder to young children that they can make the best of difficult situations.

Theme Connections

Animals
Cooperation
Exercise
Music

Lesson Objectives

Children will:
1. Experience motor movements.
2. Experience cooperative activity.
3. Explore rhythmic movement.
4. Explore onomatopoeic words.

Action Vocabulary

Catch
Dance
Flop
Jump
March
Twirl

Concepts Explored

Around
Compete
Contest
Left
Nervous
Right
Win

Developing Literacy Skills

▶ Begin Story Time by reading the title to the children. The Froggy book series is popular, so some children may be familiar with the main **character.** Introduce the author, Jonathan London, and illustrator, Frank Remkiewicz.

▶ Ask the children to predict the storyline. The front cover illustrations will offer the children clues. Ask the children what they know about marching bands. Allow a few minutes for conversation before beginning the story.

▶ *Froggy Plays in the Band* is full of **onomatopoeic** words. Invite the children to repeat the words after you. Use your voice to emphasize the words you would like the children to repeat.

▶ If the musical instruments in this story, such as triangle, recorder, and cymbals, are unfamiliar to the children, point to the pictures on the page as you read the name of the instrument. This cuing will give them a visual representation of the word and help them acquire new vocabulary.

▶ This story has a great message. After reading the book, ask the children to share experiences they have had that did not turn out exactly as planned. Invite them to talk about how Froggy and Frogilina might have felt after their mishap.

▶ Invite the children to share what they understand about the concepts listed. Ask questions such as: "Who has competed in a contest?" "Were you nervous about it?" "What kind was it?" "Was winning important to you or do you just want to have fun?"

Moving to the Story

▶ Ask the children to name their favorite instrument.

▶ What items can the children find in the classroom to play and march with? Can the children pretend to twirl a baton or dance to the beat of the music that the other children play?

▶ Just for fun, ask the children what a frog might look like marching. How could he keep a steady beat?

Developing Motor Skills

Steady Beat

Materials: CD player and any of the suggested music selections (see list to the right)

▶ This book offers a great opportunity to teach the children about a steady beat. Steady beat is the basic underlying beat of each piece of music. According to Phyllis Weikart (Weikart, 2003), steady beat competence affects a child's basic timing, language and literacy development, concentration, and overall learning.

▶ Begin by having the children clap a beat with you by counting 1−2. On the count of 1, the children bring their hands apart; on 2, they clap their hands together. The beat is steady and consistent. You might also say, "Apart, together," to help the children figure out when to clap in unison.

▶ The next step is to hold a beat while you count. For example, count 1 (clap hands together), then count 2 (hold the hands together). Repeat the clap on count 3 and hold on count 4. The children also practice saying the numbers as they clap and hold. Repeat until all the children are successful. When the children can do this successfully, you might want to have all the children join you in singing and marching around in a circle to "The Wheels on the Bus," and clap out the steady beat. Remember that you will not be clapping for every word. For example, the words wheels, bus, round, and round, would receive a clap. The words in between would not. Example: *The, on the, go, and,* and *all* receive a "hold." Additional song selections with a strong steady beat to clap or march to are "The Grand Old Duke of York" or "The Ants Go Marching." Another option is to chant "Left, right, left, right," as they march along.

Safety Tip: It is important for children to look straight ahead as they march, but tell them to be aware of the person in front of them, particularly the feet of the person ahead.

More Books to Share
A Marching Band for Bears by Eileen Benator
Our Marching Band by Lloyd Moss
Thump, Thump, Rat-a-Tat-Tat by Gene Baer

Music Suggestions
All-Time Children's Favorites by The Learning Station. Song: The Marching Song
Physical Ed by The Learning Station. Song: The Marching Game
Ready…Set….MOVE! by The Leaning Station. Song: Jump Down, Turn Around
Smart Moves by Russ InVision. Song: Play in the Band
Toddlers on Parade by Kimbo Educational. Songs: Wheels on the Bus; Grand Old Duke of York

Froggy Plays Soccer

by Jonathan London, illustrated by Frank Remkiewicz

What's the Book About?

Froggy and his teammates really want to win the City Cup. All Froggy has to do is to remember what his coach said to do (and what not to do: Touch the ball with his hands!). This could be a problem because Froggy seems to be more interested in doing cartwheels and picking daisies. Look out, Froggy, here comes the ball!

Theme Connections

Animals
Cooperation
Exercise
Imagination

Lesson Objectives

Children will:

1. Explore onomatopoeic words.
2. Explore repetitious text.
3. Experience various physical activities.

Action Vocabulary

Block	Leapfrog
Catch	Pass
Dribble	Shoot
Kick	Trap
Kneeing	

Concepts Explored

Ball control	Outside
Partner work	Inside
Personal space	

Developing Literacy Skills

▶ Begin Story Time by sharing the book cover with the children. The colorful cover will enable children to guess the storyline.

▶ Some children will want to share their personal knowledge and experiences about the game of soccer. Be sure to allow enough time for sharing stories. It will be difficult to read this book without enthusiasm!

▶ The children's experiences will help them create mental images of the game of soccer and its skills. Discussions will help children **recall** their experiences, modify their knowledge, and create new mental images. This imagery is important as children increase their vocabulary. Adding actions to unfamiliar words helps children remember newly acquired vocabulary.

▶ *Froggy Plays Soccer* has a wonderful collection of **onomatopoeic** words such as *zap, zeep, znap,* and *zoop.* When reading this story, ask the children to repeat the sounds with you. Drawing children's attention to words with fun sounds piques their interest and heightens **phonemic awareness**. Playing with words helps encourage children to use their letter-sound knowledge. Invite the children to make up their own onomatopoeic words. Create a list as the children brainstorm new words.

▶ The text also contains several opportunities for children to join in the reading by chanting repeated phrases. After reading this story, the children will want to move.

Moving to the Story

Materials: Balls, optional

▶ Very young children or children who have limited ball-handling skills may benefit by acting out the story without equipment. This will help develop their confidence and build interest in exploring the skills later.

▶ As you read the story a second time, invite each child to pretend to get dressed for the big soccer game. Encourage the children to interpret the story in a variety of ways. The goal is for each child to create movements that reflect his or her ideas. This will allow all of the children to see a number of unique interpretations as they pause to observe their classmates.

Developing Motor Skills

Leapfrog

▶ Most young children have had some experience playing leapfrog. A game of leapfrog is a great way to begin moving.

▶ Remind the children to leap over one another carefully. If a child is uncertain about participating, do not insist. Observing others is an excellent way to learn and gain confidence.
Note: This activity will be most successful outdoors or in a multipurpose room or gym.

Safety Tip: Remind the children on the ground to keep their elbows close to their sides with their hands over their tucked heads. It is important to match partners based on size, weight, and experience with this skill.

Ball Handling

Materials: Soccer balls, 8" sponge balls, or paper balls • Cones

▶ Introduce one or more of the following ball-handling skills that meet the developmental skills of the children. The skills are listed in the order of difficulty.
Note: Choose a ball that is appropriate for your space. A slightly deflated ball will be easier to control, because it will roll more slowly than one that is completely inflated.

  ▶ *Kicking:* To keep the ball under control, have the children aim toward an open space to avoid others. If you are outdoors, have the children kick the ball toward a wall.

  ▶ *Shooting:* The children can score a goal by shooting the ball between field cones that are 10′–12′ apart. The children keep track of their own score. Eliminating competition will help young children feel confident and competent as movers.

  ▶ *Dribbling:* Tell the children to find their own personal space. Give each child a ball and ask the children to practice dribbling the ball with their feet, just as Froggy did. You will notice that some children will dribble the ball with their toe, heel, inside, or outside of their foot. Encourage children to use both sides of their body (right foot, left foot).

▶ Develop the skills over a period of several weeks. When the children are ready, suggest that they organize themselves into groups of three or four to create modified soccer games. Do not worry about official rules as long as all players agree on the house rules—Froggy's rules!

More Books to Share

Game Time! by Stuart J. Murphy
K Is for Kick: A Soccer Alphabet by Brad Herzog
My Soccer Book by Gail Gibbons
Winners Never Quit! by Mia Hamm

From Head to Toe
by Eric Carle

What's the Book About?

The animals in this story show children how to exercise from head to toe. The children join animals from all over the world moving parts of the body. As always, Eric Carle's illustrations are colorful, vivid, and engaging. The text describes simple movements that children can do as you read the book. Repetitive text also encourages children to join in the reading.

Theme Connections

Animals
Parts of the body

Lesson Objectives

Children will:
1. Engage in **predictable text.**
2. Experience a variety of movements.
3. Identify parts of the body.

Action Vocabulary

Arch	Thump
Bend	Turn
Clap	Wave
Kick	Wiggle
Raise	Wriggle
Stomp	

Concepts Explored

Parts of the body

Developing Literacy Skills

▶ The title gives children a good idea about the storyline. Introduce the author and illustrator, Eric Carle. If you have read many of Eric Carle's books, your children may recognize his name or his unique illustrations. Allow a few minutes for conversation about this popular author.

▶ Before reading the book, familiarize the children with the repeated text—the question and answer on each two-page spread. Emphasize *you* in the first sentence and *can* in the second. This will encourage the children to move just as the animals in the story do.

▶ Tell the children you will point to the sentences when it is their turn to help you read. The pattern is predictable and the children will quickly catch on.

▶ Invite the children to move about as you read the book. Ask them to touch each part of their body as it is mentioned in the story.

Moving to the Story

Materials: CD player and your favorite marching music just to keep up the pace

▶ Tell the children to stand in a large circle. Stand in the middle of this circle and model two or three body movements shown in the book.

▶ Name one part of the body and focus on the ways that part of the body can move, such as turning the head from side to side, and up and down, and raising the shoulders up and down. Repeat with another part of the body.

▶ After modeling movements, give each child a turn to be the leader and come up with his or her own body movement. The children may choose to do an isolated move similar to any in the book, or they may do their own.

▶ As you step to the outside of the circle, tell the children that their turn will be in consecutive order from where you stepped out into the circle perimeter.

▶ Play instrumental marching music to keep up the movement pace.

▶ Encourage the "animals" in the center of the circle to ask the question from the book and the children to use the response from the book. This is a fun physical activity that recharges the muscles while growing pathways in the brain and developing motor skills through play and physical activity.

Developing Motor Skills

Add-On Actions

Materials: CD player and suggested music or other similar music selections

▶ Ask the children to form pairs and face their partner. One child will begin as the leader, and then the children switch roles after each movement.

▶ The focus of the activity is to add an action to each prior action. For example, if the first child raises his or her arm, the second child raises his or her arm and adds a leg lift. Then the first child raises his or her arm, lifts a leg, and adds turning around. Each pair continues to add more actions. The children may prompt one another with what comes next until they can no longer remember each sequential action.

▶ You may suggest that the children try locomotor skills, such as running in place, jumping up and down, or hopping on one foot and then the other. They can also try combinations of skip, hop, steps in place, or animal walks.

*All the children need to check their personal space
to be certain that they can move safely
without touching or bumping anyone else.*

More Books to Share

The Busy Body Book: A Kid's Guide to Fitness by Lizzy Rockwell
Exercise by Shannon Gordon
My Amazing Body: A First Look at Health and Fitness by Pat Thomas

Music Suggestions

Movin' & Shakin' by Russ InVision. Songs: First I'm Stretching; Shake a Leg; First We'll Tap Our Toes; Head, Shoulders, Knees, and Toes
Smart Moves 1 by Russ InVision. Songs: In My Body; Work Your Body; I Can Stand by Myself; I Can Sit by Myself; My Face, My Face; Can You Sit Down on Your Bum Bum?

Safety Tip: As with any activity, children should wear appropriate footwear.

Full Moon Barnyard Dance

by Carole Lexa Schaefer, illustrated by Christine Davenier

What's the Book About?

The moon is full and the barnyard animals are restless. Pig declares it is the perfect night for everyone to head down to the pond and kick up their heels under the big round moon. Each animal finds a partner, but a sudden cloud cover causes the animals to become mixed up. The wise frog convinces them that it is great to dance a friendly jig with someone new.

Theme Connections

Acceptance	Habitats
Animals	Nighttime

Lesson Objectives

Children will:

1. Explore onomatopoeic words.
2. Explore working with a partner.
3. Experience various movement skills.
4. Experience dance steps.

Action Vocabulary

Amble	Stomp
Flap	Stretch
Prance	Trot
Sashay	Twirl
Scurry	Wibble
Slink	Yawn
Step	

Concepts Explored (Dances)

Fandango	Swing
Jig	Swirl
Samba	Triple-step dip
Shuffle	Two by two

Developing Literacy Skills

▶ Introduce the author, Carole Lexa Schaefer, and illustrator, Christine Davenier, and read the book's title. Share the front cover and ask the children to predict the storyline. After several minutes of conversation, tell the children that the barnyard animals are going to dance with partners, but then the partners get all mixed up!

▶ There are several **onomatopoeic** words in the story, such as the noises that the crickets and the frogs make. Ask the children to repeat the words after you read them. Young learners will also enjoy imitating the sounds the animals make as they gather by the pond for the dance.

▶ Just as the animals moved two by two to the pond, invite the children to get up and move around the Circle Time area just like the animals. Focus on action words, such as *amble, trot,* and *scurry,* rather than the dance steps. Once you have finished reading this part of the story, have the children sit in their place for the remainder of the story.

▶ This story is about experiencing the unexpected and gaining new insight from the experience. After you finish reading the book, invite the children to share their thoughts about why they thought the animals were not comfortable with new partners. Ask the children how they would have felt.

Moving to the Story

Materials: Tape, carpet squares, or poly spots • CD player and "A Walking We Will Go" from *We All Live Together, Volume 5,* or other appropriate music

▶ Create spots on the floor by placing tape in an "X" shape on the floor, or by using carpet squares or poly spots.

▶ Have "A Walking We Will Go" from *We All Live Together, Volume 5* or another selection ready to play. The children choose a partner and stand with their partner on a spot.

▶ Tell the children they will move with a partner around the room in scatter formation, which allows the children to be anywhere in the space, unlike a line or square dance with specific formations (see Glossary pages 188-199). Stop the music at the end of two measures, or count out 16 beats or clap 16 times.

▶ Ask the partners to separate and find a different partner on a different carpet square or spot. Remind the children that only two children may share the same spot.

- Have them move with their partners and walk, stomp, skip, slide, bounce, tiptoe, or march, as they hold hands for 16 counts or beats before switching.
- To do this activity, you need to stop the music at the end of each different movement to give the children time to mix up and switch partners. The children do only one motor skill with each partner.

- You may want to have each pair practice walking around and then stopping at a different spot to switch partners before playing the music. Additionally, you may want to alert the children that they will be changing partners eight times as they move around the room.

Safety Tip: Remind the children to watch for one another when moving quickly to a different spot to find a new partner.

Developing Motor Skills

Dancing Fun
Materials: CD player and a music suggestions (see list to the right) or other music
- Put on any of the music suggestions and follow the directions. It's fun and easy for all children to do.
- You may want to explore some of the dance steps mentioned in the book. Choose instrumental music with a strong beat and join the children in learning several new dance steps.
  Note: A gym or multipurpose area is ideal. If that is not available, push your furniture to one side of the room to maximize your open floor space.

More Books to Share
Old Turtle and the Broken Truth by Douglas Wood
The Other Side by Jacqueline Woodson
The Skin You Live In by Michael Tyler
Whoever You Are by Mem Fox

Music Suggestions
All-Time Favorite Dances by Kimbo Educational. Songs: Virginia Reel; Cotton-Eyed Joe
Heel Toe Away We Go by Kimbo Educational. Song: Little Brown Jug (both vocal and instrumental)
We All Live Together, Volume 5 by Greg and Steve. Songs: Old Brass Wagon; A Walking We Will Go

Get Up and Go!
by Nancy Carlson

What's the Book About?

Author/illustrator Nancy Carlson has created a vibrantly colored book that encourages children to get up and move. The cute animals in this story explore all kinds of options for exercising: baseball, soccer, ice skating, and canoeing. The text includes fun facts about keeping the heart healthy. This book does an excellent job of celebrating uniqueness and taking care of the body.

Theme Connections

Animals   Parts of the body
Exercise   Self-esteem

Lesson Objectives

Children will:
1. Experience various movement activities.
2. Explore systems of the body.
3. Explore the benefits of exercise.
4. Learn about a variety of sports and activities.

Action Vocabulary

The children choose actions that fit one of the activities or sports in the "Concepts Explored" list, such as throwing, catching, and running for the concept of baseball.

Concepts Explored (Activities and Sports)

Baseball   Hiking
Biking   Ice skating
Canoeing   Rope jumping
Dancing   Soccer
Exercising   Swimming
Gardening   Walking
Golfing

Developing Literacy Skills

▶ Introduce the author and illustrator, Nancy Carlson, to the children. Read the book title and ask the children to predict the storyline. The front and back cover illustrations will give the children a very good idea about this active storyline.

▶ Brainstorm ideas about what the pig is doing and see if the children come up with exercise. Tell the children to watch for the many different ways the animals exercise.

▶ To set the stage for reading the book, invite the children to stand in their own personal space with plenty of space between them, and join you in doing jumping jacks. Coordinating the arm and leg movements may be difficult for the very young. As their coordination develops, they will become more efficient and fluid with their movements.

▶ Begin reading the story after the children are seated again around the Story Time circle. The text on each page is simple, so allow plenty of time for the children to focus on the illustrations.

▶ The third page spread, and most of the pages thereafter, points out the benefits of exercise. The first page that discusses exercise includes illustrations of three systems of the body: the heart and lungs (cardiovascular system), bones (skeletal system), and the muscles (muscular system). Using vocabulary that focuses on the part of the body (heart, lungs, bones, muscles), invite the children to share what they know about the body and how it works.

▶ Continue to read the book, allowing the children to respond to the statements about the benefits of exercise. The illustrations do an excellent job of supporting the text.

▶ When you are finished with the story, tell the children that you have planned several fun activities to help develop healthy hearts, lungs, bones, and muscles.

Moving to the Story

▶ As you read the book, say the name of each of the sport activities listed on the previous page and invite the children to move as if they were doing that particular sport.

▶ "Sport Dance" on the CD *On the Move with Greg and Steve* is great for acting out a variety of sports. For imaginative activities, consider "Late Last Night" on the *Late Last Night* CD.

Developing Motor Skills

Get Up and Go

Materials: Balloons, with or without yarn and a paper plate paddle • Jump ropes or yarn ropes • Utility balls • Beanbags • Baskets or buckets • Chairs • CD player and any of the music selections (see list on the right)

▶ The book encourages everyone to get up and move. If possible, try to set up six stations in a hallway or multipurpose room (see below for ideas).

▶ Divide your class into groups of about three to five children per station. The more stations you have, the fewer materials you will need per station and also provide more variety for the children. The timed interval should be between 30 seconds and one minute. The shorter the interval, the more often the children will be able to repeat the stations.

▶ Observe the children to see what time frame works best for them.

▶ Begin playing the music when all of the children are at their stations and ready to move. Encourage the children to stay active until you stop the music at the end of the interval when you tell the children to move to the next station.

▶ The stations are:

   ▶ *Balloon station:* This station can have two options, depending upon your available space. The first option is for **eye-hand tracking** and coordination and uses thick 12″ balloons with one balloon per child. The children toss the balloon up in the air and keep batting it gently until you stop the music. The second option is to tie a 12″ balloon to a paper plate or paint stick paddle with a piece of yarn (3′–4′ long). The children strike the balloon, using the paddle, in an upward motion.

   ▶ *Jump rope station:* Place the jump rope or yarn rope in a straight line on the floor and invite the children to explore ways to jump or hop over it and around it.

   ▶ *Ball bouncing station:* Each child drops and catches the ball as many times as he or she can. If the children can bounce the ball continuously with both hands, encourage them to do so.

   ▶ *Locomotor station:* The children march, walk, run, jump, and hop, all in place. You may want to put a picture of a child doing each locomotor skill as a visual aid. Have the children do 10 repetitions each.

   ▶ *Bicycle station:* The children lie on their backs with their hands under their hips, legs in the air, and "bicycle" their legs.

   ▶ *Chair station:* The object of this station is for the children to stand up and sit down on the chair as many times as they can in the time frame.

More Books to Share

Babar's Yoga for Elephants by Laurent de Brunhoff

My Amazing Body: A First Look at Health and Fitness by Pat Thomas

Walk Like a Bear, Stand Like a Tree, Run Like the Wind by Carol Bassette

Music Suggestions

Late Last Night by Joe Scruggs. Song: Late Last Night

On the Move with Greg and Steve by Greg and Steve. Song: Sport Dance

Rowdy Ropes by Dinotrax. Song: All songs are for rope jumping, so choose the ones that match the children's abilities.

Transitions to Go by The Brain Store. Songs: Ladies & Gents; Calypso on the Move

Shake, Rattle & Rock by Steve and Greg. Song: Fun to Get Fit

We All Live Together, Volume 5 by Greg and Steve. Song: Get Up and Go!

Safety Tips: Encourage the children to be mindful of one another while they are moving from one station to the next. Make certain that they each return any materials to where they belong so the next group of children can pick them up and be ready for your signal to begin.

Giraffes Can't Dance

by Giles Andreae, illustrated by Guy Parker-Rees

What's the Book About?

Gerald's long legs and wobbly knees make it difficult for him to dance, so he was dreading the Jungle Dance. Gerald watches the animals waltz, tango, and cha-cha. When Gerald works up his courage and enters the dance floor, the other animals laughed at him. A friendly cricket helps Gerald find his self-confidence.

Theme Connections

Animals	Feelings
Environments	Self-confidence

Lesson Objectives

Children will:
1. Experience rhyming text.
2. Explore emotions.
3. Learn about individuality.
4. Explore a variety of dance forms.

Concepts Explored (Actions and Dances)

Boogie	Shuffle
Bow	Skip
Buckle	Sway
Cha Cha Cha	Swish
Leap	Tango
Prance	Twirl
Rock 'n Roll	Waltz
Scottish Reel	

Concepts Explored (Emotions/Feelings)

Alone	Sad
Brave	Useless
Clumsy	Wonderful

Developing Literacy Skills

- Begin by introducing the book's author, Giles Andreae, and illustrator, Guy Parker-Rees. Read the title and ask the children to predict the storyline.
- Show the children the front and back cover. The illustrations will help set the stage for this book. Introduce the children to Gerald, the giraffe, and ask them to follow Gerald's journey as he learns more about himself.
- There are two main themes in this story. One is Gerald struggling with feelings about dancing because he cannot dance like the other animals in the jungle. The other theme is the dances the animals perform at the annual Jungle Dance. The first time you read the story, you may want to focus on Gerald and his feelings. The Emotion/Feelings list (on this page) will help with this.
- The animals' facial expressions are wonderful and clearly depict feelings and emotions. Allow enough time for the children to view the illustrations and share their thoughts about how Gerald and the other animals might be feeling.
- After finishing the book, talk with the children about how they thought Gerald felt at the end of the story and why. Invite the children to talk about times when they were unsure of themselves and how they worked through it.

Moving to the Story

- Using the action words in the story, and others if desired, provide an opportunity for the children to practice how to leap, prance, shuffle, skip, sway, swish, and twirl.
- Ask the children to choose two action words and combine the actions with arm movements to make up a dance. Give them two to three minutes to figure out the movements.
- Sit together to make a large circle. Invite each child to step into the middle of the circle to show his or her dance. It is fine if a child prefers not to dance.
- After each child has demonstrated his or her dance, ask the child to lead the other children in trying it. This may involve some problem solving. For example, if there is a leap in the dance, the children will have to figure out how everyone can leap and not crash into one another. One solution might be for everyone to leap together counterclockwise in a circle.

- Put on an instrumental piece of music with a strong steady beat, and invite the children to each be the leader when you call each name. The object is to see how quickly the children can transition from one leader to another as they change steps and moves.
- For younger children, keep it very simple. You may want to put on the children's favorite song, some lively music, or some waltz music and just let the children make up their own dances as Gerald did. Draw one child doing this.

Safety Tip: Remind the children to be careful not to bump into anyone with their arms or elbows, and to watch where they are moving.

Developing Motor Skills

Dance Fun
Materials: CD player and dance music (see suggestions on the right)
- Several of the dances in the book are cultural in nature, such as the tango, the Scottish reel, and the cha-cha.
- Invite the children to share a dance from their family or cultural background.

More Books to Share
Animal Boogie by Debbie Harter
The Dancing Tiger by Malachy Doyle
Minnie and Moo Go Dancing by Denys Cazet
Prancing, Dancing Lily by Marsha Diane Arnold

Music Suggestions
La Di Da La Di Di Dance with Me by The Learning Station. Song: If Animals Could Dance
Ready...Set...MOVE! by Greg and Steve. Song: Shimmy Shake
Rockin' Down the Road by Greg and Steve. Song: Dancin' Machine
Salsa, Soul & Swing Dances for Kids by Kimbo Educational. Songs: All, instruction guide included

The Greatest Gymnast of All

by Stuart J. Murphy, illustrated by Cynthia Jabar

What's the Book About?

Zoe is a gymnast who, in her mind, is the best gymnast of all. Zipping, zooming Zoe introduces the reader to opposites as she moves over and under, inside and outside, and back and forth. The text is simple and gives children an opportunity to move with the story as well as read along.

Theme Connections

Exercise
Opposites

Lesson Objectives

Children will:

1. Experience movement that demonstrates opposites.
2. Experience rhyming text.
3. Explore basic gymnastics skills.

Action Vocabulary

Cartwheel	Roll
Flip	Slip
Jump	Swing
Leap	

Concepts Explored (Opposites)

Forward/backward
High/low
Inside/outside
Near/far
On/off
Short/long
Under/over
Up/down

Developing Literacy Skills

Materials: Dolls or stuffed animals

▶ Children of all ages are fascinated with the sport of gymnastics. When you read the title of the book to the children, they will easily guess the storyline. Be sure to introduce the author, Stuart J. Murphy, and illustrator, Cynthia Jabar, as you set the stage for reading the book.

▶ Zipping, zooming Zoe's moves demonstrate opposites. To help children understand these concepts, invite them to participate in the story by using a small doll or plush animal to act out the part of Zoe.

▶ As you read the story, encourage the children to move their doll or stuffed animal in a way that shows they understand the action words, such as *jump* or *roll* and opposite concepts, such as *forward* and *backward* and *under* and *over*.

▶ After you read the story, allow time for the children to share their favorite movements. Ask them to use vocabulary that matches the action. For example, a child might say, "I like the way my doll can leap," and then demonstrates leaping with his or her doll.

Moving to the Story

▶ If the space allows, let all the children move to the story as you read the book. If the space is too small, select one or two children at a time to play the part of zipping, zooming Zoe to perform the skills. The rest of the children are the audience, just like in the book. Ask a different Zoe to play the part as you turn the page.

▶ As you read the story, invite the children to say the repetitive phrase in the book with you.

▶ When you read about swinging, have the children swing their arms up and down. If you have an outdoor climbing structure with a bar, later on in the day the children may want to go outdoors and practice the skill of swinging as part of this lesson (see Safety Tips).

▶ When you read about doing a flip, ask the children to flip their hands over instead of their bodies. Allow as much creativity as possible while making certain that each child stays safe.

Safety Tips: For all activities, be sure there is enough space for every child to move safely. Although Zoe does cartwheels and forward rolls, do not let the children do a cartwheel or a forward roll. Make certain that the children bend their knees and land on their feet when they swing off the bars of an outdoor climbing structure.

Developing Motor Skills

Opposites in Action

Materials: Hoops • Jump ropes • Mats, if available

▶ Review the opposite concepts with the children (see list on previous page). Ask the children to find a partner and give each child a rope and a hoop. Encourage the children to use the ropes and hoops to show opposites, such as *on* and *off,* but that it is also okay to use the ropes and hoops any way they like.

▶ Say an opposite pair, such as *up* and *down,* to the children. Then ask the children to demonstrate the opposite pair through actions or poses. The partners decide which opposite word each child will perform. Allow a minute or two for the children to explore possibilities before they share their ideas with the class.

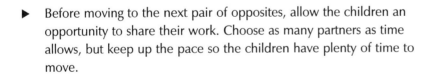

▶ Before moving to the next pair of opposites, allow the children an opportunity to share their work. Choose as many partners as time allows, but keep up the pace so the children have plenty of time to move.

More Books to Share

Black? White? Day? Night! A Book of Opposites by Laura Vaccaro Seeger

Oops! All About Opposites by Kirsten Hall

Opposites by Roger Pare

Over Under by Marthe Jocelyn

Music Suggestions

Animal Romp and Stomp for Kids by Russ InVision. Song: The Circus Dance

Can a Cherry Pie Wave Goodbye? by Hap Palmer. Song: Say the Opposite

Fun and Games: Learning to Play—Playing to Learn by Greg and Steve. Song: Opposites

Rock N' Roll Songs That Teach by The Learning Station. Song: Opposites

Walter the Waltzing Worm by Hap Palmer. Song: All the Ways of Jumping Up and Down

Harold and the Purple Crayon: Animals, Animals, Animals!

adapted by Liza Baker

What's the Book About?

Harold can go anywhere as long as he has his purple crayon and is inspired to draw. In this story, Harold draws an elephant, a camel, a herd of cheetahs, and a colony of penguins. Joining the animals means lots of action: jumping, running, sliding, and swinging. At the end of the exhausting adventure, Harold is happy to draw his way home and crawl back into his own bed.

Theme Connections

Colors   Imagination

Lesson Objectives

Children will:

1. Explore actions of various animals.
2. Explore creativity through art.
3. Explore imagination.
4. Explore a variety of movement skills.

Action Vocabulary

Dip	Race	Slide
Jump	Rest	Spray
Land	Run	Swing
Move	Skate	Walk

Concepts Explored

Back/forth	Fast	Tired
Big	Heavy	Up
Cold	Hot	Warm
Cover	On top	Wiggly
Down	Strong	

Developing Literacy Skills

Materials: Paper • Clipboards, one for each child • Purple crayons, one for each child

▶ This series of books featuring *Harold and the Purple Crayon* may be familiar to the children. Introduce the book's author, Liza Baker, and illustrators, Andy Chiang, Jose Lopez, and Kevin Murawski. Read the book's title to the children and show them the book cover. Be sure to point out the purple crayon Harold is holding. Tell the children that they will be joining Harold as he embarks on an animal adventure.

▶ Begin Story Time by giving each child several pieces of white paper, a clipboard, and a purple crayon. Invite the children to draw whatever comes to their imagination as you read the story without showing them any of the pictures. The idea is to encourage the children to create an image with their crayon before they see the illustrations in the book. Encourage the children to draw whatever they see in their minds when you read the story. Very young children will simply draw randomly on their papers. Accept all drawings.

▶ When you finish reading the story, give the children a moment to complete their last idea and then invite them to share their drawings with the class. This is a very different way of having children draw so some children might be shy about sharing their ideas. If time permits, reread the story and focus on Harold's crayon and his creations as he imagines his adventure.

Moving to the Story

▶ As you read the story a second time, invite the children to use their fingers as a purple crayon.

▶ As you read each page, allow enough time for the children to draw the animal and to act like the animal.

Developing Motor Skills

Art on the Move

Materials: Streamers, one for each child • CD player and music (see suggestions on the right), optional

▶ Give each child a streamer. If you do not have streamers, cut crepe paper into enough 4′ lengths to make two streamers for each child.

▶ Most of the action and concept words (see list on previous page) can be explored by using the streamers. If you have some favorite instrumental music that would go well with this activity, add it.

▶ After reading the story, tell the children that you are going to call out some words that were in the story. After you have called them out, the children are to move their streamers and their bodies in a way that shows they understand the meaning of each word. For example, if you say, "Jump fast!" (the first is an action word and the second is a concept word) together, all the child should jump fast. Or, if you say, "Swing back and forth" (the first is an action word and the second is a concept word) you would expect to see most of the children swinging their streamers back and forth.

▶ Begin with easy combinations and when the children are ready, challenge them with more combinations that are difficult to demonstrate.

Safety Tip: As always, it is important to remind the children to be aware of others around them and to note where their streamers are.

More Books to Share

Harold and the Purple Crayon: The Birthday Present by Valerie Garfield

Harold and the Purple Crayon: The Giant Garden by Patricia Lakin

Harold and the Purple Crayon: Harold Finds a Friend by Liza Baker

Music Suggestions

Kids in Motion by Greg and Steve. Songs: Animal Action I; The Balancing Act

Physical Ed by The Learning Station. Song: Run and Walk

Head, Shoulders, Knees, and Toes: And Other Action Rhymes

by Zita Newcome

What's the Book About?

This collection of traditional rhythms and songs features a cast of multi-ethnic children. More than fifty selections encourage hand clapping and on-your-feet action. Many selections include boxed illustrations showing finger and body movements. The book is perfect for an energetic group of children.

Theme Connections

Exercise
Parts of the body
Spatial concepts

Lesson Objectives

Children will:
1. Experience rhyming text.
2. Experience a steady beat.
3. Explore action rhymes.
4. Explore fingerplays.

Action Vocabulary

Hand clapping and imitation of body and hand motions to rhymes—the action vocabulary will depend on each rhyme. Actions may include slapping, clapping, snapping, tapping, hand rolls, and other actions.

Concepts Explored

Cooperation

Developing Literacy Skills

Materials: Chart paper • Markers

▶ Begin by introducing the book's author and illustrator, Zita Newcome. Read the title to the children and focus on the illustrations of the children, especially their actions. Ask the children to predict the storyline. They will be delighted to know that the book contains many of their favorite action songs and fingerplays. Invite the children to get up and move as you read each rhyme.

▶ Before beginning this lesson, choose three or four songs or rhymes from the book. Select ones that the children can do while sitting, standing, and with a partner.

▶ Print the chosen songs or rhymes on large chart paper. Add the illustrations that show the finger movements and body actions. Be sure to print the words and illustrations large enough for the children to see.

▶ Introduce the title of the first rhyme or song to the children. Familiarize the children with the beat of the rhyme. As you read the rhyme, use your voice to emphasize rhyming words. Point to the words as you read them and invite the children to clap along with you. Many emergent readers have memorized simple chants and songs. They will enjoy the opportunity to "read" with you.·

▶ Introduce the finger, hand, or body movements that go with the rhyme. Continue with the other rhymes that you prepared, as time allows.

▶ Save each chart so you and the children can revisit the rhymes and actions. Through repetition, children will soon memorize the rhymes, actions, and even begin to read some of the words.

Moving to the Story

Materials: Dress-up clothes, optional

▶ Many of the rhymes in this book can be acted out, such as "Head, Shoulders, Knees, and Toes," "Pat-a-Cake," "The Wheels on the Bus," and "Teddy Bear, Teddy Bear." Other rhymes, such as "The Three Bears," may be learned and performed by the children as part of a class or school performance. Young learners thoroughly enjoy choosing their favorite rhymes, chants, and songs and performing them for their parents or other classes.

▶ To add dramatic flare, bring out a box of dress-up clothes and props. Help older children make or collect simple stage props: a clock for "Hickory, Dickory, Dock," three chairs, bowls, and beds (carpet squares) for "The Three Bears," and a boat (large cardboard box) for "Here Is the Sea."

Safety Tips: Check props and dress-up clothes to make sure there are no small pieces that could pose a choking hazard. Be sure there is enough space for active learning.

Developing Motor Skills

Clap Time

Materials: CD player with suggested music • Appropriate props and dress-up clothes

▶ This book is a wonderful collection of over 50 favorite rhymes, chants, and songs with steady beats that can be clapped out individually or with a partner. Some pages have pictures for fingerplay actions.

▶ Select rhymes, chants, or poems that support your teaching goals, such as language development, gross motor activity, fine motor activity, body part identification, counting, or a topic related to a special theme or unit of study.

▶ Explore the music suggestions in this lesson plan (see list on the right). Children love to sing and the rhythmic beat of the music will help them memorize the words of each rhyme.

More Books to Share

Little Hands, Fingerplays, and Action Songs by Emily Stetson and Vicky Congdon

Off We Go! by Jane Yolen

Pocketful of Stars: Rhymes, Chants, and Lap Games by Felicity Williams

Music Suggestions

Because this book features a wide variety of classical/traditional children's rhymes and songs, the CDs suggested are those that contain the widest variety of songs that complement the book:

Here We Go Loopty Loo by The Learning Station

It's Toddler Time by Kimbo Educational

Movin' & Shakin' for Youngsters by Russ InVision

Here We Go, Harry

by Kim Lewis

What's the Book About?

Harry, Ted, and Lulu head out for an adventure on a breezy afternoon. Ted (a bear) and Lulu (a lamb) welcome the wind as they jump and tumble down a hill in the soft, summer grass. Harry (an elephant) is not able to fly like his friends. However, with the help of Ted and Lulu, Harry finally makes it down the hill. This is a wonderful story about friendship.

Theme Connections

Animals
Friendship
Self-confidence

Lesson Objectives

Children will:

1. Explore parts of the story (beginning, middle, and end).
2. Explore the concepts of encouragement and friendship.
3. Identify the story's main **characters.**
4. Experience a variety of movements.

Action Vocabulary

Blow	Hop	Run
Climb	Jump	Stop
Flap	Leap	Swoop
Float	Peer	Tumble
Fly	Roll	

Concepts Explored

Bottom	Light	Take-off
Down	Long	Top
Edge	Near	Up
Far	Small	Wide
High	Soft	

Developing Literacy Skills

Materials: Stuffed animals, one for each child

▶ Introduce the book's author and illustrator, Kim Lewis. Read the title of the book and ask the children to predict the storyline. Tell the children that the book is about three friends and their special friendship. Show the children the cover illustration as you introduce the main **characters,** Harry, Ted, and Lulu.

▶ The story's rich language, action words, and concepts are perfect for an interactive Story Time. Gather enough plush animals or puppets (bears, lambs, and elephants) so each child has one.

▶ As you read the story, emphasize the action words and concepts. Observe the children's actions as you read and make a mental note if a child does not seem to understand some of the words, such as *float, peer,* and *swoop.*

▶ When you are finished reading the story, invite the children to talk about the animals' friendship. How did they help Harry? How did Harry feel about their help? How do the children feel when a friend wants to help them learn something that they are afraid to do?

Moving to the Story

▶ Organize the children into groups of three to portray each of the three friends: Harry, Lola, and Ted.

▶ Reread the story and as you read each concept or action word, invite each character to act out the concept or action word.

▶ You may want to highlight the concept and action words in advance. Stop after reading each one to give the children time to act out that word.

Developing Motor Skills

Combining Actions

Materials: Assortment of props, such as ropes, cones, mats, hoops, scarves, climbing equipment • CD player and suggested music

▶ Ask the children to stand on one side of the room. When you say one of the following skills—hop, jump, leap, roll, tumble, or run—the children take turns doing each across the room.

▶ Help the children arrange an assortment of props around the room. Encourage the children to use the props with the actions, such as jumping with a rope, hopping over a scarf, or running around a cone.

▶ Combine each action word with several different concept words such as *jump near, jump far, jump high, jump down,* and *jump up.* Try different combinations. Allow the children to come up with their own action and concept combinations and then demonstrate the combination. Encourage their creativity.

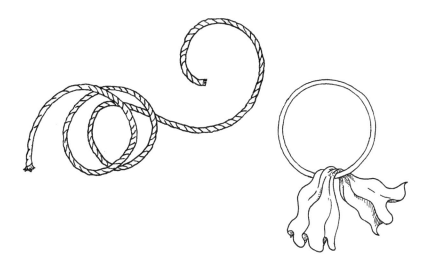

More Books to Share

Angelina's Dance of Friendship by James Mason and Katherine Holabird

Farfalina and Marcel by Holly Keller

Fox Makes Friends by Adam Relf

Little Quack's New Friend by Lauren Thompson

Music Suggestions

Musical Scarves & Activities by Kimbo Educational. Song: Let's Go Fly a Kite

Playtime Parachute Fun by Kimbo Educational. Song: Floating Cloud

Rockin' Reading Readiness by Kimbo Educational. Song: With Our Friends

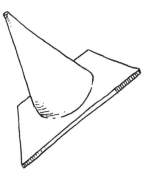

Hilda Must Be Dancing

by Karma Wilson, illustrated by Suzanne Watts

What's the Book About?

Hilda Hippo loves dancing and does it with flair. Trouble is, her dancing shook the jungle floor. The animals beg Hilda to try less-active hobbies, such as knitting and singing. Hilda, however, enjoys dancing too much to give it up. In desperation, the water buffalo ask her to try swimming. Hilda loves it because she can now do water ballet! This very noisy story is told in rhyme, with plenty of **onomatopoeia**.

Theme Connections

Animals	Self-confidence
Habitats	Self-esteem

Lesson Objectives

Children will:
1. Experience rhyming text.
2. Explore various movements.
3. Explore what it means to follow a hobby or interest.
4. Experience a variety of dance forms.

Action Vocabulary

Clap	Skip	Turn
Jump	Spin	Twist
Kick	Swim	Twirl
Leap	Trample	Whirl
Pirouette		

Concepts Explored (Dances)

Boogie	Samba
Flamenco	Tango
Rumba	Water ballet
Square dance	

Developing Literacy Skills

▶ Introduce the book's author, Karma Wilson, and illustrator, Suzanne Watts. Read the title of the book, share the illustrations on the cover, and ask the children to predict the storyline.

▶ You may want to take a few minutes to invite the children to share their dancing experiences. Take care to reinforce that dancing is for girls AND boys.

▶ Explain that the book is also about trying new things and following an interest.

▶ Before reading the story, read the words on the back cover. These words are ones that the children can repeat after you read them in the story.

▶ Whenever you read the **onomatopoeic** words (the capitalized words) and the repeated phrase, prompt the children to repeat the words after you say them.

▶ As you read the story, draw the children's attention to the wonderful illustrations, which show Hilda's joy and the frustration of the other animals.

▶ After you are finished reading the book, invite the children to share their experiences with trying new things and to talk about their interests.

Moving to the Story

▶ Invite the children to find their own place in the classroom.

▶ As you reread the story, pause after each action word long enough for each child to "try on" each of the words.

▶ Also encourage the children to express the sounds of words such as *Ka-Bump, Crash, Smash, Boom, Swisha, Clap,* and *Thump* by making those sounds with their voices or feet against the floor.

▶ After rereading the book, invite the children to make up movements to the dances in the book, such as the Square Dance, Rumba, Samba, and Tango.

Developing Motor Skills

Hilda Hippo Dance

Materials: CD player and CDs (see suggestions on the right)

▶ Review with the children each of the 13 action words (listed on the previous page). Let them demonstrate and play around with each of the 13 actions.

▶ Ask them to choose their four favorite actions and put these four actions together in any combination to make up their own Hilda Hippo Dance. Let the children work with a partner or in a group, if they prefer.

▶ After giving the children five minutes to make up their own Hilda Hippo Dance, ask everyone to sit around the circle.

▶ Let each child, pair, or group demonstrate their Hilda Hippo Dance. After the dance, the audience can call out each of the four action words that they saw being performed.

▶ Put on a CD and let everyone dance their Hilda Hippo Dance to the music.

Safety Tip: Remind the children to watch for others as they kick, twirl, pirouette, and leap.

More Books to Share

Dumpy La Rue by Elizabeth Winthrop
Lili at Ballet by Rachel Isadora
Rap a Tap Tap: Think of That! by Diane and Leo Dillon

Music Suggestions

A to Z, The Animals & Me by Kimbo Educational. Song: Hula Dancing Hippo
Dance Party Fun by Kimbo Educational. Songs: Teacher or children's choice, all are fun to try
Literacy in Motion by The Learning Station. Song: Head to Toe Dance

Hokey Pokey: Another Prickly Love Story

by Lisa Wheeler, illustrated by Janie Bynum

What's the Book About?

This is a great story about love, friendship and, as the title suggests, dancing. Cushion, the porcupine loves Barb, the hedgehog. Barb loves to dance, so Cushion asks his animal friends to teach him to dance, which is a disaster. Cushion realizes that his friendship with Barb is what helps him overcome his self-consciousness. The illustrations are full of expression and the text contains rhythmic passages and has great play with words.

Theme Connections

Animals	Friendship
Feelings	Self-confidence

Lesson Objectives

Children will:
1. Identify parts of story (beginning, middle, end).
2. Explore social skills.
3. Identify main **characters** in a story.
4. Experience various dance forms.

Action Vocabulary

Drag
Droop

Concepts Explored (Dances)

Bunny Hop	Rumba
Fox trot	Tango
Funky Chicken	Waltz
Hokey Pokey	

Developing Literacy Skills

▶ Introduce the book's author, Lisa Wheeler, and illustrator, Janie Bynum. Read the title to the children and show them the book cover. Ask the children to predict the storyline. After listening to their thoughts and ideas, tell your children that the story is about friendship and asking friends for help.

▶ Introduce the main characters. The porcupine (a boy) is named Cushion and Barb (a girl) is a hedgehog. Read the first three pages of the book to the children. Before continuing, help the children restate the problem.

▶ Invite the children to say the repeated phrase after you read it each time. This encourages children to interact with the text and helps them with language development and vocabulary building.

▶ Continue reading the story, emphasizing the names of the dances Cushion tries to learn.

▶ Because this story offers support for developing social skills, draw the children's attention to the faces of Cushion's friends after he has accidentally hurt them.

▶ When you are finished reading the story, invite the children to talk about their perceptions about how Cushion's friends felt and why. Ask the children why they thought Cushion might have been shy about asking Barb for help. Encourage the children to talk about their own experiences about asking for help and accidentally hurting a friend.

Moving to the Story

▶ Read the story again and encourage the children to explore the movements of jumping, hopping, and side **slide step** (see Glossary, page 195) when Cushion tries each of the dances.

Developing Motor Skills

Hokey Pokey, Bunny Hop, or Chicken Dance

Materials: CD player with music suggestions (see the following page)

▶ The three dances that are easiest and most developmentally appropriate for young children are the Hokey Pokey, the Bunny Hop, and the Chicken Dance. The instructions for these dances are on the insert of the *All-Time Favorite Dances* CD, or you may want to use your own instrumental variations. Consider the following variations for the Hokey Pokey and the Chicken Dance to make the activity more fun and/or easier for the children to learn.

▶ *Hokey Pokey*—For extra fun and variety, add a parachute. When you call out each body part, the children place that part of the body on top of the parachute (hands and elbows, and head), toward the parachute (hips and backside), or under the parachute (feet and whole self). When turning around, instruct the children to release the parachute with one hand, reach around behind them as they turn, and then regrasp the parachute with their second hand. When the children hear the words, "Do the Hokey Pokey" instruct them to shake the parachute up and down. You may want to practice all of the dance steps, with the parachute, before using the music.

▶ *The Funky Chicken or Chicken Dance* is fun and easy. Ask all the children to join in a circle or to scatter about the space and dance individually. The children copy you making a "beak," "wings," "tail-feathers," and then clap four times. Be certain that you know how to do the "Chicken Dance" because the children will be looking to you as the model. Some versions, such as the one suggested below, have additional instrumental music and steps. You may have the children turn in place, or all together in one large circle. Give the children the following cue words so they will have both visual and verbal cues:

  ▶ Beak (place both hands to the mouth and bring the thumb and fingers together as if "talking")
  ▶ Wings (place hands under armpits and wave with the elbows)
  ▶ Wiggle tail feathers (shake their bottoms)
  ▶ Clap (4 times)
  ▶ Circle (30 side slide steps, which may be easier when holding hands)
  ▶ Stop
  ▶ Start over with the beak.

Note: If the children do the Chicken Dance in a large circle with slide steps, it is easier to have all children hold hands and move to the beat of the music, as you count out 30 steps. There are 2 extra beats in the song (for a total of 32 beats) that give the children enough time to stop and get their hands ready to start again with the beak.

More Books to Share

Angelina's Dance of Friendship by James Mason and Katherine Holabird
Frog and Toad Are Friends by Arnold Lobel
Owen and Mzee: The True Story of a Remarkable Friendship by Isabella Hatkoff, Craig Hatkoff, and Dr. Paula Kahumbu
Porcupining!: A Prickly Love Story by Lisa Wheeler

Music Suggestions

All-Time Favorite Dances by Kimbo Educational. Songs: Hokey Pokey; Bunny Hop; The Chicken (Dance)

Hop Jump
by Ellen Stoll Walsh

What's the Book About?

Betsy is a frog who discovers dancing! Her frog friends are curious about Betsy's new discovery and soon join her. This little story packs a big message about tolerance and following your heart. Read this delightful story to the children and invite them to think of how they might dream to be different.

Theme Connections

Acceptance
Animals
Friendship
Imagination

Lesson Objectives

Children will:
1. Explore the concept of curiosity.
2. Explore the concept of uniqueness.
3. Explore various movement skills.

Action Vocabulary

Dance
Float
Hop
Jump
Leap
Turn
Twist

Concepts Explored

Personal space
General space
Spatial awareness

Developing Literacy Skills

▶ Introduce the book's author and illustrator, Ellen Stoll Walsh. Read the title of the book and show the children the illustrations on the cover. Invite the children to predict the book's storyline.

▶ The simple title and clear illustration will lead most children to conclude that the story is about frogs hopping and jumping. Allow enough time for the children to share their experiences with frogs.

▶ Draw the children's attention to the blue frog on the cover of the book. Ask the children if they can guess why that frog is blue. Explain that this frog's name is Betsy and they should watch her closely throughout the story.

▶ Engage the children in this story by inviting them to create hand motions for the action vocabulary words in the book: *hopping, jumping, leaping, turning, twisting, dancing,* and *floating.* For example, before reading the story, ask the children to make one of their hands a "lily pad" and the other hand a "frog." Two fingers will act as the frog's hind legs. As you read the story, the children make their "frogs" practice each skill. This requires that the children quickly determine the meaning of the words and create actions that interpret the words.

▶ After you have finished reading the story, ask the children what they thought made Betsy unique. Encourage the children to share their experiences and feelings about doing something different from their friends. Point out the variety of responses so the children get a sense that not everyone thinks or acts the same way, and that is okay!

Moving to the Story

Materials: CD player and instrumental music of your choice, optional

▶ Divide the children into groups of four or five. One child in each group acts out the part of Betsy, and the other children in the group play the parts of the other frogs. After they act out the story, ask the children which part is more fun, Betsy's or the other frogs'. Does Betsy need more room to float, turn, twist, and dance than the other frogs? Do the other frogs want Betsy to do what they do or something different?

▶ In the story, Betsy wants to float like the leaves. Ask the children if she can really do that. Can she pretend to float? Invite the children to move lightly in a floating manner, just like the leaves. Help the children bring meaning and understanding to the action vocabulary words by acting them out.

Developing Motor Skills

Ready, Set, Move!

Materials: Tape, poly spots, carpet squares, or another way to help children identify their own place • Classroom objects, such as a stuffed animal or beanbag • Piece of paper, a towel, or a length of rope • Leaf, feather, balloon, bubbles, or scarves, optional

▶ This story is full of **locomotor skills** (see Glossary pages 188-199) for the children to learn and practice for better coordination. Before you read the story again, invite the children to hop, jump, leap, turn, and twist, allowing enough time for them to explore these skills, or after reading the story, stand up with the children and together try each locomotor skill, chanting the word three times. For example, "Hop, hop, hop," or "Jump, jump, jump." This is a brain-friendly activity that helps integrate the action with the sound and the rhythm or cadence of the word.

▶ If the children are not certain how to leap, demonstrate the action for them, if possible. If you are unable to do the action yourself, have a child demonstrate the action. Place an object, such as a carpet square, stuffed animal, or beanbag on the floor. Show them (or have someone else show them) how to leap over the object. Ask the children if they need more room to leap, turn, and twist than they do to hop and jump. Why?

▶ Invite the children to stand up, hold their arms out, and turn around, or to lie down with their arms crisscrossed over their chest, and roll over, and over, and over. You may notice that the children will experience different degrees of dizziness when rolling compared to turning. This difference is because of the position of the head. This important movement stimulates the balance (**vestibular**) system and helps to ground or calm a child.

▶ Demonstrate the action of twisting by twisting a piece of paper, a towel, or rope. Ask the children to demonstrate what body parts they can twist, and in what directions. Invite the children to try twisting as they turn.

▶ If you have some leaves, feathers, balloons, bubbles, or scarves, you might use these items to demonstrate the word "float." Ask the children if the objects move slowly or quickly when they float. Say the names of one of these objects and ask the children to pretend to float just as these objects would.

More Books to Share

Hop, Hop, Hop! by Ann Whitford Paul
Jump, Kangaroo, Jump! by Stuart J. Murphy
Jump Up! by Dan Zanes
The Kangaroo Who Couldn't Hop by Robert Cox

Music Suggestions

Kids in Action by Greg and Steve. Song: Can You Leap Like a Frog?
Kids in Motion by Greg and Steve. Song: All the Ways of Jumping Up and Down
Rowdy Ropes by Dinotrax. Song: I Can Jump Like a Big Green Frog
"So Big" Activity Songs for Little Ones by Hap Palmer. Song: Five Little Monkeys

Safety Tips: Developing the awareness of personal space and general space requires practice. Remind the children that when they share space they must be aware of others. Remind the children also to be careful when turning around and around. They may get dizzy and fall.

Hopscotch Around the World

by Mary D. Lankford, illustrated by Karen Milone

What's the Book About?

This book is a wonderful collection of hopscotch games from 16 countries. The illustrations accompanying each game depict young children from their country playing hopscotch. A few interesting details about the countries and a world map extend the learning opportunities. You can adapt the games easily as the children develop motor skills.

Theme Connections

Exploring cultures
Numbers

Lesson Objectives

Children will:
1. Explore number concepts.
2. Explore spatial concepts.
3. Experience movement skills.
4. Explore language from other cultures.

Action Vocabulary

Hop
Jump
Toss

Concepts Explored

Balance
Hopscotch

Developing Literacy Skills

▶ Introduce the book's author, Mary D. Lankford, and illustrator, Karen Milone, to the children. Read the title and share the front cover.

▶ Be prepared for lively discussion about this book! Many children will instantly recognize the hopscotch grid on the cover. Tell the children that the book describes hopscotch games played by children around the world.

▶ Before beginning the Story Time, read the information about playing hopscotch. Consider the developmental level of the children and make a few notes of interest about the game.

▶ Share the world map, at the front of the book, with the children. Although the map is out of date, it is a great way to show children that children all over the world play hopscotch. Although most young children do not understand where each country is in the world, they will be able to get a sense that many, many children play hopscotch and children from different countries play it in different ways.

▶ Share information about playing hopscotch. The children may enjoy knowing how many different objects children use for a puck and what the variety of names are for the lines and boxes in a hopscotch grid.

Moving to the Story

▶ Because this book describes hopscotch games from around the world, the words of the various languages offer the children a chance to learn a few words from a variety of cultures with the common tie of hopscotch.

▶ Depending on the children's developmental level of understanding, read and/or share the pictures on a few of the pages. You may want to select several foreign language words to teach the children.

▶ When you are finished looking at the book with the children, invite them to play a game of hopscotch with you.

Developing Motor Skills

Beanbag Toss

Materials: Beanbags • Hoops

▶ It is best to do this activity on a sidewalk, on a gym floor, or in a multipurpose room.

- This activity allows children to practice throwing an object (a beanbag) in a specific place (a hoop), a skill needed to play hopscotch.
- Help the children create groups of four. Provide four beanbags and two hoops for each group. Space the two hoops about 5' apart from each other.
- Position two children at one hoop (the receiving end) and two children at the other hoop (the tossing end). Place all four beanbags at the tossing end, so that each child gets two beanbags.
- After the two children at the tossing end finish tossing their two beanbags into the hoop, the children at the receiving end pick up the beanbags and toss them back in the hoop at the opposite end. Continue the activity for several minutes. Each child may want to count the number of successful beanbag tosses into a hoop.
- If some children need an additional challenge, replace the hoops with smaller hoops. Hopscotch squares are small, so the children will benefit from tossing beanbags into successively smaller hoops.

Hopscotch
Materials: Chalk or tape • A puck (beanbag, flat stone, or other object that does not roll) for each child

- Depending on the setting, use chalk or tape to create hopscotch patterns.
- Begin by making certain that all of the children in your class know how to hop, jump, and toss a puck. Give each child a chance to hop and jump through the entire pattern without a puck before playing the game. Remind the children that they must also be able to balance on one foot as they reach down for their puck or beanbag, so they might also want to practice that action.
- Show the children the hopscotch pattern used in Great Britain, Poland, or the United States. Help the children form groups of two or three. Each group has its own hopscotch pattern drawn on the playground or taped on the floor.
- Begin by teaching the children one of the hopscotch games found on pages 22, 32, and 42, respectively. In general, these variations are easier than most, and can be learned quickly.
- Provide sidewalk chalk for your children so they can experiment with drawing their own hopscotch grids. Provide copies of their favorite version. This is a terrific game to play and hand down to future generations. After all, it has lasted at least 2000 years!

More Books to Share
Chicken Chickens by Valeri Gorbachev
Sidewalk Games Around the World by Arlene Erlbach

Safety Tip: Remind the children that when tossing their puck they must always be mindful of others and to aim as best as they can to hit the target, and not other children.

I'm a Little Teapot
by Iza Trapani

What's the Book About?

This version of "I'm a Little Teapot" includes expanded verses. The teapot shares its dreams with a young boy and girl. The dreams take them many places, to China, to Mexico, to an opera, and to another planet. The story ends back in the kitchen where teapot makes tea for everyone. The rhyming verses are delightful and the illustrations are beautiful.

Theme Connections

Exploring cultures
Friendship
Imagination

Lesson Objectives

Children will:
1. Experience rhyming text.
2. Explore imitation.
3. Explore the concept of "imagine."
4. Experience singing a traditional song.

Action Vocabulary

Float	Row
Fly	Sway
Pour	Tip
Race	

Concepts Explored

Bull fighting	Kite flying
Fox hunting	Out
Hide-and-seek	Peek-a-boo
High	Short
Imagining	Stout

Developing Literacy Skills

▶ Introduce the book's author and illustrator, Iza Trapani. Read the title to the children and ask them to predict the book's storyline. Most youngsters will be familiar with this action song and rhyme.

▶ Stand and lead the children in singing the original verse by Clarence Kelley and George Sanders. Invite them to perform the actions with you. When you are finished, ask the children to sit down and get ready to hear the rest of the story. Tell them to listen for variations from the original.

▶ As you read the book, focus on the rhyming words. You may want to pause at the end of each phrase so the children can suggest a word that completes the rhyme. Point to various illustrations to help cue the children as you read.

Moving to the Story

▶ Invite the children to stand and perform the original action song one more time. This repetition will help the children remember the words.

▶ Short songs offer an opportunity to foster emergent reading skills. You may want to copy the song on large chart paper, add illustrations for the actions, and hang it on the wall near the Circle/Story Time area. Once the children memorize the words, they will have an easier time "reading" along with you, as you point to the words on the chart.

Developing Motor Skills

The Magic Scarf

Materials: Scarves • CD player and Can Cockatoos Count by Twos? CD by Hap Palmer, with the song "Magic Scarf" on it, optional

▶ Although "I'm a Little Teapot" is a traditional children's song, this particular version is also about imagination. Give each child a scarf. Ask them to imagine things they could do or pretend to be with their "magic" scarf.

▶ If you have the CD by Hap Palmer, tell the children that the activities that the teapot did in the story are also things that the scarf in Hap Palmer's "Magic Scarf" does. Play the music and see if the children can pick out the imagined activities in the song that are similar to those dreamed by the teapot in the book.

Safety Tip: Remind the children that if they look up to toss and catch their scarf to also be aware of those around them.

Steady Beat

Materials: CD player and CDs (see suggestions on the right)

▶ This is a perfect song/story to explore steady beat. Invite the children to sing the song along with you as you clap out the underlying steady beat. Phyllis Weikart's book (see page 206) explains steady beat if this term is unfamiliar to you.

▶ After the children have clapped out the steady beat of the song, invite them to stand up and jump the steady beat as they clap and sing the song. Ask the children to explore other movement activities such as marching or hopping to the steady beat as they clap and sing.

▶ Find the steady beat of other traditional songs. Ask the children if they can keep the steady beat tempo the same for all traditional songs, or can they make the tempo change to become faster or slower? Allow the children time to play with the steady beat tempo to develop an understanding of the constancy of the steady beat.

More Books to Share

How Much Is That Doggie in the Window? by Iza Trapani
Mary Had a Little Lamb by Iza Trapani
Shoo Fly by Iza Trapani
Twinkle, Twinkle, Little Star by Iza Trapani

Music Suggestions

All-Time Children's Favorites by The Learning Station. Song: Medley: Twinkle, Twinkle, Little Star; I'm a Little Teapot
Can Cockatoos Count by Twos? by Hap Palmer. Songs: Magic Scarf; Toss It High, Let It Fly
Get Funky and Musical Fun by The Learning Station. Song: From Your Seat

Imagine
by Alison Lester

What's the Book About?

Two children pretend to be in different places, such as a jungle, the ocean, and a safari. The following two-page spread is an intricate drawing of the places they imagine. Along the border are the names of the animals found in that environment. The children will want to spend lots of time searching for the creatures. There is a key in the back of the book to help you and the children locate all the animals.

Theme Connections

Animals
Imagination

Lesson Objectives

Children will:
1. Experience rhyming text.
2. Explore a variety of environments in the world.
3. Explore animal movements.
4. Explore the concept of "imagining."

Action Vocabulary

Attack	Lurk
Crash	Prowl
Dash	Rock
Dig	Stampede
Drift	Stomp
Glide	Swoop
Gallop	Thump
Hide	Toboggan
Jump	Wave

Concept Explored

Imagination

Developing Literacy Skills

▶ The story takes the children through eight environments. Read the book's title to the children and invite them to imagine exploring each environment in the book.

▶ Introduce the book's author and illustrator, Alison Lester. Explain to the children that Alison Lester carefully illustrated each environment.

▶ Begin by reading the book and using your voice to emphasize the rhyming text. The fifth and seventh lines of each verse rhyme. Pause before reading the last word of each verse so the children can try to complete the rhyme.

▶ As you read the story, point out the illustrations on the page after each verse. The illustrations depict children at home, engaged in imaginative play.

▶ Show the children the names of the animals in the borders around the two-page spreads of each environment. Read the names of two or three animals and invite children to find the animal on the page. Be sure you give every child a turn.

▶ At the end of the story, tell the children they will be using their imaginations to move like some of the animals in the book.

Moving to the Story

▶ Reread the book and invite the children to act out the verses as you read them.

▶ Show the environment page spreads but do not spend time naming all the animals. This will allow the children's creativity to flow uninterrupted.

Developing Motor Skills

Under the Sea

Materials: Scarves (jellyfish) • Streamers or crepe paper cut into 4' lengths (seaweed) • Headbands with pipe cleaners attached (crab antenna with eyes) • Parachute (ocean) • CD player with ocean music, if possible

▶ Take a look at the sea life page with the children and invite them to choose to be a crab doing a crab walk, a jellyfish making up and down movements, seaweed swaying back and forth, a dolphin or other fish swimming, or the ocean gently waving (parachute).
Note: Be sure you have children to hold the parachute.

- The parachute is the ocean. The children hold the edges and gently move the parachute up and down to resemble ocean waves.
- Give the remaining children the appropriate props. If possible, play music that has ocean sounds in it.
- The children around the parachute hold it high over their heads and gently raise and lower it no more than a foot or so.
- The seaweed sways gently back and forth under the parachute. The other sea creatures move in a circle around the outside perimeter of the parachute, waiting for you to call them under the parachute.
- When you call the crabs, they all go under the parachute and crabwalk around the seaweed and then come back out. Then call the dolphins that jump, twist, play around the seaweed, and then come back out. Then call the jellyfish that hold the scarves overhead, bob up and down under the ocean (parachute) and around the seaweed, and then come back out. Continue with each different group of sea life until all have had a turn.
- The children trade places so all children have a turn to move under the sea.

Arctic Animal Tag
- Invite the children to try to waddle like a penguin; walk on just their hands (flippers) and drag their legs like a seal, sea lion, or walrus; bear walk like a polar bear; glide like an albatross; or swim like a whale.
- After everyone has had a chance to explore each of the various animal walks, they are now ready to play Arctic Animal Tag. All of the children move to one side of the room.
- Choose one child to be "IT." IT stands in the middle of the room or space. Each one of the rest of the children decides which Arctic animal he or she wants to be.
- IT calls out an animal (polar bear, penguin, seal, whale, or albatross), and the children who have chosen to be that animal try to get from one side of the room to the other without being tagged by IT.
- IT can move in any of the five ways listed and can change any time. Once a child has chosen an animal, he or she must remain that animal until he or she crosses over to the opposite side. The children may change after each cross over if they choose to.
- If IT calls out "Arctic Play," *all* the animals must move from one side of the room to the other and try not to be caught.
- There are two possible ways to play. One is that all children who are tagged join IT in the center until all animals have been tagged, or whoever IT tags first becomes the new IT.

More Books to Share
Alexander's Pretending Day by Bunny Crumpacker
Edward and the Pirates by David McPhail
Grandma Helps Us Pretend by Carol Burns

Music Suggestions
Another World by The Brain Store. Songs: Entire CD
Fun and Games by Greg and Steve. Song: Hello World (instrumental)

Safety Tips: Keep the area safe by removing everything that children might run into. Remind IT to do a two-finger tag, or use a small sponge or foam ball to tag the Arctic animals.

Imagine a Day
by Sarah L. Thomson, illustrated by Rob Gonsalves

What's the Book About?
The artistic talent of illustrator Rob Gonzales really carries this book. His stunning, surreal acrylic paintings make an ordinary day extraordinary. *Imagine a Day* will spark children's creativity and transport them beyond the limits of their everyday world.

Theme Connections
Cooperation
Imagination

Lesson Objectives
Children will:
1. Explore the concept of imagining.
2. Experience verbalizing thoughts and ideas.
3. Explore interpretive movement.
4. Experience a variety of movement skills.

Action Vocabulary
Balance	Ride
Build	Rock
Climb	Soar
Dive	Swim
Fall	Swing
Float	Touch

Concepts Explored
Above	Gentle
Around	High
Between	Imagining
Bridging	Tangle
Down	Underneath
Explore	Up

Developing Literacy Skills

▶ Introduce the book's author, Sarah L. Thomson, and illustrator, Rob Gonsalves. Read the title to the children and ask them to predict the book's storyline.

▶ The illustrations in this book are remarkable so be sure to give the children ample time to explore the book's front and back covers.

▶ Discuss the concept of imagination with the children. Refer to the cover again and ask the children to imagine what it would be like to be on top of the cliff, building a large sandcastle. Encourage the children to share their thoughts. Invite the children to continue their imagining as you read the story.

▶ The illustrator's paintings are captivating. To engage the children in this story, invite them to sit next to a friend. Pause after you read each page and show the two-page spread to the children. Allow the friends to share their thoughts and ideas about how they would feel if they were in the picture.

▶ If you are short on time, pause after every other illustration. The conversation does not have to be a long time, just a minute or so. Remind the children to take turns so each child is able to speak.

▶ The story is full of action words, such as *balance, build,* and *climb,* and concepts, such as *above, around,* and *between.* Emphasize these words as you read and point to the illustrations that support the words. This will help children understand actions or concepts that may be new to them. It will also prepare them for a more active lesson using their new vocabulary.

Moving to the Story

▶ Read the book again and as you show the children each page spread, encourage them to figure out how they want to demonstrate the action or image. They can work with a partner, with a group, or by themselves.

▶ As they act out the story, encourage them to be creative. There are no right or wrong thoughts or ideas.

Developing Motor Skills

Body Bridge Building
▶ Ask the children to form groups of three.
▶ With the children, look at the second picture in the book (the human bridge).
▶ Ask each group of three children to make a human bridge.

Safety Tip: Be sure the children do *not* try to stand on one another's shoulders as in the picture.

The Tangle Game
▶ Ask all of the children to stand in a circle and hold hands.
▶ Choose two children to be the "untanglers." Those two children stand outside the circle, turn around, and hide their eyes while the children in the circle go *under, over, inside*, and *outside* the circle to tangle themselves up. The only rule is that no one can let go of hands. You may need to help the children with this step.
▶ After everyone has tangled the circle as much as they can, call the two untanglers to come and untangle the children. They figure out how to reverse the tangle of children and bring the circle back to everyone standing and holding hands.
▶ This game is great for developing children's creativity, **spatial awareness**, and problem solving. Allow enough time for everyone to be an untangler.

Concept Exploration
Materials: Carpet square or hoop for each pair of children
▶ Ask the children to each find a partner. Give a carpet square or hoop to each pair.
▶ Tell the children that when you say a concept (see list on previous page), such as *above, down,* or *underneath*, they are to demonstrate that particular concept using their bodies and the hoop or carpet square. For example, if you say *underneath* the partners might sit underneath the carpet square and hold it over their heads, or they might lie down underneath the carpet square.
▶ Describe for the class how each pair has demonstrated the concept. For example, "Rosie and Jose are holding their hoop *high* above their heads."

More Books to Share
Edward in the Jungle by David McPhail
Edward and the Pirates by David McPhail
Imagine a Night by Sarah L. Thomson
A Quiet Place by Douglas Wood

Music Suggestions
Another World by The Brain Store. Songs: Entire CD
Music for Thinking by The Arcangelos Chamber Ensemble and the Center for Psychoacoustic Research. Songs: Entire CD

In the Small, Small Pond
by Denise Fleming

What's the Book About?
This Caldecott Honor book about a pond is filled with vibrant illustrations and energetic, rhyming text, full of **alliteration** and **onomatopoeia**. The colorful pictures take the pond animals from spring, through summer and fall, and into winter. The action words will have the children wiggling and jiggling in no time.

Theme Connections
Animals   Seasons
Habitats

Lesson Objectives
Children will:
1. Experience rhyming text.
2. Explore alliteration.
3. Explore onomatopoeic words.
4. Explore interpretive movement.

Action and Sound Vocabulary
Wiggle/jiggle/wriggle
Waddle/wade/parade
Hover/shiver/quiver
Drowse/doze/close
Lash/lunge/plunge
Splitter/splatter/scatter
Circle/swirl/twirl
Sweep/swoop/scoop
Click/clack/crack
Dabble/dip/flip
Splish/splash/flash
Pile/pack/stack
Chill/breeze/freeze

Concepts Explored
The concepts are imbedded in the Action and Sound Vocabulary.

Developing Literacy Skills
▶ Introduce the book's author and illustrator, Denise Fleming. Read the title to the children and ask them to predict the book's storyline.
▶ After a brief conversation, suggest that the children imagine an adventure that takes them to a pond. As they peer through the reeds at the edge of the pond, the pond comes to life!
▶ Tell the children that when you read the book, they are to imagine being the critter in each picture. As you read, use **voice inflection** to emphasize the rhyme, **alliteration**, and onomatopoeic words.
▶ Reread the story a second time and invite the children to use their hands, bodies, or voices to act out the movements and sounds the creatures in the story are making.
▶ Pause at the end of each phrase so the children can say the word that completes the rhyme.

Moving to the Story
▶ Reread the story and invite everyone to stand and act out the action and sound words and review the pond creature that goes with each set of rhyming words.

All terms in bold are explained in greater detail in the Glossary on Appendix pages 188-199.

Developing Motor Skills
Pond Critter Charades
Materials: None
▶ The Action and Sound Vocabulary listed on the left is grouped according to rhyme and alliteration. Review with the children the names of each of the animals, along with each animal's three descriptive words. Now they are ready for Pond Critter Charades.
▶ Ask each child to find a partner. Without the other children hearing, assign each pair one of the animals in the book: the tadpoles, geese, dragonflies, turtles, herons, minnows, whirligigs, swallows, crabs, ducks, raccoons, and the muskrats.
▶ Invite one pair at a time to come to the middle of the room and act out the actions and sounds of their assigned creature. The other children guess which pond critter the pair is acting out.

▶ To make it more challenging, divide the class into two teams and alternate taking turns to see how much time it takes the opposite team to guess the pond critter.

▶ You may also want to talk with the children about other critters that live in or around a pond. Put rhyming words together for those creatures and act them out.

More Books to Share
Are You a Dragonfly? by Judy Allen
It's Mine! by Leo Lionni
Little Quack's New Friend by Lauren Thompson
Splash! by Ann Jonas

Music Suggestions
Charlotte Diamond's World by Charlotte Diamond. Song: Splishin' and Splashin'
Rockin' Reading Readiness by Kimbo Educational. Song: Rhyming Word Shuffle (Rhyming Word Families)
Tony Chestnut & Fun Time Action Songs by The Learning Station. Song: Way Down Yonder
The Wide-Mouthed Bullfrog by Mar Harmon. Song: The Wide-Mouthed Bullfrog

In the Tall, Tall Grass
by Denise Fleming

What's the Book About?

A young child peering through the tall grass sees the sun is high in the sky, as animals crunch, munch, dart, dip, strum, and drum. As bats loop and swoop, the stars come out and the full moon rises. The animals bid the tall, tall grass "goodnight." The colors are bold and bright and the simple, but language-rich text bursts with vibrant verbs and boisterous **onomatopoeia**.

Theme Connections

Animals
Habitats
Imagination
Opposites

Lesson Objectives

Children will:
1. Experience rhyming text.
2. Explore **alliteration.**
3. Explore **onomatopoeic words.**
4. Explore interpretive movement.

Action and Sound Vocabulary

Crunch/munch/lunch
Dart/dip/sip
Strum/drum/hum
Crack/snap/flap
Pull/tug/lug
Slip/slide/glide
Ritch/ratch/scratch
Skitter/scurry/hurry
Zip/zap/snap
Hip/hop/flop
Stop/go/glow
Lunge/loop/swoop

Developing Literacy Skills

▶ Introduce the book's author and illustrator, Denise Fleming. Read the title to the children and ask them to predict the book's storyline. Invite the children to imagine lying in tall grass on a sunny morning, taking a nature tour by using their imagination.

▶ Before reading the book to the children, tell the children to imagine being the animal in each picture as they listen to the story. Use **voice inflection** to emphasize rhyme, **alliteration**, and onomatopoeic words.

▶ Reread the story a second time and invite the children to use their hands or voices to act out the movements and sounds the animals are making. Ask the children to say the words as they dramatize each one.

▶ Pause at the end of each phrase so the children can say the word that completes the rhyme.

▶ The end of the story is a great invitation to curl up, take a deep breath, and rest before moving to the next activity.

Moving to the Story

▶ This story is similar to *In the Small, Small Pond*, also by Denise Fleming. Take each set of three words from the action and sound vocabulary list. Give the children a few seconds to think about the words and perhaps to remember the animals that did the action.

▶ Ask the children to demonstrate how to move using the words together.

▶ Invite the children to make up their own animal or other movement possibilities.

Developing Motor Skills

Animal Charades

Materials: CD player with suggested music (see list on the next page)

▶ The Action and Sound Vocabulary is grouped according to its rhyming/alliteration partners. Review the names of each of the animals, along with the three words associated with each one. Now the children are ready for Animal Charades.

▶ Ask each child to find a partner. Without the other children hearing, assign each pair one of the animals in the book: the caterpillars, hummingbirds, bees, chicken, ants, snake, mole, beetles, frogs, rabbits, fireflies, and bats.

More Books to Share

Camping Out by Mercer Mayer
The Happily Ever Afternoon by
    Sharon Jennings
The Monster in Harry's Backyard by
    Karen Gray Ruelle
One Wide Sky: A Bedtime Lullaby
    by Deborah Wiles

Music Suggestions

Rockin' Down the Road by Greg
    and Steve. Song: The Green
    Grass Grew All Around
Rockin' Reading Readiness by Kimbo
    Educational. Songs: Tongue
    Twister Twist; Rhyming Word
    Shuffle
Walter the Waltzing Worm by Hap
    Palmer. Song: Walter the
    Waltzing Worm

▶ Invite one pair at a time to come to the middle of the room and act
   out the actions and sounds of their assigned animal. The other children
   guess which animal the pair is acting out.

▶ For an additional challenge, divide the class into teams and alternate
   taking turns to see how much time it takes the opposite team to guess
   the animal.

▶ You may also want to talk with the children about other animals that
   live in or around a grassy meadow. Put rhyming words together for
   those creatures and act them out.

The Itsy Bitsy Spider

by Iza Trapani

What's the Book About?

Iza Trapani takes this classic tale and adds more verses with obstacles for the little spider to overcome. The verses provide additional fun and action to the story. Trapani's watercolor illustrations are beautiful and bring the story to life.

Theme Connections

Cooperation
Imagination
Spiders

Lesson Objectives

Children will:

1. Experience singing a traditional song.
2. Explore imitation.
3. Explore rhyming text.
4. Experience various movement skills.

Action Vocabulary

Climb	Plop
Creep	Ran
Fall	Rest
Flick	Slip
Jump	Spin
Knock	Wash
Land	Weave

Concepts Explored

Down	Out
Off	Up

Developing Literacy Skills

▶ Introduce the story's author and illustrator, Iza Trapani. Share the book's front cover with the children and ask them to predict the storyline.

▶ Many children will be familiar the traditional song and will be delighted to hear a story about Itsy Bitsy Spider. Tell them that Itsy Bitsy Spider is determined to climb, because that's what spiders do!

▶ Begin Story Time by asking the children to sing the first part of the book with you. The first few pages follow the traditional song. Invite the children to act out the parts of the song, using hand and body movements:

  ▶ climb (the spider)—use finger movements that show upward movement

  ▶ down (the rain)—make hand movements from up high to down low

  ▶ sun (dried the rain)—hold arms up in a circle and sway from side to side

▶ The children can sit or stand as you read. The exact hand motions are not important, as many children will have prior experience with this action song and may want to show you what they have learned.

▶ Continue reading the story, pausing just before the end of sentences so the children can complete the sentence with a rhyming word.

▶ Draw the children's attention to the various objects that Itsy Bitsy Spider attempts to climb. Be sure to allow enough time for the children to enjoy the beautiful watercolor illustrations.

▶ After reading the story, invite the children to share their ideas about Itsy Bitsy Spider's climbing adventures and ask the why they think the spider was able to accomplish her climbing goals.

Moving to the Story

▶ Suggest that the children get down on the floor in a spider walk position.

▶ Remind them that they have already acted out the parts with their hands. Read the story again and encourage them to spider walk throughout the story.

▶ Spider walking takes lots of muscle strength, so when Itsy Bitsy falls down in the story, they can sit on their bottoms, and put their feet up in the air until she begins to climb again. The difficulty of spider walking is similar to the difficult time Itsy Bitsy Spider had getting to a place where she can build her web.

Developing Motor Skills

Spider Tag

Materials: None

- ▶ Ask all of the children to gather on one side of the activity area. This area is the "base."
- ▶ Choose one child to be Itsy Bitsy. That child stands on the opposite end of the room.
- ▶ This game is similar to "Mother, May I?" Itsy Bitsy will say something such as, "Jump four times toward me." The children respond, "Itsy Bitsy, may I?" If Itsy Bitsy says, "Yes," the children move forward.
- ▶ Itsy Bitsy changes the movements, such as walk backward two steps, hop five steps, run in place six steps, skip two steps, and so on. As the children get closer to Itsy Bitsy, the spider may respond, "No, you may not," at any time.
- ▶ When Itsy Bitsy says, "No, you may not," this is the signal that Itsy Bitsy will try to tag as many children as he or she can before they are safely back on "base."
- ▶ Continue playing until everyone who wants to be Itsy Bitsy has had a turn.

Safety Tip: Remind the children to tag gently.

Cooperative Spider Walks

Materials: None

- ▶ Help the children form groups of four. Tell the children that spiders have eight legs, and that four children in a group (two legs each) will add up to eight legs.
- ▶ Ask the children to stand one behind the other. Each child bends over and extends one hand between his or her legs to the child standing behind him or her. The child behind grasps the extended hand.
- ▶ Each group of four children that created a connected "spider" uses cooperation to move around without breaking apart.
- ▶ Another way to do cooperative spider walks is to pair each child with a partner. The two children are on their hands and knees with the child behind holding onto the ankles of the child in front. Each pair crawls cooperatively around the room.

More Books to Share

Diary of a Spider by Doreen Cronin
Little Miss Spider by David Kirk
Miss Spider's Tea Party by David Kirk
The Very Busy Spider by Eric Carle

Music Suggestions

All-Time Children's Favorites by The Learning Station. Song: Itsy Bitsy Spider
Bugsters Tunes & Tales by Russ InVision. Song: Spiders Life
It's Toddler Time by Kimbo Educational. Song: Itsy Bitsy Spider

Jumping Day

by Barbara Juster Esbensen, illustrated by Maryann Cocca-Leffler

What's the Book About?

Children will jump for joy when you read this book about a little girl who jumps from the moment she wakes up until she jumps in bed at night. The little girl is as cheerful as the vibrant colors on each page. The rhythmic verses are as energetic as the little girl.

Theme Connections

Exercise
Opposites

Lesson Objectives

Children will:

1. Experience rhyme in text.
2. Explore a variety of ways to jump.
3. Explore directional concepts.
4. Explore interpretive movement.

Action Vocabulary

Jump

Concepts Explored

Down
In
Into
Out
Over
Under
Up

Developing Literacy Skills

▶ This book is perfect for very young children. Introduce the book's author, Barbara Juster Esbensen, and illustrator, Maryann Cocca-Leffler, and read the title. Tell the children to keep their eyes on the little girl in the book as she jumps all day long from the moment she wakes up until she goes to bed at night.

▶ Invite the children to participate in the story by jumping their fingers up and down on their legs. The children can use their fingers to jump *up, down, into, over,* and *under* an imaginary object. This will help children understand location or placement prepositions.

▶ The rhyming text is simple, which makes it easy for the children to follow along when you read the story. Ask the children to help you "read" the book by suggesting words to complete the rhyming phrase.

▶ When you finish reading the story, ask the children if they would like to have a Jumping Day. The following activities give them an opportunity to be active all day long. They will have so much fun that they might ask for a Jumping Day every week!

Moving to the Story

▶ Invite the children to jump throughout the day. Tell them that jumping is harder than walking, so jumping exercises their heart muscle and makes their leg muscles stronger.

▶ Suggest that the children jump down the hall, jump to snack and lunch, jump outside, and jump everywhere they go. At the end of the day, ask the children what it was like to jump everywhere. Was it easy or difficult? Was it fun?

Developing Motor Skills

Jumping Day

Materials: Use any equipment you have available for the children to explore the skill of jumping, using the concepts explored. For example:

- ▶ Hoops (out or into)
- ▶ Parachute (under)
- ▶ Ropes (over)
- ▶ Soft Steps (up and down)
- ▶ Stack mats (up and down)

▶ In an open space in your room or in the largest space that you can find, set up a jumping obstacle course that explores the concepts listed.
  Note: If a large movement space is not an option, put on music, such as "All the Ways of Jumping Up and Down" from *Walter the Waltzing Worm*, and follow the words of the song.

▶ Within the obstacle course, set up "jumping stations" for the children to jump in ways that help them understand different concepts. For example, set up a hoop station where the children can jump *out of* the hoop, *into* the hoop, or *over* the hoop. At a rope station, they can jump *over* the rope or *under* the rope. At a mat station, they can jump *over* the mat, jump *from* one mat to another, or jump *down* from a small height onto the mat.

▶ There should be no more than three children at each station. The children rotate through each station at least three times to understand the concepts.

Safety Tips: Children who have not had very much experience jumping down from a height, jumping in a hoop, jumping over a rope, or jumping up may not know how to land with their knees slightly bent and on the balls of their feet. Please make certain that your landing areas have mats when the children are jumping down from a height, and provide a safe landing for the children. Remind the children that they must always land on their feet.

More Books to Share

J Is for Jump Shot by Mike Ulmer
Jump, Frog, Jump! by Robert Kalan
No Jumping on the Bed! by Tedd Arnold
The Story of Jumping Mouse by John Steptoe

Music Suggestions

Action Songs for Preschoolers by Kimbo Educational. Song: Movin' Every Day
Playtime Parachute Fun by Kimbo Educational. Song: Bumping and Jumping
Ready...Set...MOVE! by Greg and Steve. Song: Jump Down, Turn Around
Walter the Waltzing Worm by Hap Palmer. Song: All the Ways of Jumping Up and Down
We All Live Together, Volume 2 by Greg and Steve. Song: The Boogie Walk

Just the Thing!

by Damian Harvey, illustrated by Lynne Chapman

What's the Book About?

Big Gorilla has a terrible itch. The advice from other jungle animals does not help a bit! He tries wriggling, squirming, scritching and scratching, rubbing and scraping, and nothing helps. Children will delight at the silly efforts Big Gorilla makes to satisfy his itch. This book has humorous illustrations and wonderful action language.

Theme Connections

Animals
Habitats
Families

Lesson Objectives

Children will:

1. Experience rhythmic text.
2. Experience a variety of movements.
3. Experience interpretive movement.

Action Vocabulary

Bump	Rub	Squirm
Flop	Scoot	Stretch
Hop	Scrape	Tumble
Jump	Scratch	Twist
Press	Scrunch	Wallow
Push	Slide	Wiggle
Reach	Slither	Wriggle
Roll	Sprawl	

Concepts Exlored

Gummy	Relief	Wearily
Itchy	Slippery	Worse
Middle	Sloppy	

Developing Literacy Skills

▶ Introduce the book's author, Damian Harvey, and illustrator, Lynne Chapman. Read the title and show the children the front cover and illustration. Ask the children to predict the storyline. This invitation will prompt lots of discussion because the illustration and the title do not seem to go together. After several minutes of conversation, ask the children to sit back and enjoy the story.

▶ Begin reading the story. Suggest that the children say the repeating line with you. Each time it appears, pause to give the children time to say it with you.

▶ After you finish the story, reread the title. Ask the children to share their ideas about why the author chose the title. What was "just the thing"?

Moving to the Story

▶ Reread the story and invite the children to act out being Big Gorilla. Along with acting out the action words, as you read the story, encourage the children to show the concepts of *gummy* (with their feet), *sloppy* (with their hands), *slippery* (spin or slide on their bottoms or stomach), and *wearily* (by walking).

▶ After each incident of not being able to scratch the itch, the children try to scratch the middle of their backs while saying the repeating phrase with you.

▶ At the end the children can scratch the back of another child and then act out their relief.

Safety Tip: If you have a small space, you may want to do this with a small group of children, with each taking a turn acting out concepts.

Developing Motor Skills

Big Gorilla Says

Materials: None

▶ This game is very much like Simon Says using the action vocabulary listed on the left. When you say, "Big gorilla says..." and follow it with an action, the children do the action.

▶ Explain that if you say an action without first saying, "Big gorilla says…," they are not to move. If any children move when you do not first say, "Big gorilla says…." those children must jump up and down five times, and then the game begins again.

▶ Tell the children that you might try to trick them, so they must listen very carefully.

Group Back Scratch
Materials: None

▶ Tell the children to listen very carefully to your instructions. Have all of the children line up in one long line, facing in one direction. Each child places his or her finger on the middle of the back of the child in front.

▶ When you say, "Go," the children move their fingers up and down to gently scratch the back of the child in front of them.

▶ Then tell the children to stop, turn around, and place their fingers on the back of the person who just scratched their back. Again, when you say, "Go," the children move their fingers up and down to reciprocate the back scratch from their classmate.

▶ Remind the children to give each other a gentle back scratch, one that they would enjoy getting. This is great **tactile (touch)** input and can help to ground (calm) some children.

More Books to Share
Good Night, Gorilla by Peggy Rathmann
Gorillas by Julie Murray
Little Gorilla by Ruth Lercher Bornstein
My Friend Gorilla by Atsuko Morozumi

Music Suggestions
A to Z, The Animals & Me by Kimbo Educational. Song: Itchy Iguana
Bugsters Tunes &Tales by Russ InVision. Song: Itch & Scratch
La Di Da La Di Di Dance with Me by The Learning Station. Song: Scratch My Back
Late Last Night by Joe Scruggs. Song: Wiggle in My Toe

Monkey See, Monkey Do

by Marc Gave, illustrated by Jacqueline Rogers

What's the Book About?

This book is perfect for emergent readers. The text is simple, rhyming, and contains lots of "get up and move" verbs to encourage active learning. The illustrations are delightful and help support the storyline, which is filled with monkey business!

Theme Connections

Animals
Opposites
Spatial concepts

Lesson Objectives

Children will:

1. Experience rhyming text.
2. Explore opposites through movement.
3. Explore movement through imitation.

Action Vocabulary

Bend	Swim
Reach	Swing
Row	Walk
Run	

Concepts Explored

Bunch	Middle
Fast	Play
Go	Right
Imitate	Slow
Left	Stay

All terms in bold are explained in greater detail in the Glossary on Appendix pages 188-199.

Developing Literacy Skills

▶ Begin Story Time by introducing the story's author, Marc Gave, and illustrator, Jacqueline Rogers. Read the title and ask the children to predict the storyline. The book's cover will give a visual clue. Draw the children's attention to this, as it is important that children learn that pictures and illustrations carry messages.

▶ The text on each page is simple. This will give the children ample time to create their own "monkey business" as you read.

▶ Tell the children to stand up and find their own personal movement space. The rhyming text gives children an opportunity to complete the sentences with a rhyming word. Encourage the children to act out the story and to complete the sentences. This is a great way to increase comprehension and **recall**.

▶ The story is very active. At the end of the story, you may want to ask the children to curl up in a ball as they say "goodnight." This will help the children settle down for the next activity.

Moving to the Story

▶ Ask each child to find a partner. One child will be the monkey that copies the other child.

▶ Read the story again and ask each pair to act out the story.

▶ On another day, you might choose one of the music selections listed below and have fun doing the activities in the song along with any other actions that the children think of.

Developing Motor Skills

Follow Me!

Materials: CD player and music

▶ Model the following actions so the children can imitate you.

▶ The text and actions in *Monkey See, Monkey Do* lend itself to helping children developing the eight critical movement patterns for **sensorimotor development**, which are listed below:

  ▶ deep breathing (inhale and exhale as deeply as possible)
  ▶ **tactile**/sensory input (tapping, patting, clapping, slapping with interesting rhythmic or musical patterns)
  ▶ core/distal movements (in/out movements, such as open arms wide then give self a hug, or legs apart then together)
  ▶ head/tail movements (up/down movement)

- alternating upper/lower body movements (animal walks, such as Bunny Jump, inchworm, or creative dance moves)
- alternating left/right side body movements (animal walks, such as the bear walk, or creative dance moves)
- **cross-lateral** movement patterns (**midline** crossing, such as a crawl or a hug, or creative dance moves)
- **vestibular** activities (rocking, spinning, turning, bouncing, leaping, inverted hanging)

▶ Teach the children each of the eight parts separately. These eight patterns are used as body/brain energizers in many classrooms. Once the children learn the patterns, it takes only five minutes to go through them, and the children can take turns being the leader. Use any of the music suggestions with this activity.

- For **deep breathing**, have the children pretend to blow up a huge balloon, breathing in through the nose and out through the mouth. They show how big the balloon is with their arms. When the balloon gets too large, they pop it with a clap of their hands. Try inhaling and exhaling, with four counts inhale, and four counts exhale. This activity provides oxygen for the brain to think more clearly.

- For **tactile/touch**, the children tap as many body parts as possible, beginning with the head and tapping all the way down to their toes, and back up again.

- For **in/out movements**, ask the children how many different ways they can make their arms and legs open wide and close tight, bringing everything to the center of the body.

- **Up/down movements** require the children to think of ways and directions that they can stretch their arms away from their feet and then bring them close again.

- For **alternating upper/lower body movements**, invite the children to make up a dance in which they only move their arms; their legs are frozen. Now ask them how they would only move their legs; their arms are frozen.

- Now tell the children to make up **alternating left/right side movements** for their arm and leg on one side of the body at a time, making their arm and leg on one side move together. Do the same on the opposite side.

- **Cross lateral** means that the children try in many ways to criss-cross their arms and legs, such as high overhead, in the middle of their bodies, or low down, close to their feet.

- Lastly, the children add **spinning, rocking on their back or bottom, jump** and turn around in the air, such as a quarter jump turn, half jump turn, full jump turn, or any combination. These are **vestibular** activities.

More Books to Share
The Copy Crocs by David Bedford
Copy Me, Copycub by Richard Edwards
The Copycat Fish by Marcus Pfister
Me Too! by Jamie Harper

Music Suggestions
Animal Romp and Stomp for Kids by Russ InVision. Song: Monkey See Monkey Do
Can a Cherry Pie Wave Goodbye? by Hap Palmer. Song: Following You
Kids in Motion by Greg and Steve. Song: Shadow Dancing
Perceptual Motor Rhythm Games by Jack Capon and Rosemary Hallum. Song: The Shoemaker (Shoemaker's Dance)
Physical Ed by The Learning Station. Song: Monkey in the Middle

Safety Tip: Remind the children to share the space with others and be aware of each other's personal space.

Moonbear's Shadow

by Frank Asch

What's the Book About?

Moonbear's Shadow will appeal to all youngsters who have wondered about their constant companion—their shadow. As Bear moves through his day, he cannot get rid of his shadow. The illustrations are simple and uncomplicated and allow the listener to focus on the story.

Theme Connections

Animals
Opposites

Lesson Objectives

Children will:
1. Identify the story's **characters**.
2. Explore parts of the story (beginning, middle, and end).
3. Explore the concept of shadows.
4. Experience interpretive movement.

Action Vocabulary

Climb
Dig
Hammer
Nod
Run

Concepts Explored

Beginning, middle, end
Shadow

Developing Literacy Skills

Materials: Chart paper • Markers

▶ Begin story time by introducing the children to the author and illustrator, Frank Asch. Read the title and ask the children to share their thoughts and ideas about shadows. If the children do not know what is needed to make a shadow, talk about this with them.

▶ You might want to create a **KWL chart** with three columns—What Do We **K**now About Shadows?; What Do We **W**ant to Know?; and What Did We **L**earn? Ask the children the first two questions and write down their answers in each column.

▶ This book is written so even young children can verbalize the story's beginning, middle, and end. Focus on details that describe what Bear was doing at the beginning of the story. Continue this thread as you read the story so the children can develop a sense of the story problem and Bear's solution.

▶ After reading the story, go back to the KWL chart. Ask the children what they learned about shadows.

▶ Ask the children to identify the story's **character**(s). Most of the children will know that the main character is Bear. Some children will identify Bear's shadow as a character. This is sure to spark a great conversation.

▶ Invite the children to talk about the story's beginning, to describe the problem that Bear faced, and to say how the story ended. You will find that some children will want to report every detail. Help them focus on one or two ideas by reframing their words.

Moving to the Story

Materials: Overhead projector • sheet • stuffed bear, optional

▶ Use an overhead projector or an opaque projector to cast a shadow on a white backdrop, such as a sheet or poster board. Use a stuffed bear to create a shadow on the white board. Let the children take turns using the bear to make shadows as you read the story.

▶ Give each child a turn as the "shadow maker." Read the story slowly so the children have ample time to create the shadows.

▶ The very best way for young children to understand shadows is to take them outside on a sunny day and let them run, jump, hop, skip, and participate in other activities so they can see their shadow doing the same.

▶ This is a terrific opportunity to discuss how and why the shadow is long sometimes and short at other times.

Developing Motor Skills

Shadow Tag

Materials: None

▶ It is best to do this activity outside on a sunny day or inside in a brightly lit room.

▶ Ask each child to find a partner. One of the two children in each pair is "IT."

▶ IT tries to step on the other child's shadow. IT says, "Gotcha!" when he or she steps on the other child's shadow. Then the other child becomes IT and tries to step on the first child's shadow.

▶ This game usually lasts about five minutes, or until everyone appears very tired.

Guided Discovery

Materials: Sidewalk chalk

▶ This activity requires that the children go outside on a sunny day during the morning, at noon, and then in the afternoon.

▶ Ask each child to find a partner.

▶ Give each pair a piece of sidewalk chalk. Ask each partner to first trace the feet of his or her partner and then trace an outline of the partner's shadow.

▶ Write each child's name or first and last name initials on each of the shadows.

▶ The feet mark the spot where each child was standing. At each of the time intervals (morning, noon, afternoon), bring the children back outside to observe how their shadows have changed size and shape by having them again stand in their initial spot and retrace the shadow.

▶ Have the children mark the morning shadow as number 1, the noon shadow as number 2, and the afternoon shadow as number 3 to note how the shadow changes during the day. You may want to extend the lesson by making a science study of this.

More Books to Share

Gregory's Shadow by Don Freeman
The Little Book of Hand Shadows by Phila H. Webb
Shadows by Deanna Calvert
What Makes a Shadow? by Clyde Robert Bulla

Music Suggestions

Action Songs for Preschoolers by Kimbo Educational. Song: Follow the Leader
Can a Cherry Pie Wave Goodbye? by Hap Palmer. Song: Following You
Kids in Motion by Greg and Steve. Song: Shadow Dancing

Move!

Steve Jenkins and Robin Page, illustrated by Steve Jenkins

What's the Book About?

Caldecott Honor winner Steve Jenkins has created a wonderfully illustrated book about the movement of animals. The sparse illustrations, using mixed-media collage technique, accentuate the movement of the animal on each page. Some animals have four legs, some have two, some have wings, some just slither their bodies. At the end of the book, you will find brief, interesting facts about each of the featured animals.

Theme Connections

Animals
Spatial concepts

Lesson Objectives

Children will:
1. Explore the animal kingdom.
2. Imitate the movement of animals.
3. Make predictions about the animals featured in the book.
4. Understand how a variety of animals move.

Action Vocabulary

Climb	Leap	Swing
Dance	Run	Waddle
Dive	Slide	Walk
Float	Slither	
Fly	Swim	

Concepts Explored

Across	Down	Through
Away	Far	Up
Below	In	

Developing Literacy Skills

Materials: Stuffed animals or puppets, one for each child

▶ Share the book's front cover with the children. Introduce the book's authors, Steve Jenkins and Robin Page, and illustrator, Steve Jenkins. Focus on the title and the rabbit. Ask the children to share their ideas about how a rabbit might move and to use their fingers to show different movements. Explain that they are going to learn about some animals and how they move in different ways.

▶ To encourage the children's active engagement with the story, give each child a stuffed animal or puppet of one of the animals in the story. Depending on the number of children in your class, you may need several of each animal. The format of the book describes two different ways that each animal moves. The gibbon, for example, swings and walks.

▶ As you read each page, begin by pointing to the action word. Ask the children to guess the word.

▶ Read the text and suggest that the children verbalize and demonstrate (using their toy animal) how the animal moves. For example, if a child says, "swing" while swinging the gibbon, it will help him or her remember the action vocabulary.

▶ Before you turn the pages, ask the children who are holding that particular animal to predict how the animal will move on the next page.

▶ The action vocabulary is written in a spiral design on the back cover. After reading the story, point to the words on the back cover and invite the children to move their animals as you say the words. Without the **picture cues**, the children will have to **recall** what they learned from the story.

▶ If time and the children's attention permits, share with the children the interesting facts about each animal that are listed at the end of the book. This provides a natural extension into non-fiction reading and science.

Moving to the Story

▶ Explore the action words with the children. Ask the children to choose an animal from the story to imitate. Be sure all of the animals are chosen!

▶ As you read the story again, invite the children to stand up, find their own personal space, and act out the movements of their animal.

- As you read the story, ask the children to keep moving as you introduce the remaining animals. The child acting out the gibbon, which is at the beginning of the story, will have lots of movement time compared to the child acting out the penguin, which is at the end of the story, so repeat this activity several times with the children choosing different animals to imitate each time.
- Suggest that the children add animal sounds to their movements.

Developing Motor Skills

Imagine How They Move

Materials: None

- After reading the story, ask the children to find their personal space for movement.
- Read each action word and invite the children to show you how people would perform that movement skill.
- At the end of the story, ask the children to sit in their personal space. Invite them to share their thoughts about how some movements might be easier or more difficult for some animals than others and why.
- Ask the children if it would be easy for snakes to run or crocodiles to fly, or children to slither. How important is an animal's body in how it moves?

Safety Tips: Remind the children to move safely in the space available. The action words *dive, run,* and *slide* may encourage some children to move too quickly for the space. Remind the children to watch for others to avoid collisions. You may want the children to participate in small groups with one child moving at a time.

More Books to Share
Animals on the Go by Jessica Brett
Can You Move Like an Elephant? by Judy Hindley
Little Quack by Lauren Thompson
My Visit to the Zoo by Aliki

Music Suggestions
A to Z, The Animals & Me by Kimbo Educational. Songs: Teacher's or children's choice (any song will be appropriate)
Can a Cherry Pie Wave Goodbye? by Hap Palmer. Songs: Animal Quiz Part One; Animal Quiz Part Two
Get Funky and Musical Fun by The Learning Station. Song: Crab Walking
Rowdy Ropes by Dinotrax. Song: I Can Jump Like a Big Green Frog

My Many Colored Days
by Dr. Seuss, illustrated by Steve Johnson and Lou Fancher

What's the Book About?

Dr. Seuss and illustrators Steve Johnson and Lou Fancher created a stunning book depicting feelings and moods. The text and colors bring these emotions to life with truth and clarity. The children in the story are drawn simply, which allows any child to identify with them. The font and style of the text makes the words dance across the pages, adding to the emotional energy of this wonderful book.

Theme Connections

Colors
Feelings
Imagination

Lesson Objectives

Children will:
1. Experience rhyming text.
2. Explore feelings and emotions.
3. Explore how colors depict moods.
4. Explore interpretive movement.

Action Vocabulary

Buzzy	Flap	Walk
Change	Jump	Watch
Drag	Kick	

Emotional Expression and Concepts Explored

Alone	Different	Mad
Angry	Down	Quiet
Bright	Energetic	Sad
Busy	Good	Sudden
Confused	Happy	Slow
Cool	Loud	Surprise
Deep	Low	

Developing Literacy Skills

▶ Introduce the book's author, Dr. Seuss, and the illustrators, Steve Johnson and Lou Fancher, who created the paintings for the story. Read the title to the children and ask them to predict the storyline. The vivid colors used in the illustrations are integral to the story so you will want to spend some time exploring the drawings on the book's cover.

▶ Tell the children that people often use color words to describe their moods. This discussion will help set the stage for Story Time.

▶ Dr. Seuss uses a number of colors to convey moods and feelings. Invite the children to think about how the following colors make them feel: black, blue, brown, gray, green, orange, pink, purple, red, and yellow, and then share their thoughts.

▶ After a few minutes of discussion, begin reading the story. Use your voice to emphasize the feelings and emotions in the text. You may want to pause before reading the word that completes the rhyming text so the children can provide a rhyming word.

▶ When you read about a Mixed-Up Day, ask the children how they might feel if they experienced all of the colors in one day. The words on the last page have a reassuring message.

Moving to the Story

Materials: CD player and music, optional

▶ Now that the children have had some exposure to color and mood, reread the story and invite the children to stand and move to the colors and moods in the book.

▶ If available, music adds another component to the experience. Suggestions include classical music such as Beethoven's "Ode to Joy" and the music listed on the next page.

Developing Motor Skills

Color the Mood
Materials: Index cards colored or painted in each of the 10 colors in the book

▶ Hold up a colored card (one of the 10 colors highlighted in the story).

▶ When the children see the color, they move the way the color makes them feel, and show a facial expression that expresses that same feeling. For example, if the color red makes a child feel happy, then he or she might run, jump, and laugh. You may want to use dogs as an example for "happy." When dogs are happy, they wag their entire bodies!

▶ Although the book shows specific moods related to specific colors, many children in your class may not identify with the colors in the same way. It is important to tell the children that they are free to act out the color in exactly the way that it makes them feel.

▶ Quickly alternate the cards among each different color, based upon the interest level of the children. Some color mood expressions will be shorter than others.

Emotional Expression Dance
Materials: CD player and suggested music (see list on the right), or any instrumental or classical music

▶ Divide the children into groups of two or three children. Review the list of 20 emotions by reading the emotional expressions and concepts listed on the previous page to the children and provide time for the children to act them out. Remind the children that a fast or slow movement, along with jumps, hops, and skips, and other movements and body positions that they choose show emotion.

▶ Ask the children to combine movements showing three emotions to form a "dance."

▶ Now the children are ready to practice their "dances" (the combination of acting out three emotions). After a few minutes of practice, each group or pair can perform their dance for the rest of the class.

More Books to Share
Feelings by Aliki
The Giving Tree by Shel Silverstein
Hooray for Diffendoofer Day! by Dr. Seuss
Knuffle Bunny: A Cautionary Tale by Mo Willems

Music Suggestions
Can Cockatoos Count by Twos? by Hap Palmer. Songs: Colors in Motion (Basic); Colors in Motion (Mixing Colors)
Getting to Know Myself by Hap Palmer. Songs: Feelings; What Do People Do
"So Big" by Hap Palmer. Song: When I'm Down, I Get Up and Dance
We All Live Together, Volume 2 by Greg and Steve. Song: The World Is a Rainbow

One Duck Stuck: A Mucky Ducky Counting Book

by Phyllis Root, illustrated by Jane Chapman

What's the Book About?

This engaging counting book brings to life 10 animals who try to help Duck, who is stuck in the muck in the march. The **predictable text** is rich with fun sounds and rhyme. The illustrations are very colorful and quite silly.

Theme Connections

Animals
Cooperation
Habitats
Numbers
Sounds

Lesson Objectives

Children will:
1. Count to 10.
2. Experience rhyming text.
3. Explore **onomatopoeia**.
4. Explore a variety of movements.

Action Vocabulary

Climb	Plod
Crawl	Slide
Hop	Slither
Jump	Swim
Leap	Whir

Concepts Explored

Helping
Stuck

Developing Literacy Skills

▶ Introduce the book's author, Phyllis Root, and illustrator, Jane Chapman. Read the title to the children and ask them to predict the storyline.

▶ Many children may not be familiar with a marsh or the animals found in a marsh. Take a few minutes to discuss this environment. Tell the children that there are 10 different animals in the story and they all try to help their friend, Duck.

▶ You may also want to ask the children if any of them has ever been stuck in or on something. What did they do to solve the problem?

▶ This book offers an opportunity for the children to count on their fingers as you read.

▶ Locate and read the repetitive phrases in the book ("No luck. The duck stays stuck deep in the muck down by the … marsh," and "Help! Help! Who can help?"). Tell the children that when you point to these words, they can read the words with you. You may also want the children to read the numerals on each page spread.

▶ Begin reading the story. The text is full of **onomatopoeic** words such as *clomp, pleep, plop, plunk, slink, slosh, splish, spluck,* and *zing.* Use your voice to emphasize these words. Encourage the children to play with the sounds these words make as they move their fingers to the action words.

▶ After you have finished reading the book, randomly name the animals in the story, and ask the children if they can remember the number there were of each animal. This will help develop the children's ability to **recall** information from a story.

Moving to the Story

▶ This story is fun to act out by focusing on the action vocabulary words, which are listed on the left.

▶ Reread the story to the children. As you come to each action or concept word on each of the pages, pause a moment to give the children time to act out each of the words.

Developing Motor Skills

Stuck Duck Tag

Materials: Carpet squares • Blindfolds, optional

▶ This game, which involves strategizing, dodging, and timing, is most successful in a large Circle/Story Time area, a hallway, a multipurpose room, or a gym.

▶ Divide the class into two equal groups. One group stands along each of the four sides of the game area, and the other is scattered randomly through the center of the game area. To determine how far apart the children in the center should stand, have them put their arms out. They should be within 2'–3' of touching their neighbors in any direction. Each child in the middle of the area stands with one foot "stuck" on a carpet square. These children are the Stuck Duck taggers.

▶ Set up boundaries so the children in the center are all an equal distance from the sidelines. The children in the center are allowed to switch a stuck foot in order to capture someone from the other group, as long as one foot remains on the carpet square.

▶ The children in the center close their eyes or wear a blindfold. When you say, "Ready, go!" the children around the edges try to sneak through without being tagged. They can walk or crawl through the maze of stuck ducks. The Stuck Duck taggers listen carefully for sounds that let them know that someone is near them. Once a child is tagged, the tagger opens his eyes and trades places with the child that he tagged. Play continues.

▶ Young children may do better playing with their eyes open; however, older children should play with eyes closed. Continue play until most everyone has been tagged at least one time.

Safety Tip: Remind the children to tag gently.

More Books to Share

Anno's Counting Book by Mitsumasa Anno
Fish Eyes: A Book You Can Count On by Lois Ehlert
Hat Tricks Count: A Hockey Number Book by Matt Napier
Mouse Count by Ellen Stoll Walsh

Music Suggestions

Get Funky and Musical Fun by The Learning Station. Song: Ants Go Marching
Kids in Motion by Greg and Steve. Song: Count Bounce
Rowdy Ropes by Dinotrax. Song: 1, 2, 3, 4, 5, 6, 7, 8

All terms in bold are explained in greater detail in the Glossary on Appendix pages 188-199.

Our Marching Band

by Lloyd Moss, illustrated by Diana Cain Blumenthal

What's the Book About?

A group of children decide to form a band. They soon discover that dedication, perseverance, and lots of practice enable them to attain their goal—to march in a band. This story is written in rhyme, with lots of lively language. The zany watercolor illustrations are large, making this a perfect book for Story Time.

Theme Connections

Celebrations
Cooperation
Sounds
Spatial concepts

Lesson Objectives

Children will:
1. Experience rhyming text.
2. Explore the concept of teamwork.
3. Introduce a variety of musical instruments.
4. Explore participating in a marching band.

Action Vocabulary

March
Serenade

Concepts Explored

Parade
Practice
Teamwork

Developing Literacy Skills

Materials: Chart paper • Markers

▶ Introduce the book's author, Lloyd Moss, and illustrator, Diana Cain Blumenthal. Read the title of the book and ask the children to predict the storyline.

▶ Because the title and cover illustration closely match the story, you may want to invite the children to share what they know about bands. Talk about bands having many members and that all the musicians need to work together—teamwork—so the music sounds good. Ask them to watch how the children in the story try their hardest to make their band a success.

▶ Young children may not be familiar with the instruments presented in this story. This is a great opportunity to develop a **KWL chart** (What Do We **K**now?; What Do We **W**ant to Know?; and What Did We **L**earn?) about musical instruments. List the names of all of the instruments with which the children are familiar. If they do not mention instruments that are presented in the story, add these to the "W" list as things about which they will want to know.

▶ As you read the story, use your voice to emphasize the names of the musical instruments. This will help the children remember the unfamiliar names of some of the instruments.

▶ To emphasize the rhyming text, pause before reading the last word of each phrase so the children can provide rhyming words.

▶ After you finish reading the story, refer to the KWL chart. Review the names of the instruments in the "K" column. Read the names of the instruments in the "W" column and ask the children what they learned about these. Add this information to the "L" column on the chart. The children are now ready to participate in their own marching band.

Moving to the Story

Materials: CD player and "Play in the Band" on *Smart Moves 2 Preschool thru 1st* or any music about playing in a band

▶ Put "Play in the Band" on *Smart Moves 2 Preschool thru 1st* or any song about playing in a band. It's fun, upbeat, and has individual parts for the children to pretend to play each instrument.

Developing Motor Skills

Marching Musical Parade

Materials: Cymbals, drums, triangles, xylophones, or other percussion instruments • CD player and marching music (see suggestions on the right) • Cones • Picture of a square

▶ Do this activity anywhere in the room, school hallway, gym, or outside if it allows easy marching.

▶ Ask each child to choose a percussion instrument.

▶ Provide a space for the children to march. Allow them to march freely until they can march in a steady beat to the music and accompany the marching music with a steady beat.

▶ After the children have mastered marching to a steady beat while playing an instrument, talk to them about marching in a pattern. Show them a picture of a square and then arrange four cones in a square formation.

▶ Have the children follow you marching around each of the four cones, without instruments or music to start. Next, add their percussion instruments and the marching music. They will thoroughly enjoy the experience. Depending upon the age and ability of the children, you can add math concepts, such as dividing the square in half vertically (making two rectangles) or in a diagonal (making two triangles) and marching around these patterns. You can also have the children change the direction in which they march. By changing directions and the sides and angles on the square, you can create a variety of marching patterns.

Safety Tip: Sometimes children get very confused with direction changes. Take time to direct them or cue them to make certain that they are moving in the correct direction to avoid confusion or collisions.

More Books to Share

Charlie Parker Played Be Bop by Chris Raschka

The Jazz Fly by Matthew Gollub

My Family Plays Music by Judy Cox

Zin! Zin! Zin! A Violin by Lloyd Moss

Music Suggestions

All-Time Children's' Favorites by The Learning Station. Song: The Marching Song

Movin' & Shakin' for Youngsters by Russ InVision. Song: Do You Know How To…?

Rock N' Roll Songs That Teach by The Learning Station. Song: Read a Book

Smart Moves 2 Preschool thru 1st by Russ InVision. Song: Play in the Band

Over in the Pink House: New Jump Rope Rhymes
by Rebecca Kai Dotlich, illustrated by Melanie Hall

What's the Book About?
This is a new collection of jump rope rhymes, 32 in all. The rhythmic poems are catchy, and the illustrations, which are a combination of watercolors, pastels, and ink, add to the lyrical quality of the collection.

Theme Connections
Cooperation
Exercise
Humor

Lesson Objectives
Children will:
1. Experience rhyming text.
2. Experience rhythm in text.
3. Explore poetry.
4. Explore rope jumping.

Action Vocabulary
Jump
Rope Jumping

Concepts Explored
Cooperation
Steady beat (jumping) combined with rhyme

Developing Literacy Skills

▶ Introduce the book's author, Rebecca Kai Dotlich, and illustrator, Melanie Hall, to the children. Read the title and ask the children to predict the storyline.

▶ Explain to the children that for many years boys and girls have enjoyed jumping rope to rhymes. You may want to tell the children that the title of the book is also the name of one of the jump rope rhymes in the book.

▶ Before you read the book, select a few of the rhymes that are catchy and easy to memorize.

▶ Tell the children that they can "jump" along as you read by using two fingers as their "legs." They can use the palm of their other hand as a surface for jumping.

▶ Begin by reading the title of one of the poems you selected, and then read the rhyme to the children. Reread the selection and, using your own fingers, tap to the rhythm of each syllable. Read it again slowly, and invite the children to chant the poem with you and tap their fingers.

▶ Read the remaining poems you selected, following the same procedure. If time allows, repeat each selection so the children can begin to memorize the words. The rhythmic text of each poem will help the children learn the timing necessary for rope jumping.

Moving to the Story

▶ Select a few rhymes to read aloud and encourage the children to act them out.

Developing Motor Skills

Flat Rope Jumping
Materials: Nylon, cotton, or braided yarn ropes
▶ Place the rope in a straight line on the floor.
▶ Encourage the children to jump back and forth over the rope.
Note: Even very young children can learn flat rope jumping, which is using a rope that is stationary on the floor or ground. The *Rowdy Ropes* CD listed below includes a guide to help you teach children the step-by-step process of jumping rope. Children as young as four can learn to jump, and

eventually learn to turn the rope. When the children are ready to begin turning the rope overhead, the CD and guide offer progressive rope-jumping steps.

Pretend Rope Jumping

Materials: None

▶ Read a rhyme and have the children clap a steady rhythm to the rhyme. That steady beat will then transfer to their feet for jumping.

▶ Invite the children to stand up with their pretend jump ropes. This time, as you read the rhyme, they jump in rhythm to the rhyme.

Jumping Lightly

Materials: Nylon, cotton, beaded, or speed (licorice) jump ropes

▶ For this activity, you need a space large enough for the children to turn their ropes over their heads.

▶ The first hurdle in learning how to jump rope is jumping lightly on the feet.

▶ Ask the children to stand up tall and show you their best posture. Now, ask them to show you how lightly and quietly they can jump on the balls of their feet.

▶ Ask them to jump in rhythm as you clap out 20 jumps.

▶ After the children have learned to jump in rhythm to a beat, they are ready to begin turning the rope over their head, and lift up their toes to capture it. They will then lift up their heels to allow the rope to go behind them. This activity should be practiced until you can see that most of the children have the **eye-hand/eye-foot coordination** to begin turning the rope overhead and to allow the rope to pass under their feet.

Note: Jumping while turning the rope over the head is more difficult for children under the age of five. Younger children will enjoy having you hold the rope and moving it back and forth for them to jump over, or wiggling it on the floor for them to jump over the "wiggle worms." Remind the children that every time they jump, the rope needs to go under their feet.

More Books to Share

A, My Name Is Alice by Jane Bayer
Anna Banana: 101 Jump Rope Rhymes by Joanna Cole
Hot Day on Abbott Avenue by Karen English

Music Suggestions

Rowdy Ropes by Dinotrax. Songs: Entire CD for "Flat Rope" jumping, partner jumping, and long rope jumping

Safety Tip: To see all the children in the group, arrange them in two rows. Ask the children to stand side by side at a double arms' length apart. Have every other child take three giant steps backward. This will give you two rows that are offset. If you need to make four rows, divide the children accordingly.

Pretend You're a Cat

by Jean Marzollo, illustrated by Jerry Pinkney

What's the Book About?

This beautifully illustrated book depicts children from a variety of ethnic backgrounds pretending to be a cat, a dog, a pig, and several other animals. The children are shown wearing costumes and using props that will spark the imaginations of young learners.

Theme Connections

Animals
Imagination
Sounds

Lesson Objectives

Children will:
1. Experience rhyming text.
2. Explore interpretive movement.
3. Explore the concept of pretend.
4. Experience a variety of movement skills.

Action Vocabulary

Balance	Jump	Slide
Beg	Leap	Slither
Climb	Peck	Soar
Dig	Peck	Stretch
Dive	Perch	Swim
Fetch	Roll	Twirl
Flee	Root	Wiggle
Fly	Run	
Glide	Scat	
Hop	Scratch	

Concepts Explored (Animal Sounds)

Bark	Hiss	Roar
Buzz	Moo	Snort (oink)
Chatter	Neigh	Tweet
Cheep	Peep	
Chirp	Purr	

Developing Literacy Skills

▶ Introduce the book's author, Jean Marzollo, and illustrator, Jerry Pinkney. Read the title to the children and show them the book's front and back covers.

▶ Ask the children to predict the storyline. Tell the children that the boys and girls in the story are pretending to be many different animals. Invite the children to watch for their favorite animals.

▶ Because the book is written in rhyme, it is easy for the children to participate as you read. Pause just before completing the rhyme so the children can complete the phrase with a rhyming word.

▶ Many page spreads show children using simple props while they pretend to be the animals. The facial expressions and body movements of the children are also important to point out. Draw children's attention to the illustrations, as these ideas will help them understand the concept of pretend.

▶ When you are finished reading the book, ask the children to **recall** the animals mentioned in the book (there are 13). Invite the children to talk about the actions and sounds of their favorite animals.

Moving to the Story

▶ This book begs to be acted out as you read it to the children! After the children have listened to the story one time and have had time to discuss their favorite actions and sounds of each animal, invite them to act out each sound and movement as you read the story a second time.

▶ When you read the last question of each page, invite the children to demonstrate other ways that the animals might move.

Developing Motor Skills

Animal Sound Sing Along

Materials: CD player with recommended CDs or your own music

▶ Divide the class into five equal groups. Each group chooses a different animal sound to "sing." Take any classic children's song such as "Old MacDonald Had a Farm" or "Twinkle, Twinkle, Little Star."

▶ Tell the children that you will be the "choir director" for the "animal choir."

- Each group takes a turn barking, baaing, oinking, neighing, or making an animal noise for one line of the song when you point to a group. For example, group one may bark the first line, group two may baa the second line, group three may oink the third line, and so on.
- The idea is to see how long the children can sing in the tempo, tune, rhythm, and voice of their animal. Try this in a round if the children don't get too silly, although it will certainly end up being quite humorous.

Animal Statues

Materials: CD player with recommended CDs (see list on the right) or your own music

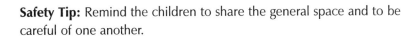

- Put on your favorite lively instrumental song.
- Tell the children that you when you call out the name of an animal, they are to move like that animal until you stop the music. When the music stops, they are to stop and freeze into a statue of that animal.
- Start the music and again and call out a different animal. When the music stops, the children must turn into statues of that animal.
- Say one of the action vocabulary words listed on the previous page when you stop the music so the children have to stop in a different way each time.

Safety Tip: Remind the children to share the general space and to be careful of one another.

More Books to Share

Alexander's Pretending Day by Bunny Crumpacker
Grandma Helps Us Pretend by Carol Burns
Dick and Jane: We Play and Pretend by Grosset and Dunlap
Wee Sing and Pretend by Pamela Conn Beall and Susan Hagen Nipp

Music Suggestions

Literacy in Motion by The Learning Station. Song: Old MacDonald
Tunes for Tiny Tots by Music with Mar. Song: My Fat Cat
We All Live Together, Volume 5 by Greg and Steve. Song: Down on the Farm
The Wide-Mouthed Bullfrog by Music with Mar. Song: I Have a Cat

Quick as a Cricket

by Audrey Wood, illustrated by Don Wood

What's the Book About?

In this classic book, a little boy imagines going through the day being just like the animals he imagines. The colorful illustrations are large and inviting. The inspiration for this daydream adventure is the bulletin board in the child's room.

Theme Connections

Cooperation
Imagination
Insects and bugs
Opposites

Lesson Objectives

Children will:

1. Experience rhyming text.
2. Explore opposites.
3. Explore the concept of imagining.
4. Explore interpretive movement.

Action Vocabulary

The vocabulary is imbedded in the concepts.

Concepts Explored (Opposites)

Brave/shy
Cold/hot
Lazy/busy
Loud/quiet
Mean/nice
Quick/slow
Sad/happy
Small/large
Tame/wild
Tough/gentle
Weak/strong

Developing Literacy Skills

▶ Introduce the book's author, Audrey Wood, and illustrator, Don Wood. When you read the title, focus the children's attention on the cover illustration. Tell the children that, like the child on the cover, they can use their imaginations to dream about how they could become the animals in the story.

▶ Begin Story Time by reading the first three pages. The ways in which the child represents the animals are presented in opposite pairs: quick and slow, small and large, and so on. Point this out to the children so they can predict responses to the text that show their understanding of the concept of opposites.

▶ When you are finished reading the story, ask the children to **recall** the different animals in the story. Can they remember the words used to describe how the animals moved? This develops the children's recall ability.

Moving to the Story

▶ Read the story a second time, and this time, invite the children to act out the meaning of the opposite words as you read along.

▶ Tell the children to pretend to be each animal in the pair of opposite words.

READ! MOVE! LEARN!

Developing Motor Skills

Opposites

Materials: Carpet squares • CD player and recommended music, optional

▶ Review the opposite concepts with the children. Ask the children to find a partner. Give each child a carpet square. Explain that the partners are going to act out opposites on or around the carpet squares. Tell them they can act out the opposites or simply position their bodies like statues to show opposites.

▶ Read one of the words in a pair of opposites (see previous page, Concepts Explored). The partners decide the word each child will demonstrate through movement or poses. Allow a minute or two for the children to explore possibilities before they share their ideas with the class.

▶ After the children share their ideas with the class, ask them to do the same with another opposite pair. Keep the pace speedy so the children have plenty of time to move.

▶ If you have any of the CDs listed on the right, play one or more "opposites in action" tunes for additional fun.

Safety Tip: Remind the children to stay within their personal space on or close to their carpet square.

More Books to Share
Pinduli by Janell Cannon
The Skin You Live In by Michael Tyler
Whoever You Are by Mem Fox

Music Suggestions
Fun and Games, Learning to Play— Playing to Learn by Greg and Steve. Song: Opposites
Rock n' Roll Songs That Teach by The Learning Station. Song: Opposites
Smart Moves 1 by Russ Invision. Songs: In My Body

Rolie Polie Olie
by William Joyce

What's the Book About?
Rolie Polie Olie is a very round robot. After helping to clean the house, Rolie Polie Olie and his sister spend the rest of the day skipping and gliding, bumping and bouncing, swinging and sliding. At the end of the day, Rolie Polie Olie is so wound up that he goes into high gear, clanking and crashing, and turning rooms into rubble. He apologizes to his family and all is well before they say goodnight.

Theme Connections
Exercise
Families
Shapes

Lesson Objectives
Children will:
1. Experience rhyming text.
2. Explore a variety of movements.
3. Explore interpretive movement.

Action Vocabulary
Bounce	Race
Bump	Scratch
Brush	Skip
Curl	Slide
Dance	Spin
Glide	Stamp
Hop	Stomp
Jump	Swing
Roll	Turn

Concepts Explored
Curve	Round
Hide-and-seek	Swirl
Playing	Think

Developing Literacy Skills

▶ Introduce the book's author and illustrator, William Joyce. Read the title and share the front cover illustration with the children. Ask them to predict the storyline.
▶ The children will be fascinated by the illustrations. Tell them to watch Rolie Polie Olie closely as he bounces through his busy day.
▶ Explain that the story is written in rhyme. Pause at the end of each rhyming phrase so the children can suggest a word that rhymes.
▶ As you read the story, allow enough time for the children to look at the illustrations. If appropriate, ask the children to identify round or curved objects in Olie Land.

Acting Out the Story

▶ Tell the children that almost everything in Rolie's life is round or has curves. Talk about what "curve" and "round" means.
▶ Ask the children to form curves with their arms, hands, and fingers. In their personal space, ask the children to form their bodies into a round shape, just like Rolie's shape. This activity will help the children understand the concepts of "curve" and "round."

Developing Motor Skills

Carousel
Materials: Parachute
▶ Play this circular game outside on a grassy area or in a gym or multipurpose room.
▶ All the children find a place around the parachute. As they move around in a circle, walking, side sliding, jumping, hopping, skipping, and so on, they dip down and up, moving as though they are animals on a carousel.
▶ Switch directions or change the movement for variety.

Roller Ball

Materials: Parachute • Balls

▶ Play this game outside on a grassy area or in a gym or multipurpose room.

▶ Have the children stand and hold onto the edge of the parachute at about waist high.

▶ Put one or two utility balls or sponge balls on the parachute. The idea is for the children to move cooperatively to keep the balls rolling around the parachute without rolling off.

▶ The children on one side of the parachute lower it as the children on the other side of the parachute raises it.

▶ After the children have mastered this, challenge them to figure out how to make the balls go around the parachute in a circle.

Note: During this activity use as many action vocabulary words (see list on previous page) as possible.

Rolie Polie Race Away

Materials: Parachute • Balls • CD player with complementary music suggestions (see list on the right)

▶ Play this game outside on a grassy area or in a gym or multipurpose room.

▶ Have all the children find a place around the parachute and hold the parachute at waist height. Create pairs of children by dividing the class in half. For example, if there are 20 children, count each child up to 10, and then begin at one again. This way, the child directly across from each child will be his or her partner.

▶ Tell the children that you will call out a number. The two children with that number let go of the parachute, run half way around the outside of the parachute to the other child's spot, jump up and down four times, and then duck under the parachute going across the middle to get back to their home place before their racing partner gets to his or her home spot.

▶ If appropriate, ask the children to use the action vocabulary from the story (listed on the previous page) to decide how to move or to change the action after each child's turn.

Safety Tip: Remind the children to watch for one another when they go under the parachute.

More Books to Share

Hello, Robots! by Bob Staake

I Spy a Runaway Robot by Liz Mills (editor)

Robots: Rodney and the Rusties by Kate Egan

Robots Slither by Ryan Ann Hunter

Music Suggestions

It's Toddler Time by Kimbo Educational. Songs: Up, Down, Turn Around; Round and Round We Go; Merry-Go-Round

Sally the Swinging Snake by Educational Activities. Song: Watch Me

Rosie's Walk
by Pat Hutchins

What's the Book About?

The storyline is simple—Rosie the hen goes for a walk and is followed by a rather clumsy fox. Rosie, of course, is unaware of the fox but completes her walk without so much as losing a feather. The same cannot be said for the fox! Pat Hutchins focuses on prepositions to send Rosie walking through the farm and back again.

Theme Connections

Animals
Farms
Habitats
Spatial concepts

Lesson Objectives

Children will:

1. Explore prepositional phrases.
2. Explore relationships between **characters**.
3. Describe the actions of the fox.

Action Vocabulary

Walk

Concepts Explored

Across
Around
Over
Past
Through
Under

Developing Literacy Skills

▶ Introduce the book's author/illustrator. Read the title to the children and ask them to predict the storyline. Draw the children's attention to the cover illustration. Point out the hen and the fox. Tell the children to watch the fox as he follows Rosie!

▶ This story's text is very simple and the type is large enough for the children to read along with you. As you read, point to each word, emphasizing the prepositions.

▶ The simplicity of the text leaves much to the imagination. After reading the story, invite the children to talk about the relationship between Rosie and the fox. Are they friends? Does Rosie know that the fox is following her? What happens to the fox at the end of the story? The children will be ready to get up and act out the part of Rosie or the fox.

Moving to the Story

▶ Show each page to the children again. This time ask them to provide a word that describes the action that the fox is doing. For example, hiding, leaping, getting hit with the rake, jumping, landing, and so on.

- Ask each child to find a partner. One child will take the part of acting out Rosie and the other will take the part of acting out the fox.
- Read the story again and invite the children to act out each of the preposition concepts (listed on the previous page) and walking activities of Rosie and the actions of the fox.
- If there is time, let the children switch parts.

Safety Tip: Remind the children to move safely when acting out the part of the fox.

Developing Motor Skills

Going on a Walkabout
Materials: Classroom objects, such as cones, rope, desks, chairs, a balance beam (or a line on the floor made with tape), and so on

- Tell the children that they will be exploring different ways to "walkabout" like Rosie did.
- When you say an action concept (listed on the previous page), the children use an object in the classroom to demonstrate the concept. For example, if you say, "around," they might walk *around* an object, such as a table, chair, or bookcase.
- Ask them to change how they are walking in the following ways:
  - directions, such as forward, sideways, backward, left, or right
  - pathways, such as zigzag, curved, or straight
  - levels, such as high, middle, or low
- If appropriate, ask the children to walk on their heels, toes, or the sides of their feet.
- If available, include the suggested music or other on hand that will complement the walking activity.
  Note: This activity may be done with or without equipment. Take a look at the Concepts Explored list and decide if you have simple items in the classroom that might be incorporated into a walkabout for the children. If not, encourage the children to use their imaginations.

More Books to Share
The Chicken Sisters by Laura Numeroff
Chicks and Salsa by Aaron Reynolds
Hattie and the Fox by Mem Fox
The Problem with Chickens by Bruce McMillan

Music Suggestions
We All Live Together, Volume 5 by Greg and Steve. Song: A Walking We Will Go

Saturday Night at the Dinosaur Stomp

by Carol Diggory Shields, illustrated by Scott Nash

What's the Book About?

Scott Nash, the illustrator, uses humorous drawings to bring the rockin' dinosaurs in this book to life. The dinosaurs boogie at a Saturday all-night extravaganza, creating the first earthquake! Author, Carol Shields, uses rhythm and **alliteration** that will surely delight young audiences.

Theme Connections

Dinosaurs
Humor

Lesson Objectives

Children will:
1. Explore alliteration in text.
2. Experience interpretive movement.
3. Experience rhyme in text.
4. Experience various dance forms.

Action Vocabulary

Jump
Plod
Romp
Shuffle
Trample
Tromp
Twirl

Concepts Explored (Dances)

Bump
Conga Line
Rock n' Roll
Twist

Developing Literacy Skills

▶ Introduce the book's author, Carol Diggory Shields, and illustrator, Scott Nash. Read the title to the children and ask them to predict the storyline.

▶ If some children do not know what *stomp* means, discuss its meaning so they understand what happens in the story.

▶ Share the pages (at the front of the book and the very end of the book) that show the dance steps from the some of the dances.

▶ Ask the children what they think the footprint patterns, arrows, and letters and numbers mean. Ask them if the markings might be helpful for learning the different dances.

▶ The text is written in rhyme and the author uses catchy **alliteration**. Use your voice to emphasize the rhyme. To focus on the alliteration, you may want the children to repeat the phrases after you.

▶ The illustrations do a great job of depicting movement. As you read the story, draw the children's attention to the pictures showing the dinosaurs dancing. This will increase their interest in learning the dinosaur dances.

Moving to the Story

▶ This is a fun story for the children to pantomime.

▶ Invite the children to stand up and get ready to act out the actions of the dinosaurs, from slicking back their scales to scrubbing necks and curling tails.

▶ Read the book again, moving quickly when there is nothing to pantomime, but pausing after each action word or phrase to give the children time to act out the words.

All terms in bold are explained in greater detail in the Glossary on Appendix pages 188-199.

Developing Motor Skills

Dancing Fun

Materials: CD player with suggested music (see list on the right) or other music of your choice

▶ It's dance time, and just like the dinosaurs, the children can do a Conga Line!

▶ Have the children line up one behind the other in groups of three. Each group stands next to the other groups and faces you. (Working in smaller groups will create more success for the children.)

▶ Standing with your back to the children, demonstrate walking three steps, then stop and stick one foot out to the side. Walk three more steps and put the other foot out to the side. Continue by repeating the same pattern. If the children understand that this is a pattern, it may be easier for them to understand and learn.

▶ Have everyone begin stepping forward with the left foot. The pattern would be left, right, left, place the right foot to the side, step forward with the right, left, right, and then place the left foot to the side and begin the pattern over again.

▶ Stand in front of the children with your back to them, and go through the pattern several times until most get it. You may have to back everyone up to start over when you get to the wall, or you might tell the children to turn and keep going.

▶ After the children get comfortable with the pattern, older children can try the dance with their hands on the hips of the child in front of them. Younger children can simply follow their leader.

▶ Put on music and have fun.

Safety Tip: Let the children know that they may have to change direction or take smaller steps to avoid colliding with another group.

More Books to Share
Dinosaur ABC by Roger Priddy
How Do Dinosaurs Say Goodnight? by Jane Yolen
Oh, Can You Say Di-no-saur? by Bonnie Worth

Music Suggestions
All-Time Favorite Dances by Kimbo Educational. Songs: All are fun to try—Conga Line; The Twist; The Hokey Pokey; The Chicken
Kids in Action by Greg and Steve. Songs: Bop 'Til You Drop; Get Ready, Get Set, Let's Dance; The Conga Line
Rockin' Reading Readiness by Kimbo Educational. Song: Five Huge Dinosaurs

Schoolyard Rhymes: Kids' Own Fun Rhymes for Rope Jumping, Hand Clapping, Ball Bouncing, and Just Plain Fun

by Judy Sierra, illustrated by Melissa Sweet

What's the Book About?

This amazing collection of playground rhymes includes rhymes that are new and rhymes that have been used for generations. Included are wonderful rhymes for rope jumping, hand clapping, ball bouncing, and skipping. The illustrator uses watercolors and fabric collages to capture the energetic spirit of the verses.

Theme Connections

Cooperation
Exploring cultures
Humor

Lesson Objectives

Children will:
1. Experience rhyming text.
2. Experience chanting rhymes.
3. Explore rhythmic movement (clapping, jumping, ball bouncing).

Action Vocabulary

Ball bouncing
Chanting
Clapping
Rope jumping

Concepts Explored

Steady beat
Patterns in movement

Developing Literacy Skills

Materials: Chart paper • Markers

▶ Introduce the author, Judy Sierra, who selected the rhymes, and illustrator, Melissa Sweet. Read the book's title to the children, including the subtitle. Ask the children for their predictions about the book.

▶ The cover illustrations and the words written in the jump rope will spark conversations about jump ropes rhymes. If appropriate, share the information in the introduction about the history of playground rhymes from several countries.

▶ Tell the children that they are going to learn how to chant rhymes and then explore moving their bodies to the beat of the rhymes.

▶ Before reading the book to the children, familiarize yourself with the rhymes in the book. Find your favorites from your childhood. Considering the children's interests and developmental level, choose three or four rhymes that you feel your children will enjoy.

▶ Write the rhymes on large chart paper so the children can read them with you.

▶ Ask the children to sit in pairs. Read the first rhyme, using a chanting or singsong inflection. Invite the children to repeat the rhyme with you several times.

▶ When you feel the children are ready, have them sit facing their partner, knee-to-knee. Demonstrate a simple clapping pattern that they can perform together. As you say the rhyme the children clap to the rhythm of the rhyme. Encourage the children to say the words as they clap hands. Practice several times before moving onto the next rhyme. If appropriate, you may want to change the clapping pattern or ask the children to change partners.

▶ When you have presented all of the rhymes on the chart, the children are ready to explore the rhymes again, but this time on their feet!

Moving to the Story

Materials: Jump ropes, balls

▶ After you have read several rhymes that are appropriate for your children, ask each child to name his or her favorite.

► Invite them to do partner hand clap patterns, flat rope jumping, or ball bouncing to the rhyme. After each child is sitting so each has enough space to move, on your cue, they all chant the rhyme and try to keep their hands moving to the beat.

Developing Motor Skills

Rhythmic Ball Bouncing
Materials: Playground balls, one for each child
► Provide a ball for each child. Allow the children time to learn some ball control and explore steady beat ball bouncing. It is best for them to use both hands in bouncing the ball for both sides of the body to work together or **bilateral integration** (see page 197 in the Glossary). It may be easier for many children to simply drop the ball and catch it each time in order to develop a steady beat.
► After the children have practiced, say a rhyme with them as you clap out the beat.

Flat Rope Jumping
Materials: Braided yarn rope, jump rope, or thick string, one for each child
► Flat Rope Jumping is done with a thick rope or a string on the floor.
► Each child needs a large area in which to place his or her rope in a straight line with everyone facing the same direction. For safety of movement, be sure that there is sufficient space between each rope and between each row. If your space will not accommodate the whole class, do this activity with small groups of children.
► Give the children time to explore ways they can jump, hop, or leap over their rope, or move around their rope. They may want to try jumping side-to-side, apart-together straddle jumps, scissor jumps, or forward and backward jumps. Introduce the next steps in learning how to jump rope when the children have mastered the beginning steps and are ready to learn more.
► After some exploration time, have the children clap a steady beat as you read a jump rope rhyme from the book. Next have the children clap and jump at the same time. Remind the children that the jumps are to be small, light, and on the balls of their feet.

More Books to Share
Ant, Ant, Ant! An Insect Chant by April Pulley Sayre
Gimme a Break, Rattlesnake! Schoolyard Chants and Other Nonsense by Sonja Dunn
Trout, Trout, Trout! A Fish Chant by April Pulley Sayre

Music Suggestions
The *Rowdy Ropes* CD is designed for children who do not know how to jump rope. It has a guide book for teaching children the skills of jumping rope.

Rowdy Ropes by Dinotrax. Songs: All, although the following are recommended: 1, 2, 3, 4, 5, 6, 7, 8; March Around Our Ropes; Follow the Leader; Teddy Bear
Tony Chestnut & Fun Time Action Songs by The Learning Station. Songs: Tony Chestnut; Five Little Monkeys

Safety Tip: It is best for children to wear athletic shoes when jumping. Remind the children to check their personal space to make certain that others are not too close.

"Slowly, Slowly, Slowly," Said the Sloth
by Eric Carle

What's the Book About?

Eric Carle has written a wonderful story about another way to move through life—slowly. This adventure, featuring a sloth, takes place in the Amazon rain forest where the sloth meets a host of animals that are curious about why the sloth moves so slowly. Eric Carle's illustrations will capture and slow down even the fastest-moving children.

Theme Connections

Animals	Habitats
Feelings	Imagination

Lesson Objectives

Children will:
1. Experience repetitive text.
2. Explore animals of the Amazon rain forest.
3. Explore new vocabulary of synonyms.
4. Experience interpretive movement.

Action Vocabulary

Awaken	Hang	Think
Crawl	Sleep	Yawn

Concepts Explored

Boring	Lazy	Relaxed
Calm	Lethargic	Slow
Impassive	Mellow	Sluggish
Lackadaisical		Stoic
Laid-back	Placid	Unflappable
Languid	Quiet	Upside down

Developing Literacy Skills

Materials: Chart paper • Markers

▶ Introduce the book's author and illustrator, Eric Carle. Many children are familiar with Eric Carle's books. Some children may not recognize Eric Carle's name but they may be familiar with the style he uses to illustrate his works.

▶ Read the title of the book and show the cover illustration to the children. Ask them to predict the storyline. Tell the children that the animals in this story live in the Amazon rain forest. For more information about sloths, refer to the book's foreword, written by Jane Goodall.

▶ To add to the enjoyment of Story Time and to increase comprehension and understanding of new words, begin by sharing the inside of the back cover with the children. There are 24 animals featured on last page spread, along with their names. The animals appear throughout the story. Tell the children to watch for the animals as you read the book.

▶ On the left side of a large piece of chart paper, write "Sloth." Tell the children that, with their help, you are going to make a list of the words used by the animals in the story to describe the sloth.

▶ After you read each page spread, pause for a moment so the children can tell you the word each animal uses when it talks to the sloth. Add each word to the list. When you get to the page where the sloth describes itself, add these words to the list as well. Encourage the children to repeat the words after you. Engage the children in a discussion about how the words are similar in meaning.

▶ Read the book again. Ask the children to identify the animal (other than the sloth) on each page spread and write that animal's name on the right side of the chart paper.

▶ Ask the children to say two or three words that describe how that particular animal moves. Continue with the rest of the book. After you are finished reading the book, ask the children to share their thoughts about how all animals move uniquely.

Moving to the Story

▶ Explain to the children that they will take turns pretending to be a photographer in a rain forest. Choose one child, who goes to the opposite end of the room and turns his or her back to the rest of the children.

▶ Invite the remaining children to pick an animal from the book or any other rain forest animal that may not be in the book to act out.

▶ Choose one child to be the sloth. Remind the sloth to move very, very slowly. The children all act out the movements of their chosen animals, moving slowly on all fours, if at all possible, so the photographer will have a harder time finding the sloth among them.

▶ The photographer says, "Camera, action!," turns to face the children, and looks through a pretend camera, trying to find the sloth. The children will soon learn not to make animal sounds or to move too fast, so it is more difficult for the photographer to identify the child who is the sloth.

▶ When the photographer guesses correctly which child is the sloth, that child becomes the new photographer and the remaining children choose a new sloth.

Developing Motor Skills

Animal Show

Material: Chart paper and marker • CD player with suggested music (see list on the right) or music of your own choice

▶ Tell the children that they are animals in a show and you are the show master. Introduce each "animal" to a pretend audience. After each child has had a chance to move or walk like an animal, ask the children to choose their favorite animal for one last parade.

▶ Write down each chosen animal on a chart. As you call out the name of each animal, the child representing that animal moves like that animal and then tells something that is unique about his or her animal. For example, if you say, "elephant," the child might first move like an elephant and then say that the elephant has a long nose (trunk).

▶ After each animal (child) has been introduced, invite all of them to move in their own way around the activity space.

Safety Tip: Remind the children to share general space as they all move around.

More Books to Share
Anita Takes Notes by Osvaldo P. Amelio-Ortiz
Just Think! by Bette Killion

Music Suggestions
Jungle Jazz Band by Mark Oblinger. Songs: All or any, children/teacher's choice
Jungle Jazz Joint Jam by Play It Cool Records. Songs: All or any, children/teacher's choice
Jungle Jazz Joint Jump by Play It Cool Records. Songs: All or any, children/teacher's choice
More Music with Mar by Music with Mar. Song: Jungle
Walter the Waltzing Worm by Hap Palmer. Song: Song About Slow, Song About Fast

The Snail's Spell

by Joanne Ryder, illustrated by Lynne Cherry

What's the Book About?

This short story is about a child who imagines life as a snail. The language is slow-paced and dream-like and takes place in a garden. The guided imagery is excellent! The detailed illustrations in the garden are brilliant, and extend this book into the area of science. This story is perfect for encouraging children to slow down their bodies and focus their thoughts.

Theme Connections

Animals
Habitats
Imagination

Lesson Objectives

Children will:
1. Explore the concept of imagining.
2. Explore characteristics and the habitat of snails.
3. Explore interpretive movement.

Action Vocabulary

Curl	Pull
Glide	Stretch
Lying	Touch

Concepts Explored

Down	Slowly
Fast	Small
Feel	Smaller
Hide	Soft
Imagine	Up
Long	Upside down
Shrink	

Developing Literacy Skills

Materials: Chart paper • Markers • CD player and soft, instrumental music, optional

▶ Introduce the book's author, Joanne Ryder, and illustrator, Lynne Cherry. Read the title to the children and show them the cover illustration. Take a moment to point out the animals that are on the cover and ask the children to predict the storyline. This might be difficult for very young children so you may want to tell them that the child in the story is going to use his imagination as he pretends to be a snail moving through a vegetable garden.

▶ This story provides just the right words for a wonderful lesson based on guided imagery.

▶ Before reading the story, help the children create a **KWL chart** about snails (What Do We **K**now About Snails?; What Do We **W**ant to Know? and What Did We **L**earn?). Write the three headings in columns at the top of a piece of large chart paper. Encourage the children to offer ideas for the first and second columns. Allow several minutes for this activity. When the children are finished, tell them that they will complete the chart after you read the story.

▶ You may want to play soft instrumental music to help set the stage for reading the book.

▶ Begin Story Time by inviting the children to curl into a small shape just like the child in the first illustration.

▶ Read the pages slowly to emphasize how a snail moves. Pause at the end of each page so the children have an opportunity to explore different ways to move as they imagine being a snail. Be sure to point to the child in each illustration. As he immerses himself in the story, he imagines himself becoming smaller and smaller.

▶ When you are finished reading the story, invite the children to talk about how it felt to move like a snail. Focus on the KWL chart and review the first two columns. Help the children make changes to the first column, based on what they learned. Complete the last column as you guide the children's discussion.

Moving to the Story

▶ Tell the children that they are going to glide, in snail-like manner, across the floor.

▶ Divide the class into four groups. Line them up side by side with lots of room between each group. This allows them enough room to move without bumping into one another.

▶ The first child in each of the four lines curls up just like the child in the book. Then these children slide their arms forward, stretching out as far as they can. The next step is to pull the legs back up under the body by shifting the weight of the body to the forearms, and sliding the knees forward. After the first child in each group slides forward, each child behind will, in turn, do the same. The waiting children may want to practice how a snail moves by moving their fingers up and down their arm or leg as a snail would move.

▶ After each group of children has had a turn to try to move like a snail, ask them to do it again with their eyes closed. Let the children know that snails do not see like we see. They can sense light and dark, and must feel their way along. Their hands (feelers) may touch things as they move along, and they will have to decide whether to continue in that direction or change directions. This activity enables the children to explore all of the action words listed on the previous page.

Developing Motor Skills

Snail Tracks

Materials: Lengths of tape, floor balance beams, or balance strips

▶ Review the page in the book where it says that the snail makes its own sticky path to glide on.

▶ Put painters' tape, masking tape, duct tape, a balance beam, or balance strips on the floor.

▶ Ask the children to move like snails along the tape, balance beam, or balance strips.
Note: Make sure that there are only four or five children moving at a time unless you are in a gym or have a large space in your classroom.

▶ Suggest that the children close their eyes and try to stay on their path.

Safety Tips: If the floor is hard on the children's elbows or knees, ask them to think of a way that they could move like a snail and not hurt their knees or elbows. Sometimes all it takes is putting on a sweater or sweatshirt to cover the elbows, and making sure that their pants cover their knees. The children will be more successful at being snails if they take off their shoes.

More Books to Share
Let's Make-Believe by P. Taylor Copeland
Free Fall by David Weisner

Music Suggestions
Leaping Literacy by Kimbo Educational. Song: The Sounds of Nature
Singing in Our Garden by Banana Slug String Band. Song: No Bones Within
We All Live Together, Volume 3 by Greg and Steve. Song: Nocturnal (Instrumental)

Snowball Fight!

by Jimmy Fallon, illustrated by Adam Stower

What's the Book About?

"Snow day!" is music to the ears of children. In this delightful story, a boy and his young sister awake to the news that school is closed. They immediately plan a snowball fight and anxiously await the arrival of neighborhood friends. Attack! An all-in-fun snowball fight ensues. This story celebrates a time-honored, childhood winter delight.

Theme Connections

Friendship
Seasons

Lesson Objectives

Children will:
1. Experience repetition in text.
2. Experience rhyming text.
3. Explore interpretive movement.

Action Vocabulary

Attack
Run

Concepts Explored

Competitive activities

Developing Literacy Skills

▶ Introduce the book's author, Jimmy Fallon, and illustrator, Adam Stower. Read the title to the children and ask them to predict the storyline.

▶ The title is sure to excite children who look forward to winter every year as well as children who have never experienced snow. Invite the children to use their imaginations as you read so they, too, can experience a snowball fight.

▶ Before reading the story, engage the children in a discussion about competition. Many teachers like to use the term "friendly competition" to help young children understand that the goal for competitive activities at this age is to have fun. Tell them that the children in the story play so everyone stays safe.

▶ Read the repeated phrase in the book and ask the children to repeat the phrase after you say it. Invite them to say the phrase with you every time you read it in the book.

▶ After you finish reading the story, ask the children to share their experiences playing in the snow. If you live in a mild climate, ask the children what they would do if school closed because of snow. Encourage the children to share their thoughts and ideas.

Moving to the Story

Materials: Masking tape • Old newspapers or magazine pages

▶ Divide the children into two groups that are evenly matched physically. One group is on one side of the room and the other half on the other side of the room.

▶ Place a piece of tape on the floor in the middle of the space. Place several piles of old newspapers or magazine pages on each side of the room.

▶ When you say, "Go," the children quickly make paper balls (snowballs) and toss them at the children on the other side of the room. When a child is hit with a snowball, he or she must move over to the opposite side.
   Note: With young children, make the paper snowballs ahead of time.

▶ After two minutes or so, stop the game to see who has gathered the most players. Have the players return to their original side and begin again.

Developing Motor Skills

Snowball Target Toss

Materials: Targets, such as cardboard boxes or buckets, hoops, or cutout snowflakes • Foam balls, beanbags, or paper balls • Hoops

▶ Arrange several target stations around the room. Provide at least five targets of various heights and distances. The targets can be buckets or boxes arranged at different distances from the throw line, hoops, cutout snowflakes taped at different levels to the wall, or anything else that will work for your area.

▶ Ask the children to find a partner. Provide at least six balls or beanbags per station, or three balls per child. These are the "snowballs."
Note: At the box or bucket station, provide beanbags. At the hoop station, provide paper balls, foam balls, or other balls.

▶ The children throw the "snowballs" at each station and try to hit the target. One child throws three balls or beanbags, and then the other child has a turn to throw three balls or beanbags.

▶ Provide a hoop at each station for the children to throw from and to return their "snowballs" to when completed. Allow approximately one minute for the children to throw their three balls, return them to the start line, and be ready to move to the next station.

▶ If some children need more time, then adjust accordingly for the entire group. Remind the children to put the opposite foot forward from their throwing hand. For example, if they throw with the right hand, the left foot needs to be in front, and alternately for the left hand.

Safety Tip: Remind the children that beanbags are only to be thrown at targets.

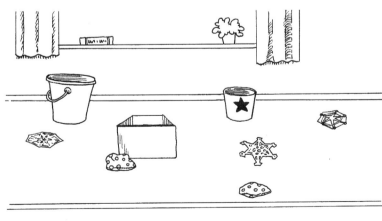

More Books to Share
All You Need for a Snowman by Alice Schertle
Downhill Fun by Michael Dahl
Snow Day! by Barbara M. Joosse
The Snowy Day by Ezra Jack Keats

Someone Says
by Carole Lexa Schaefer, illustrated by Pierr Morgan

What's the Book About?

An active group of children moves through their day at school leaping like frogs, dancing like ponies, and eating like tigers. Their play is a time for their imaginations to soar. This book is illustrated with vibrant artwork and is full of onomatopoeic language.

Theme Connections

Animals
Exercise
Exploring cultures
Imagination

Lesson Objectives

Children will:
1. Experience **onomatopoeia**.
2. Experience rhyming words.
3. Explore interpretive movement.

Action Vocabulary

Build
Dance
Draw
Eat
Fly
Leapfrog
Line up
Sing
Walk

Concept Exploration

Cooperation
Dream
Imagine
Pretend

Developing Literacy Skills

▶ Introduce the book's author, Carole Lexa Schaefer, and illustrator, Pierr Morgan. Read the title to the children, show them the front and back cover illustrations, and ask them to predict the storyline.

▶ The title and cover illustrations do not give clues about the story so you may want to tell the children that the book is about a group of schoolchildren who really like to use their imaginations. Encourage the children to remember all of the activities that the children in the book participate in during their day.

▶ Before reading the story, tell the children that the book's illustrator drew an image over and around the children to give us a sense of their imaginations. For example, the little girl on the cover who is pretending to fly has a sketch of a bird around her. That is her imagination at work!

▶ As you read the story, draw the children's attention to the illustrations. Because the story is short, you may want to spend time having the children repeat the rhyming word pairs (for example, *clip* and *clop*) and the onomatopoeic words (for example, *spring* and *boink*). This simple activity helps develop important **pre-reading** skills. When you are finished reading the story, the children will be ready to act out the storyline.

Moving to the Story

Materials: Hoop

▶ Have the children scatter around the circle time space.

▶ Place a hoop in the center of the area. Ask each child to think of an action word that everyone can do, just like the children in the story. You may start by suggesting a few of the action words from the story, such as *walk, leapfrog, line up,* and *dance*.

▶ Tell the children that you will name an action word or words after saying, "Someone says…." (For example, "Someone says clap your hands.") Select a child to stand in the hoop and demonstrate the action that everyone else will do.

- After all the children do the action, say, "Someone says…" again, and another child stands in the hoop and demonstrates the new action. Continue until everyone has had a turn to be leader.
- If appropriate, depending on the skills and interest of the children, another option would be for you to say, "Someone says…," and a child steps into the hoop, and says and does an action for everyone to follow.

Developing Motor Skills

Imagination
Materials: Scarves • CD player and instrumental music • Hoops or ropes
- Give each child a scarf. Begin by asking the children to imagine different ways they can use the scarf. Examples include as a superhero's cape, a hula skirt, or the wings of a bird. The possibilities are endless.
- Invite each child to imagine a way to use the scarf. Put on some instrumental music and let each child come up with a suggestion.
- Try imagining with hoops or ropes. Observe how the children's actions change.

More Books to Share
Countdown to Kindergarten by Alison McGhee
D.W.'s Guide to Preschool by Marc Brown
Miss Bindergarten Gets Ready for Kindergarten by Joseph Slate
Preschool to the Rescue by Judy Sierra

Music Suggestions
Any instrumental music piece with a mellow beat is appropriate.

Sometimes I Like to Curl Up in a Ball

by Vicki Churchill, illustrated by Charles Fuge

What's the Book About?

Wombat spends his day as most young children do—playing! Wombat loves to move and make sounds, just because it feels good. As Wombat moves through his day, he entertains himself and his friends. This book is an enjoyable reminder that children's play does not always need a purpose. "Just because" is good enough!

Theme Connections

Friendship
Humor

Lesson Objectives

Children will:
1. Experience rhyming text.
2. Explore the concept of play.
3. Explore a variety of motor movements.

Action Vocabulary

Curl
Fall
Jump
Land
Jog
Run
Walk

Concepts Explored

Personal space
Travel

Developing Literacy Skills

▶ Some children might not be familiar with wombats, so an explanation about this playful animal is a great way to start the lesson. This stocky, burrowing creature is about three feet long and lives in Australia. It is in the marsupial family.

▶ Ask the children to share their thoughts and ideas about playing to set the stage for this book. For example, ask, "Do you like to play alone?" "Do you always have fun when you play?" "How do you decide what you want to play with?"

▶ Ask the children to see what inspires Wombat's play. The illustrations in this book are delightful and really convey Wombat's pleasure while playing.

▶ As you read the story, draw the children's attention to the rhyming words. Pause at the end of a sentence to encourage the children to come up with a rhyming word that completes the sentence. Some children will choose a word that not only rhymes, but also makes contextual sense. Other children will search for a word that rhymes but is very silly. Accept both responses. Children love to play with words.

▶ Use the pictures to help children predict parts of the story and foster their comprehension.

Moving to the Story

▶ *Sometimes I Like to Curl Up in a Ball* begs for active interpretation by the children as you read it.

▶ The pictures and the rhyme in the story will encourage the children to be more dramatic as the story comes to life. If you allow plenty of time for the children to interpret the story in their own way, you will see the creative ways children interpret the story.

▶ Praise the children for their imaginative actions to encourage them to take risks and move in new ways.

▶ This is a great story to read as a transition. Ask the children to stay curled up after you finish reading the story. During this restful moment, tell them the next activity of the day.

Developing Motor Skills

Moving Like Wombat

Materials: Carpet mats, one for each child • CD player for music • Mat for practicing falling and landing

▶ This activity focuses on locomotor skills. Explain to the children that Wombat loves to move in many different ways, including *curling up, falling, jumping, walking,* and *running.*

▶ Review the definition of *personal space,* and ask the children to stay within their personal space and not travel around the room as they move. (Carpet mats are a great way to identify a child's space.) Although Wombat runs in the story, ask the children to jog in place. The skill of falling also needs to be controlled. Ask a child to model falling in slow motion so all the children have a clear idea about how to practice this skill.

   Note: Be sure to provide a mat for the child to do this.

▶ Ask the children to find their personal space in which to move. "Show me how you can…" is a great way to guide their movement. Complete the sentence by adding one of the action words from the story, such as *curl, jump,* or *walk.* This is a great way to assess the developmental level of the children's motor skills.

▶ Spend just enough time with each skill so you can observe each child but still keep a quick pace. Make a mental note if any of the children have difficulty with a particular skill, and plan lessons that allow children time to practice these skills.

Safety Tips: Remind children to always land on their feet when jumping. If you allow the children to be noisy and yell as Wombat did, you may want to prepare them, because some children may become startled or upset by loud noises.

More Books to Share

Diary of a Wombat by Jackie French
Found You, Little Wombat! by
    Angela McAllister
Swim, Little Wombat, Swim! by
    Charles Fuge
Wombat Divine by Mem Fox

Music Suggestions

Any Australian music featuring a didgeridoo (similar to a kazoo)

The Squiggle
by Carole Lexa Schaefer

What's the Book About?

With a little creativity, a piece of string can be anything. This book tells the story of a class of children taking a walk to the park. They are all in a slow, tight, straight line except for the little girl at the end of the line. She finds a piece of string and the fun begins. To extend the book, the author includes several activities.

Theme Connections

Exploring cultures
Imagination
Shapes
Spatial concepts

Lesson Objectives

Children will:
1. Explore the concept of imagining.
2. Explore interpretive movement.

Action Vocabulary

Dance	Slither
Grab	Snap
Pat	Tug
Push	Turn
Shuffle	Walk

Concepts Explored

Around	Outside
Beside	Over
Between	Path
Big	Slow
Bunched up	Ripple
Full	Rise
Inside	Squiggle
Last	Straight Line
Long	Tight

Developing Literacy Skills

Materials: Pieces of string or yarn, each about a yard long, one for each child

▶ Introduce the book's author, Carole Lexa Schaefer, and illustrator, Pierr Morgan, to the children. Read the title and share the cover illustration. Ask the children to predict the storyline.

▶ Very young children might not be familiar with the meaning of the word *squiggle* (a wavy line) so you may want to spend a few minutes discussing their ideas.

▶ Tell the children that the little girl on the cover takes an imaginative walk.

▶ The story includes words to describe the shapes or objects the girl designs. When you are finished reading the story, encourage the children to create words or sounds to complement their shapes.

Moving to the Story

Materials: Streamers, or pieces of yarn, rope, or string, one for each child

▶ Give children a streamer or a piece of yarn, rope, or string.

▶ Reread the story and invite the children to pretend that they are the little girl in the story. As you read each action or concept word, ask the children to look at the pictures in the book and move their strings, streamers, or yarn ropes in the same ways as the little girl, and encourage them to come up with their own ideas.

▶ At the end of the story, ask the children for other ideas of things they can pretend with their strings.

Developing Motor Skills

String/Rope Shapes

Materials: Paper shapes (triangle, rectangle, square, circle) • Streamers, braided yarn jump rope, or lengths of string (4' long)

▶ Give each child a piece of string or a yarn jump rope. Encourage them to explore movement possibilities with their string. Ask the children what things they can do or shapes they can make using their string or yarn rope.

▶ After the children have had a chance to explore the possibilities, hold up a common shape cut out of paper, such as *triangle, square, rectangle,* or *circle*, and ask the children to make the shape on the floor with their string or yarn rope.

More Books to Share
Alice the Fairy by David Shannon
Jumanji by Chris Van Allsburg

Music Suggestions
Ball, Hoop, and Ribbon Activities for Young Children by Kimbo Educational. Songs: Choose any or all of the ribbon songs or instrumentals
Rowdy Ropes by Dinonastics. Songs: Jump Rope Shapes; Letter Movements

▶ After making each individual shape, invite the children to explore the concepts of *over, around, beside, between, inside,* and *outside* of their shape. For even more movement, have the children do some of the following:
- ▶ hop up and down inside the shape;
- ▶ leap over the shape;
- ▶ gallop around the shape;
- ▶ make letters of the alphabet such as L, V, W, N, O, or P; and
- ▶ do a variety of other locomotor movements and other concepts.

Starry Safari
by Linda Ashman, illustrated by Jeff Mack

What's the Book About?

The girl in the story takes an imaginative safari driving a bright orange jeep. Children will love to act out this adventure, from interacting with the animals to pitching a tent at the end of the day. The scary night challenges the courageous girl, just before she is tucked in by the Big Safari Ranger. The large, brightly colored acrylic illustrations will keep children engaged in the story.

Theme Connections

Animals
Feelings
Imagination
Self-confidence
Sounds

Lesson Objectives

Children will:
1. Experience rhyming text.
2. Explore **onomatopoeia**.
3. Learn about safaris and animals of the African plains.
4. Explore interpretive movement.

Action Vocabulary

Bump	Gaze	Race
Chase	Go	Somersault
Circle	Hide	Swing
Crawl	Pass	Trail
Curl	Pounce	Wallow

Concepts Explored

Angry	Lanky	Scare
Detour	Listen	Tall
Inside	Overhead	Wily
Join	Roadblock	

Developing Literacy Skills

Materials: Chart paper • Markers

▶ Introduce the book's author, Linda Ashman, and illustrator, Jeff Mack. Share the front and back cover illustrations. Read the title to the children and ask them to predict the storyline.

▶ Ask the children to share what they know about safaris. Invite them to watch for their favorite animals as you read the story.

▶ On a large piece of chart paper, write "Safari." As you read the book, ask the children to help you list the names of the animals in the story.

▶ Emphasize the rhyming words. Read the rhyming phrases and pause just before finishing so the children can complete the phrases with a rhyming word.

▶ Toward the end of the story, you will find two pages of onomatopoeic words. After you finish reading the story, revisit the two pages and ask the children to think about which animals listed on the chart could have made the sounds that the little girl heard while inside her tent.

▶ Ask the children if the little girl was frightened by anything. Encourage the children to talk about what might frighten them and why.

Moving to the Story

Materials: Hoops, one for each child

▶ Give each child a hoop and explain that it is the steering wheel of their jeep.

▶ Have the children scatter around the room.

▶ Tell the children that as you read the story a second time, they are to do the following actions when you emphasize each of the following words:

  ▶ racing = run in place, lifting the knees high
  ▶ passing fields = walk
  ▶ trailing herds = take long giant steps in a zigzag pattern
  ▶ gazing = baby steps
  ▶ bump = stop
  ▶ chase = follow someone
  ▶ race = jog
  ▶ roadblock = jump up and down in place
  ▶ detour = hop on one foot
  ▶ wallow = turn around in a circle
  ▶ somersault = stop, put hoop down to the floor, step in it and bring it up over their body and head and back to their hands

▶ Because there are so many words in the story, remind the children of the action that goes with each word.

Note: Depending on the age and abilities of the children in your class, you might want to begin with three to five actions and let the children make up their own actions for the rest of the words in the story. After the children have mastered the actions, add more.

Safety Tip: When jogging, remind all the children to move around the room in the same direction.

Developing Motor Skills

Animal Tag
Materials: None

▶ Have all of the children move to one side of the room.

▶ Select one child to be the "animal catcher," who stands in the middle of the room. The remaining children choose which safari animal they want to be. The animals in the story are zebra, wildebeest, giraffe, rhino, ostrich, buffalo, hippo, crocodile, chimpanzee, gorilla, elephant, and lion. The children must remain that animal until they cross over to the opposite side of the room.

▶ When the animal catcher says the name of an animal, everyone who is that animal must try to run to the opposite side of the room without being caught.

▶ Whoever is tagged becomes the new animal catcher.

▶ Play continues until everyone has run across the room at least two times.

More Books to Share
Adventures of Riley: Safari in South Africa by Amanda Lumry and Laura Hurwitz
Magic Color Skeleton: Safari Animal Adventure by Shaheen Bilgrami
Meerkat's Safari by Claudia Graziano
On Safari by Diane James
Way Far Away on a Wild Safari by Jan Peck

Music Suggestions
Jungle Jazz Band by Mark Oblinger. Songs: All or any, children/teacher's choice
Jungle Jazz Joint Jam by Play It Cool Records. Songs: All or any, children/teacher's choice
Jungle Jazz Joint Jump by Play It Cool Records. Songs: All or any, children/teacher's choice
Literacy in Motion by The Learning Station. Songs: Swahili Counting Song; Kwanzaa

Susan Laughs

by Jeanne Willis, illustrated by Tony Ross

What's the Book About?

This sweet book shares the emotions and activities of Susan, a little girl who uses a wheelchair. Through rhyming couplets, the book focuses on Susan's abilities rather than her disabilities, showing that Susan and other children have much in common. The crayon and pencil illustrations portray a spirited Susan.

Theme Connections

Feelings
Friendship
Self-esteem

Lesson Objectives

Children will:
1. Experience rhyming and **predictable text**.
2. Explore a variety of movements.
3. Explore feelings and emotions.
4. Explore similarities and differences in people.

Action Vocabulary

Dance	Paint	Swing
Fly	Ride	Throw
Grin	Row	Trot
Hear	Sing	Wave
Hide	Spin	
Hug	Splash	
Laugh	Swim	

Concepts Explored

Angry	Happy	Shy
Bad	Loud	Strong
Fear	Proud	Wrong
Feel	Right	Weak
Good	Sad	

Developing Literacy Skills

Materials: Cutout paper dolls, one for each child

▶   Introduce the book's author, Jeanne Willis, and illustrator, Tony Ross. Read the title of the book and share the cover illustration. Ask the children to predict the storyline. Tell the children that Susan is like most other children in so many ways but she has one difference. Listen carefully!

▶   The story is full of action words and words that describe Susan's feelings and emotions. For an interactive Story Time, give the children cutout paper dolls and ask them to pretend the paper doll is their friend, Susan.

▶   As you read the story, invite the children to act it out with their paper doll. Draw the children's attention to the illustrations on each page. Encourage the children to talk about how they might be like Susan, in actions or feelings.

▶   The book is written in simple rhymes. Pause before finishing each rhyming couplet so the children can complete the sentence with a rhyming word.

▶   When you are finished reading the story, invite the children to talk about their experiences with children who have disabilities. Allow enough time for young learners to talk about their thoughts and to ask questions.

Moving to the Story

▶   Susan is just like any other active child. She does what her friends do, just differently.

▶   Say each of the action vocabulary words (see the list on the left) and ask the children how they might pretend to do some of the things that Susan does, such as *flying* and *swinging*. For example, they might explore how many of their body parts can swing back and forth, and ways they could pretend to fly.

▶   Suggest that the children use different parts of their bodies to explore emotional concepts. For example, ask the children how their bodies would look if they were showing *sadness* or *fear*. Encourage your class to try a variety of facial expressions to go with the emotional concepts.

Developing Motor Skills

Popcorn

Materials: Parachute or large sheet
• Playground balls, balloons, sponge balls

▶ Ask each child to move a chair around the perimeter of the circle/story time area.

▶ Bring out a parachute or large sheet. Instruct the children to all grab a handle (if a parachute) or material along the edge (if a sheet), sit down, and shake the wrinkles out.

▶ Toss some balloons, sponge balls, and playground balls onto the parachute. The children try to shake all of the balloons and balls off the parachute.

▶ Ask some children to retrieve the balls and balloons, and put them back on, after everything has been shaken off. Continue until interest wanes.

It is important to adapt play to children's special needs. To help children develop a greater understanding of children with disabilities, and in Susan's case lower body disabilities, the following games are modified so all children can play them.

Balloon Striking

Materials: Paint sticks • Paper plates • Glue • String or yarn • Balloons

▶ Ask the children to each find a partner.

▶ Each child sets up his or her chair directly in front of his or her partner's chair, which is approximately 5' away.

▶ Make a paddle by gluing a paint stick between two paper plates. If necessary, tie one end of a piece of string or yarn that is about 8' in length around a balloon and the other end to one of the paddles for quick retrieval.

▶ The children try to volley the balloon back and forth as many times as possible. The idea is to try to do more strikes than their previous count.

More Books to Share

Arnie and the New Kid by Nancy Carlson
Don't Call Me Special: A First Look at Disability by Pat Thomas
Friends at School by Rochelle Bunnett
We Can Do It! by Laura Dwight

Music Suggestions

We All Live Together, Volume 2 by Greg and Steve. Song: Popcorn
We All Live Together, Volume 5 by Greg and Steve. Song: Friends Forever

Teddy Bear, Teddy Bear: A Classic Action Rhyme

illustrated by Michael Hague

What's the Book About?

This version of the classic rhyme includes notes and illustrations at the end of the book so teachers can learn the actions to the rhyme if they are not familiar with them. The colorful illustrations are outstanding! The little bear and his mother are adorable and there are just enough details on every page to keep young children interested in the book.

Theme Connections

Exercise
Imagination

Lesson Objectives

Children will:

1. Experience rhyme in text.
2. Interact with **predictable text**.
3. Explore a variety of movements.

Action Vocabulary

Balance (Show Your Shoe)
Bend (Touch the Ground)
Climb (Stairs)
Turn (Around)

Concepts Explored

Off
On

Developing Literacy Skills

Materials: Teddy bears, one for each child

▶ Introduce the story's illustrator, Michael Hague. Read the title of the book to the children and show them the cover illustration. Ask the children to predict the storyline. This rhyme is very popular with children so many of them may be familiar with it. Explain that this rhyme has been around for many years, and the original author is unknown.

▶ If possible, gather enough teddy bears so each child has one. This helps create a fun, interactive Story Time. Set the bears aside for a moment.

▶ Tell the children that the first time you read the story they are going to help you read the words. The print is large enough so the children can follow along. Point to the words as you read them and encourage the children to join you. They will quickly learn the **predictable text**.

▶ Before reading the story a second time, share the last pages of the book (Note to Parents) with the children. You will find illustrations and directions for movements for each of the rhyming phrases.

▶ Give each child a bear and allow a minute or two for the children to practice the actions with their bear. As you read the story, invite the children to help their teddy bear act out the words to the story. The children may want to do this several times. They are now ready to get on their feet and pretend to be the teddy bear!

Moving to the Story

▶ This is a fun action rhyme that the children can act out as you read.

▶ If the children are older and know how to jump rope, you might want to take this activity to a large open space and have the children jump rope. If appropriate, try long rope jumping, which means groups of three children, with two turners and one jumper. If the children are not yet ready to jump with the rope turning, the two turners can gently swing the rope to and fro for the jumper to learn to jump over. This is a basic rope jumping progression. The children can take turns being turners and jumpers.

Safety Tip: Remind the children to stay safe by keeping far enough away from turning ropes.

Developing Motor Skills

Teddy Bear Antics

Materials: None

▶ Invite the children to make up their own action rhymes and act them out.

▶ After reading each page to the children, ask them what other movement possibilities they might add to the story that would also rhyme. An example might be "Teddy Bear, Teddy Bear jump up and down. Teddy Bear, Teddy Bear leap with a bound."

More Books to Share

The Teddy Bear by David McPhail
Teddy Bear Tears by Jim Aylesworth
Teddy Bears' Picnic by Jimmy Kennedy
Where's My Teddy? by Jez Alborough

Music Suggestions

Fun and Games by Greg and Steve. Song: The Teddy Bear Song
It's Toddler Time by Kimbo Educational. Song: Teddy Bear
Rowdy Ropes by Dinotrax. Song: Teddy Bear
Shake, Rattle, and Rock by Greg and Steve. Song: Teddy Bears Picnic
"So Big" Activity Songs for Little Ones by Hap Palmer. Song: Teddy Bear Playtime

All terms in bold are explained in greater detail in the Glossary on Appendix pages 188-199.

Ten in the Den

by John Butler

What's the Book About?

Ten in the Den revisits a popular counting rhyme. The 10 cuddly animals are snug in their den but the little mouse asks the animals to "roll over." Out of the den and down the grassy hill they go! Finally, the little mouse finds himself all alone in the den and scampers after his friends. They all snuggle together and fall fast asleep. The soft, pastel watercolors make the plush animals look real.

Theme Connections

Animals
Friendship
Numbers
Parts of the body

Lesson Objectives

Children will:

1. Experience rhyming text.
2. Experience **predictable text**.
3. Explore counting down.
4. Explore a variety of movements.

Action Vocabulary

Bounce	Slide
Bump	Slip
Fall	Snuggle
Flop	Thump
Hop	Tumble
Pounce	Wiggle
Roll	Yawn
Scamper	

Concepts Explored

Little	Squiggle
Over	Swirl
Prickly	Tickly
Rumble	Whirl

Developing Literacy Skills

▶ Introduce the book's author and illustrator, John Butler. Read the title to the children and show them the book cover. The children will enjoy counting the cute animals on the cover.

▶ Point to the mouse in the illustration and tell the children that the little mouse creates a big problem. Can the little mouse solve the problem at the end of the story?

▶ Just like the popular rhyme, "Ten in the Bed," the rhyme in this book allows children to count down from 10 to none. If the children know the rhyme, encourage a few minutes of conversation about counting down.

▶ Ask the children to hold up their hands and show 10 fingers. Invite them to count down, using their fingers, as you read the story.

▶ Ask the children to help you read the repetitive phrase and to repeat the rhyming words that describe how the animals moved down the hill.

▶ When you finish the story, engage the children in a discussion about the friendship the animals have. Consider talking about how it might feel to roll down a hill. After this discussion, the young learners will be ready to act out the part of the little animals in the story.

Moving to the Story

Materials: Tape

▶ Divide the class into groups of 10. Explain that they will be acting out the parts of the animals.

▶ Use tape to designate an area on the floor as the den. Each group of 10 children lies down on their backs next to each other in this space.

▶ Before you reread the story to the children, have them count off by 10, so each child knows his or her number. The little mouse is number one.

▶ If appropriate for your group, have the children practice either all rolling over together or one at a time, beginning with number 10. They can all shout, "Roll over!" together. Make certain that the children understand that they are to roll over only one time, beginning on their back and ending on their back.

▶ As you read the story, when you come to the new total in the den, do not tell them, but have each of the children count out their number beginning with the mouse to come up with the remaining number. The children may also want to act out the action words as they fall out of bed and then *roll, bounce, flop, hop, bump,* or *tumble* across the floor.

Safety Tips: To prevent "space invasion," ask the children to roll over keeping their legs "glued" together and their arms stretched overhead hiding their ears. Ask the children to all roll over together as they say, "Roll over."

Developing Motor Skills

Body Part Count
Materials: Hoops or individual carpet squares, one for each child

▶ Give each child a hoop or carpet square. The children place the hoop or carpet square on the floor and then stand in the middle of it, making certain that they have their own personal space.

▶ Explain that you will call out a number of body parts to remain inside the hoop and a certain number to be outside the hoop. No other body parts are to touch the floor except those called out. For example you might say, "Place four fingers inside the hoop and your bottom and five toes outside the hoop. How many body parts should be touching the floor?" Go no higher than 10 body parts, and limit the number according to the level of understanding of your children.

▶ Acknowledge the children's speed and accuracy of addition and, at the same time, note the children who need to learn to identify the parts of the body or to practice addition skills.

More Books to Share
Cha-Cha Chimps by Julia Durango
Click, Clack, Splish, Splash: A Counting Adventure by Doreen Cronin
The First Day of Winter by Denise Fleming
Over in the Meadow: A Counting Rhyme by Olive A. Wadsworth

Music Suggestions
Can Cockatoos Count by Twos? by Hap Palmer. Songs: Jumping to Add and Subtract; Numbers Can Tell About You
Kids in Motion by Greg and Steve. Song: Count Bounce
Leaping Literacy by Kimbo Educational. Songs: The Rhyme Family (Rhyme); Chim Chimmy Chimpanzee (Sentence Segmentation); Animal Cookies (Syllable Segmentation)

Ten Terrible Dinosaurs

by Paul Stickland

What's the Book About?

This title could not be more appropriate. Ten very feisty dinosaurs stomp, dance, push, and shove their way from a gang of ten, until one last dinosaur is left standing. His friends do not give up easily and come back for one last "roar." Children will love acting out this colorful counting book.

Theme Connections

Dinosaurs
Feelings
Numbers

Lesson Objectives

Children will:

1. Experience rhyming text.
2. Explore new vocabulary.
4. Explore subtraction.
4. Experience a variety of movements.

Action Vocabulary

Dance	Sneak
Flap	Stamp
Pop	Stand
Push	Stomp
Shove	Swing

Concept Exploration

Crazy	Tangle
Elated	Terrible
Enormous	Testy
Fearless	Thundering
Feisty	Weary
Silly	

Developing Literacy Skills

Materials: Plastic dinosaurs (10 for each child)

▶ Introduce the book's author and illustrator, Paul Stickland. Read the title to the children and show them the cover of the book. Ask the children to predict the storyline.

▶ The children will be eager to listen to this story, as many children love dinosaurs.

▶ To make Story Time interactive, give each child 10 plastic dinosaurs. **Note**: You can purchase inexpensive plastic dinosaur counters or markers from most teachers' supply catalogs.

▶ As you read the story, encourage the children to subtract one dinosaur at a time from their dinosaurs so they see a representation of the numerals on each page. You may want to pause half way through the story so the children can count the remaining dinosaurs to make sure they have subtracted correctly.

▶ Prompt the children to read the repetitive line by running your finger under the words as you read. They will quickly learn this line. The children will also enjoy shouting "Roar!" at the end of the story.

Moving to the Story

▶ Divide the class into groups of 10, one on each side of the Circle/Story Time area.

▶ Help the children count off from one to 10. Remind the children that dinosaurs are big and rowdy. They should stay in their personal space and move like dinosaurs, being careful not to touch the other dinosaurs.

▶ Start with 10, and then count off the remaining numbers. As you say each number, the child from each group who is that "number" moves to a designated spot. (Let the children decide where that place will be.)

▶ The remaining dinosaurs continue to act out the rhymes in the book until one "snoring" dinosaur in each group remains. The other dinosaurs sneak up on the sleeping dinosaurs and awaken them with a ROAR!

Developing Motor Skills

Dinosaur Tag

Materials: CD player with complementary music suggestions

▶ Just as in the story, the children will dance, stomp, stamp, flap, and move across the room. Ask the children to come up with additional creative ways to move across the room besides the four listed above.

▶ Choose a child to be "IT." IT calls out an action word such as *stomp*, and the children all stomp from one side of the room to the other. IT also moves in the same way as he or she tries to tag the other children.

▶ Every child who is gently tagged joins the IT in the center to try to tag the other children. The last child to be tagged becomes the new IT.

Safety Tip: Remind the children to use a gentle touch when tagging. You may also want to have IT tag with a sponge ball.

More Books to Share

How Do Dinosaurs Count to Ten? by Jane Yolen

How High Can a Dinosaur Count? by Valorie Fisher

March of the Dinosaurs by Jakki Wood

Ten Little Dinosaurs by Pattie Schnetzler

Music Suggestions

Rockin' Reading Readiness by Kimbo Educational. Song: Five Huge Dinosaurs

"So Big" Activity Songs for Little Ones by Hap Palmer. Songs: Ten Wiggle Worms (Part I); Ten Wiggle Worms (Part II)

Thesaurus Rex

by Laya Steinberg, illustrated by Debbie Hart

What's the Book About?

Thesaurus Rex is a busy explorer. He spends his day stretching, reaching, extending, bending, and then his pants need mending! This book provides many opportunities for movement while introducing children to synonyms. Children never tire of dinosaurs, so Thesaurus Rex will be a big hit. The watercolor and pen illustrations are bright and humorous.

Theme Connections

Dinosaurs
Families

Lesson Objectives

Children will:

1. Explore alliteration.
2. Explore onomatopoeia.
3. Explore rhyming text.
4. Explore synonyms.
5. Explore movement concepts.

Action Vocabulary (Synonyms)

Synonyms for call, clean, drink, eat, explore, land, leap, mud, play, slip, stretch, and wrap

Concepts Explored

Exploring
Playing

Developing Literacy Skills

▶ Introduce the book's author, Laya Steinberg, and illustrator, Debbie Harter. Read the title and show the front cover to the children. Ask them to predict the storyline.

▶ Most young children are not familiar with a *thesaurus*. Because the word ends in "saurus" and the main **character** is a dinosaur named Rex, many children will think that the story is about a "thesaurus dinosaur!" How you explain the meaning of *thesaurus* will depend on the developmental level of your children.

▶ This book is primarily about synonyms. Additionally, the text is written in rhyme and the words are great examples of **alliteration** and **onomatopoeia**. The text is simple so you will have ample time to focus on the rich language opportunities in this book.

▶ Before reading the book, ask the children to stand up in their own personal space. Read the first two pages and invite the children to follow Thesaurus Rex as he begins his day by exercising. Have the children sit down for the rest of the story.

▶ Read the first line on each page spread. Emphasize the key word and ask the children to think of words that have the same or similar meanings. When the children are finished sharing their thoughts, read the remainder of the text and draw attention to the synonyms. Emphasize the rhyme, alliteration, and onomatopoeia as you read. When reading the last page, invite the children to curl up in their personal space and say, "goodnight." This is a great way to transition to another activity or another part of the day.

Moving to the Story

▶ Invite everyone to stand up and this time as you read the story, ask the children to pantomime or act out as many words as they can in the story.

▶ By looking at the pictures in the book, and with you pointing out each word next to the picture, the children will be able to act out the words more effectively.

Developing Motor Skills

Dinosaur Stomp

Materials: *Rockin' Reading Readiness* CD and CD player

▶ Play the instrumental version of "Five Huge Dinosaurs" or your own instrumental music with a slow, heavy, dinosaur-like beat.

▶ As the children begin to move to the music, call out a word and its synonyms for them to act out.

▶ Give the children time between each of the synonyms to think about slight differences among each of the words. After they have mastered the skills necessary for this activity, they can progress to learning Synonym Charades.

Synonym Charades

Materials: Chart paper and marker • CD and suggested music selections

▶ Write the 12 key words from the book and their synonyms on chart paper.

▶ Divide the children into two teams. Each team sits across from each other in the Circle/Story Time area.

▶ Explain that when you call a child from one of the teams, you will whisper a word that the child acts out for his or her team. Remind the children that they may want to use the movements from Dinosaur Stomp to make the game easier to guess the correct word or synonyms. Whisper one of the 12 key words and its synonyms to the child. The child may choose any of the words within that word grouping to act out. (The book does not give any words to go with *land*, so we have added three synonyms for it—*alight, get down*, and *touch down*.)

▶ If anyone on the child's team says the word or any of its synonyms, they get credit for the word. Agree upon amount of time for each team to figure out what the word or its synonyms are. If the player's team cannot determine the word, the opposite team will have a chance to say the word or any of its synonyms. If the opposite team guesses correctly, they get to keep the opposite team's player. If the opposite team cannot immediately come up with the word or a synonym, it goes to the back of the pile that you are holding.

▶ This is a friendly competition to see who can "capture" the most players from the opposite team by correctly guessing the keyword or any of its synonyms.

Safety Tip: When acting out the synonyms remind the children that they are sharing general space.

More Books to Share

How Do Dinosaurs Eat Their Food? by Jane Yolen
How Do Dinosaurs Get Well Soon? by Jane Yolen
When Dinosaurs Go to School by Linda Martin

Music Suggestions

Movin' & Shakin' for Youngsters by Russ InVision. Song: First I'm Stretching
Rockin' Reading Readiness by Kimbo Educational. Song: Five Huge Dinosaurs

All terms in bold are explained in greater detail in the Glossary on Appendix pages 188-199.

Three Cheers for Tacky

by Helen Lester, illustrated by Lynn Munsinger

What's the Book About?

In this rambunctious story, Tacky the penguin joins his rather proper penguin friends in practicing for a cheerleading contest. Try as they might, the proper penguins cannot get quirky Tacky to perform the simple cheer. The day of the contest arrives and, within minutes, Tacky's missteps have the audience and judges laughing and begging for more. This book sets the stage for children to explore a good-natured group activity.

Theme Connections

Cooperation	Self-confidence
Friendship	Self-esteem
Humor	

Lesson Objectives

Children will:
1. Experience rhyming text.
2. Identify main **characters** and setting in a story.
3. Identify the problem and solution in a story.
4. Explore a variety of movements.

Action Vocabulary

Bow	Roll
Cheer	Sit
Clap	Stand
Crash	Trip
Flop	Waddle
March	Wave

Concept Exploration

Bored	Properly
Cooperate	Right
Exactly	Softly
Left	Teamwork
Practice	Wildly

Developing Literacy Skills

Materials: Chart paper • Markers

▶ Before reading the story, take a few moments to write the penguins' cheer on a large piece of chart paper.

▶ Introduce the book's author, Helen Lester, and illustrator, Lynn Munsinger. Read the title to the children and show them the cover illustration. The back cover will also be of interest to the children. Ask the children to predict the storyline.

▶ Some children may be familiar with the pompoms the penguins are holding and the word *cheer*. Tell the children to watch Tacky because he has a unique way of moving and cheering.

▶ Explain what a cheer is and familiarize the children with the cheer that the penguins will perform. Tell the children that as they sit and listen to the story, they can do the hand movements every time the penguins practice their cheer.

▶ Draw the children's attention to the penguins' cheering costumes. Each penguin has his or her initial on his or her sweater. This may help the children remember the names of the main characters in the story.

▶ Read the story with enthusiasm, particularly the cheer. Allow enough time for the children to look at the illustrations. Tacky's antics are funny! After you finish reading the story, ask the children to share their thoughts and ideas about cooperation and practicing as a team. The children may want to create their own cheers.

Moving to the Story

Materials: Streamers

▶ Divide the class into groups of five or six children per group. Give each child a streamer. The groups pretend they are going to be in a cheer contest, just like Tacky and his friends. Ask them to:
   ▶ Practice marching.
   ▶ Create a special pattern using left and right activities, either in marching, moving their streamer, or both.
   ▶ Make up a short cheer.

▶ Give the children an agreed-upon time limit to prepare their march and cheer. After they come up with their cheer, give them about five minutes to practice.

▶ Invite each group to present the group cheer. Remind everyone what being a respectful audience means.

▶ Award blue ribbons to everyone!

Developing Motor Skills

Follow the Leader with Streamers

Materials: CD player with suggested music • Ribbon streamers or crepe paper streamers • Scarves, if ribbons or streamers are not available

▶ Do this activity in a group, indoors or outdoors.

▶ Gather all of the children into a large circle formation with plenty of room for streamer movement.

▶ Begin by putting on one of the songs for streamers from *Ball, Hoop, and Ribbon Activities for Young Children*, or any similar music. Music is important for this activity.

▶ Encourage the children to explore movement possibilities with their streamers. Suggestions include circles overhead (helicopter), side or front arm circles, horizontal circles (stir the cookies), sweeping actions, rainbow arches, up and down movements, spirals, and twirling actions.

▶ Tell the children that they each will have a chance to be the leader. If the children are in one large circle, each new leader will step into the center to show off his or her special streamer pattern.

More Books to Share

The Enormous Potato by Aubrey Davis

Nicole's Boat by Allen Morgan

The Perfect Clubhouse by Daniel J. Mahoney

Working Together by Pam Scheunemann

Music Suggestions

Animal Romp and Stomp for Kids by Russ InVision. Song: Penguin Waddle

Ball, Hoop, and Ribbon Activities for Young Children by Kimbo Educational. Instrumental song versions: The Muppet Show Theme; Ding Dong the Witch Is Dead; "Chinese Dance" from The Nutcracker

Dinonastics Bean Bag Songs Activity Songs by Dinotrax. Song: Bean Bag "Walk Walk Walk (Like a Penquin)

Preschool Playtime Band by Kimbo Educational. Instrumental song versions: Alexander's Ragtime Band; Yankee Doodle Dandy/You're a Grand Old Flag; Come Follow the Band; Entry of the Gladiators; Hey, Look Me Over; McNamara's Band; Stars and Stripes

Safety Tip: Remind the children to give themselves and their streamers enough room for movement.

Tumble Bumble

by Felicia Bond

What's the Book About?

The story begins with a tiny bug that goes for a walk and meets other animal friends. A little boy discovers all the animals in his room at the end of the story. Felicia Bond's watercolor illustrations are inviting and uncomplicated. The text is predictable and written in rhyme.

Theme Connections

Animals
Friendship
Numbers
Spatial concepts

Lesson Objectives

Children will:

1. Experience rhyming text.
2. Explore counting to 10.
3. Identify the main **characters** in the story.
4. Explore interpretive movement.

Action Vocabulary

Bounce	Stretch
Bump	Stroll
Dance	Tiptoe
Hop	Walk

Concepts Explored

Apologize	Squashed
Introduce	Startle
Jig	Tumble bumble
Open	Yawn
Scare	Zigzag

Developing Literacy Skills

Materials: Index cards • Markers

▶ Before reading the story, write one of the numerals from 1–10 on an index card.

▶ Introduce the book's author and illustrator, Felicia Bond. Read the title and show the cover illustration to the children. The illustration on the cover makes predicting the storyline difficult. You may want to tell the children that the animals seen dancing on the lawn go on an adventure.

▶ Ask the children to watch closely so they can learn how the boy in the illustration discovers the animals.

▶ Because the story is written in rhyme, emphasize this by reading the rhyming phrase and pausing before the last word. Allow the children to complete the rhyme with an appropriate word.

▶ At the end of the story, count the animals and the boy together with the children to see if there are 10 characters. The children will now be ready to get up and act out the story themselves.

Moving to the Story

▶ Gather the children into two circles of 10 children each, or adapt the size of the groups based upon the number of children in your class.

▶ Invite the children to act out the story. One child is the "tiny bug" and walks around the outside of the circle, while all of the other children walk counter-clockwise in a circle. As you read the story, the tiny bug chooses a "cat" and they stroll in the opposite direction (clockwise) around the outside of the circle as you continue to read.

▶ For each animal (child) added to the group, the last animal chosen will then choose the next animal. For example, the cat chooses the alligator, the alligator chooses the bee and so on, until there is no longer a counter-clockwise circle.

▶ This activity prepares the children for Rig-a-Jig-Jig (on the next page).

Developing Motor Skills

Rig-a-Jig-Jig

Materials: Masking tape • CD player with "Rig-a-Jig-Jig" on *KinderMusik: Rig-A-Jig Jig,* or chant the words without music

▶ Use masking tape to make a circle on the floor.

▶ Engage the children in a discussion about meeting and greeting people. A wonderful song that is about meeting, greeting, and making new friends and is fun for children to act out is the following old English folk song:

Rig-a-Jig-Jig

As I was walking down the street,
Down the street, down the street,
A friend of mine I chanced to meet,
Hi-ho, hi-ho, hi-ho.
Rig-a-jig-jig and away we go,
Away we go, away we go!
Rig-a-jig-jig and away we go,
Hi-ho, hi-ho, hi-ho.

▶ Invite each child to find a friend. Ask them to practice shaking hands to say, "Hello" or "I'm happy to meet you." Explain to the children that they will be meeting and greeting many friends.

▶ Have the children scatter around the classroom or movement space.

▶ Ask the children to begin walking and then to stop on your cue. When they stop walking, they will now be close to a new friend. Explain that when you play the music, they are to stop when they hear, "A friend of mine I chanced to meet," and shake right hands with the person closest to them. Everyone will then take their new partner's hand on the words, "Hi ho, hi ho, hi ho" and skip around the circle clockwise until they hear the words "Hi ho, hi ho, hi ho" again. At this point they are to let go of the new friend's hand, and wave goodbye as they scatter around the classroom or movement space, and continue walking as the song plays again.

▶ The fun part of this song is that the children do not know whom they will end up greeting when they hear the words, "A friend of mine I chanced to meet."

More Books to Share

Annie and the Wild Animals by Jan Brett
Do You Want to Be My Friend? by Eric Carle
Fritz and the Beautiful Horses by Jan Brett
My Friend Rabbit by Eric Rohmann

Music Suggestions

Fun and Games by Greg and Steve. Song: In My Playground
KinderMusik: Rig-A-Jig Jig by Kindermusik. Song: Rig-a-Jig-Jig
We All Live Together, Volume 5 by Greg and Steve. Song: Friends Forever

The Way I Feel

by Janan Cain

What's the Book About?

The clever verses in this book explore the world of emotions and feelings. The illustration colors change with different moods, and the children's expressions are very convincing as they express feelings, such as being scared, frustrated, happy, and sad. *The Way I Feel* allows children to explore their emotions without judgment. This book is sure to be a favorite.

Theme Connections

Feelings
Imagination

Lesson Objectives

Children will:
1. Experience rhyming text.
2. Explore feelings and emotions.
3. Explore interpretive movement.

Action Vocabulary

As you read the book, ask the children what movements would show each emotion or feeling listed in Concepts Explored. Write down what the children say in a chart from as the children explore the emotions, feelings, and action vocabulary.

Concepts Explored

Angry	Proud
Bored	Sad
Disappointed	Scared
Excited	Shy
Frustrated	Silly
Happy	Thankful
Jealous	

Developing Literacy Skills

▶ Introduce the book's author and illustrator, Janan Cain. Read the title to the children and show the cover illustration to the children. Ask them to share their thoughts about how the child on the cover might be feeling and why. Allow a few minutes for this discussion.

▶ Tell the children that they will meet several **characters** in the story who are all are experiencing different emotions and feelings.

▶ The fonts and graphics on each page spread match the emotions. Draw the children's attention to this as you read. Some children may want to explore this idea when they do their own drawing and writing.

▶ Another way to foster literacy development is to focus on the rhyming text. Pause just before the end of each phrase and allow the children to complete the phrase with a rhyming word.

▶ The book depicts 13 feelings and emotions. As you read the story, pause after each page and invite the children to talk about some things that make them feel the way the child in the story feels. Be accepting of all responses and assure the children that everyone has feelings and emotions that are neither "right" nor "wrong." They are just the way we feel at that moment. Be sensitive to children who do not want to offer their thoughts during the discussions. It is difficult for some children to talk about their feelings and emotions. Later, you may want to reread the story to a child who was particularly quiet to allow him or her to share his or her thoughts in a one-on-one setting.

Moving to the Story

▶ Read the story a second time and invite the children to act out the same emotion or feeling that the child on each page is showing.

Developing Motor Skills

Simon Says

Materials: CD player and *We All Live Together, Volume 3 CD*, optional

▶ Play Simon Says. If some of the children are unfamiliar with this game, explain how to play the game or put on the spoken version of "Simon Says," which is just before the instrumental version on the *We All Live Together, Volume 3* CD.

▶ Say, "Simon says, 'show me…'" and then say a feeling or emotion.

▶ The children express the emotion on their face and demonstrate any action that they feel should accompany each emotion or feeling.

Goofy Hat Game

Materials: Goofy hat

▶ Have the children form a circle around the Circle/Story Time area. Provide a goofy hat for the children to wear when they play the Goofy Hat Game.

▶ Give the goofy hat to one child. This child stands in the center of the circle and acts out an emotion. Everyone around the outside of the circle copies the hat wearer.

▶ The child wearing the hat gives the hat to another child in the circle and that child puts on the hat, comes to the center of the circle, and acts out another emotion or feeling for everyone to imitate.

▶ Play until every child has had a turn to wear the goofy hat.

Safety Tip: After the children have formed a circle, have them take one step backward to assure that each person has enough personal space to move without bumping into their neighbor. If they are still too close, ask them to move back one more step.

More Books to Share

Go Away, Big Green Monster! by Ed Emberley
Today I Feel Silly by Jamie Lee Curtis
What Are YOU So Grumpy About? by Tom Lichtenheld
When Sophie Gets Angry—Really, Really Angry by Molly Bang

Music Suggestions

Fun and Games by Greg and Steve. Song: Goofy Hat Dance
Kids in Motion by Greg and Steve. Song: Show Me What You Feel
Literacy in Motion by The Learning Station. Song: Sad, Bad, Terrible Day, and Angry
"So Big" Activity Songs for Little Ones by Hap Palmer. Songs: So Happy You're Here; When I'm Down I Get Up and Dance
We All Live Together ,Volume 3 by Greg and Steve. Song: Simon Says (instrumental version)

We All Went on Safari: A Counting Journey Through Tanzania

by Laurie Krebs

What's the Book About?

In this beautifully illustrated book, a group of Maasai children and adults go on safari through the grasslands of Tanzania and see 10 African animals. The graceful movement of the animals will surely encourage imitation by the children. The rhyming text is simple but lively and the counting pattern makes it predictable. The book includes facts about the Maasai people, Swahili names, and a map and information about Tanzania. You can use the book's glossary to teach children to count to 10 in Swahili.

Theme Connections

Animals	Habitats
Exploring	Numbers
cultures	Spatial concepts

Lesson Objectives

Children will:
1. Experience counting to 10.
2. Experience rhyming text.
3. Learn about animals of Tanzania.
4. Explore a variety of movements.

Action Vocabulary

Count	Ostrich walk
Dive	Spy
Elephant walk	Startle
Flamingo walk	Swim
Follow	Watch
Giraffe walk	Zebra walk
Lion walk	Zigzag
Monkey walk	

Concepts Explored

High	Past
Near	Through
Over	Up

Developing Literacy Skills

▶ Introduce the book's author, Laurie Krebs, and illustrator, Julia Cairns, to the children. Read the title, including the subtitle, and show the cover illustration to the children. Some children may be able to predict the storyline.

▶ Explain the meaning of *safari* to help set the stage for Story Time.

▶ As you read the story, invite the children to use their fingers to show you the correct number of animals as they appear in the story.

▶ The text is written in rhyme. To emphasize this, read the phrase and pause just before the end, allowing the children to complete the phrase with a rhyming word. Most children will discover quickly that the rhyming word is a number word.

▶ The back of the book includes a brief explanation of the Maasai people of East Africa. If appropriate, share this information with the children. There is also a glossary of Swahili names, qualities that the names suggest, and pronunciations. You may want to familiarize yourself with the proper pronunciations before reading the story.

▶ When you are finished with the story, encourage the children to talk about their favorite animals from the story. Refer to the glossary to include additional information about the animals as the children talk about them.

Moving to the Story

Materials: Classroom objects for children to walk *past, over, through, up, near,* and so on

▶ Set up your classroom like an obstacle course. Use the Concepts Explored vocabulary words and other prepositions to guide your setup (*through, near, over, past,* and so on). Tell them they are going on a "walkabout."

▶ Say the name of an animal along with a specific action. For example, "See the elephant walking through the grass." The children then demonstrate an elephant walking and moving through the (pretend) grass. Another example could be children doing an ostrich walk in a circular pattern.

▶ Invite the children to make up some animal walks with pathway combinations (*curved, zigzag, straight,* and so on) and spatial relationships, (*over, under, around, on off, through, beside, between,* and so on).

Developing Motor Skills

Animal Dance

Materials: Drum, rain stick, or CD player and CD of music with an African beat (see suggestions on the right).

▶ Review various animal walks (see suggestions and descriptions in the Glossary on pages 192-194) with the children.

▶ Ask the children to find a partner. Help each pair determine which child will be the leader first.

▶ Play a steady beat on the drum or with the rain stick, or play music as the children move about the room. The leader in each pair imitates the actions of an animal of their choice. Their partners copy the movements.

▶ Say, "Switch," and the second child becomes the leader and models the movements of a different animal for his or her partner to imitate. Continue play until each child has had a turn to be the leader three times.

Animal Stop and Go

Materials: None

Note: This is played similar to Red Light, Green Light.

▶ Refer to Animal Walks and Movement Patterns in the Glossary (pages 192-194) so you can show the children the animal movements. If you are unable to demonstrate the moves, choose a volunteer to demonstrate. For the lion and zebra, have the children put their hands on the floor and walk on both the hands and the feet.

▶ Ask the children to move to the back of the room. Choose one child to be the "Animal Hunter." The Animal Hunter turns his or her back to the children (animals), says, "Go," and counts to 10.

▶ The rest of the children choose an animal and move like that animal to try to get to the opposite end of the room without being seen moving. The children can change their animal movements as they make their way to the front of the room.

▶ The Animal Hunter says, "Stop," and turns around to see which animals he or she can catch stepping forward

▶ The idea of the game is for one of the animals to get to the front of the room and gently tag the Animal Hunter without being seen moving. If the Animal Hunter sees anyone take a step, that child must go back to the start line.

▶ When a child reaches the front of the room (or space), the game begins again with that child as the Animal Hunter. The children will have great fun if you begin as the Animal Hunter. You can then model the actions of the Animal Hunter for them.

More Books to Share

Honey…Honey…Lion! by Jan Brett
Jungle Drums by Graeme Base
Kiss Kiss! by Margaret Wild
Why Mosquitoes Buzz in People's Ears by Verna Aardema

Music Suggestions

Jungle Jazz Band by Mark Oblinger . Songs: All or any, children/teacher's choice
Jungle Jazz Joint Jam by Play It Cool Records. Songs: All or any, children/teacher's choice
Jungle Jazz Joint Jump by Play It Cool Records. Songs: All or any, children/teacher's choice
Literacy in Motion by The Learning Station. Songs: Swahili Counting Song; Kwanzaa

We're Going on a Bear Hunt
by Michael Rosen, illustrated by Helen Oxenbury

What's the Book About?

Children never tire of hearing this delightful story that sets them off on a great adventure—a bear hunt. Excitement and anticipation builds as the **characters** in the story encounter obstacles along the way. In the end, the characters come face to face with a bear and a fast retreat is the only way back to safety.

Theme Connections

Animals
Families
Feelings
Imagination
Spatial concepts

Lesson Objectives

Children will:
1. Experience rhyming text.
2. Experience **predictable text**.
3. Explore **onomatopoeia** in text.
4. Explore interpretive movement.

Action Vocabulary

Catch	Tiptoe
Shut	Trip
Stumble	Whirl
Swirl	

Concepts Explored

Back	Quick
Big	Scared
Deep	Thick
Down	Through
Into	Under
Narrow	Up
Open	Wavy
Over	

Developing Literacy Skills

▶ Introduce the book's author, Michael Rosen, and illustrator, Helen Oxenbury, to the children. Read the title and show the children the cover illustration. Ask the children to predict the storyline.

▶ Because this book is so popular, many children may be familiar with it. For the children who do not know the story, assure them that the family is going on an imaginary bear hunt!

▶ The story is written with a rhythm and cadence that is easy for children to follow. The repetitive phrases allow the children to help you read the story. The **onomatopoeic** words in this story help children learn about letter blends in words.

▶ Because the prepositions *over*, *under*, and *through* are used throughout the book, the book reinforces the meaning of these concepts.

▶ Before reading the story, teach the children the repetitive phrases and as you read the book, invite the children to say the repetitive phrase along with you. Use your voice to build excitement and anticipation as you read the story and relief as you end the story, safely under the bed covers. This provides important modeling for the class. As the children become writers, you will undoubtedly hear them read their own creative stories, full of colorful, descriptive vocabulary.

▶ After you finish reading the story, invite the children to talk about the parts of the story that they found interesting. Were some parts funny? Were other parts of the story frightening? Revisit the illustrations in the book and ask the children to identify how the children and the adult were feeling. Did the illustrator do a good job of conveying the feelings and emotions? Don't forget to include the dog and the bear in the discussion!

Moving to the Story

▶ Reread the onomatopoeic words in the book. An engaging way to illustrate these words and others is with hand motions. As a cooperative activity, help the children figure out a variety hand motions to perform as you read the story. The result will be a combination of voice and movement.

▶ This is a perfect rhyme book for chanting and clapping. Tell the children to echo (repeat) each line after you. Set up a "slap, clap" rhythm with the children slapping their thighs and then clapping their hands. After chanting and clapping to the rhythm of the story individually, the children may want to work with a partner—the children clap each other's hands and then slap their thighs. The children may create their own interesting handclap patterns that they can share with the rest of the class.

Developing Motor Skills

Going on a Bear Hunt

Materials: Classroom items to set up an imaginary environment that includes a door, long wavy grass, a river, a boat, a forest, wind, and a cave (**Note:** Construct a cave by draping a sheet or parachute over a table, or use a large cardboard box or collapsible tunnel.) • A stuffed bear • CD player and "Goin' on a Bear Hunt" on the *Kids in Action* CD, optional

▶ Ask the children to consider objects in the classroom that they might travel *under, over, around, through, up,* and *down.* Include things that the children might open and shut, and objects that they can pretend to stumble over or trip over. Also create places where the children can tiptoe. Help the children construct one large cave. Don't forget to place the bear in the cave!

▶ The children are now ready to act out the story. As you read the book, invite the children to move through the classroom as if they were the **characters** in the book. To keep everyone safe, tell the children that "bear hunting" requires quiet hunters who move in a very stealthy manner. Be prepared for a burst of activity as the children reverse their movement pattern after meeting the bear.

▶ If desired, add a musical twist with "Goin' on a Bear Hunt" on the *Kids in Action* CD. Gather the children in a circle and choose a leader. Have the children pantomime the actions to the song. You might ask the children what the differences are between the book and the CD.

More Books to Share

Oh, A-Hunting We Will Go by John M. Langstaff
The Secret Birthday Message by Eric Carle
We're Going on a Lion Hunt by David Axtell

Music Suggestions

Kids in Action by Greg and Steve. Song: Goin' on a Bear Hunt

Safety Tip: Remind the children to move carefully and considerately throughout their movement space. This will help keep everyone safe.

All terms in bold are explained in greater detail in the Glossary on Appendix pages 188-199.

We're Going on a Ghost Hunt

by Marcia K. Vaughan, illustrated by Ann Schweninger

What's the Book About?

Two children and their puppy set out to find a ghost in this scary Halloween adventure, a take-off on *We're Going on Bear Hunt*. The rhyming, **predictable text** is perfect for emergent readers. The text is full of action words and movement to help with language development. Many Halloween surprises await your children—skeletons, bats, and haunted houses. The colorful illustrations help to take the edge off this spooky tale!

Theme Connections

Imagination
Spatial concepts

Lesson Objectives

Children will:
1. Experience rhyming text.
2. Interact with repeated text.
3. Experience various movements.
4. Explore interpretive movement.

Action Vocabulary

Crawl	Scurry
Dance	Swirl
Dash	Twirl
Fly	Wade

Concepts Explored

Across	Low
Afraid	Out
By	Pass
Fast	Slow
High	Through
Into	Under

Developing Literacy Skills

▶ Introduce the book's author, Marcia Vaughan, and illustrator, Ann Schweninger. Read the title and show the children the front cover. Ask the children to predict the storyline.

▶ Some children will be familiar with *We're Going on a Bear Hunt* and may compare the books.

▶ Begin by teaching the children the repeated phrases in the book.

▶ Read the story and encourage the children to say or "read" the repeated phrases with you. When you are finished reading the story, the children will be ready to get on their feet and participate in a more active "hunt."

Moving to the Story

▶ Ask the children to recall the repetitive phrases in the story and to act out the storyline.

▶ Reread the story and invite the children to say the first two phrases with you. As you read the last phrase for each page, encourage the children to move around the Story Time area (or the classroom) acting out the words.

▶ The children return home—the Story Time area—at the end of the story.

Developing Motor Skills

Spooky Moves

Materials: CD player with suggested music, optional

▶ Explain to the children that they are going to practice how the children in the story moved on their ghost hunt. Practice is important before they go on their hunt!

▶ Ask the children to find their personal space, making enough room for everyone in the room.

▶ Call out each action word and encourage the children to move about their space: crawling, dancing, dashing, and so on. Allow a minute or two for the children to explore each action.

▶ You may want to add instrumental Halloween-type music.

More Books to Share

Big Pumpkin by Erica Silverman
House That Drac Built by Judy Sierra
The Little Old Lady Who Was Not Afraid of Anything by Linda Williams
Scary, Scary Halloween by Eve Bunting

Music Suggestions

Casper's Spookiest Songs and Sounds by Sony Wonder. Song: Spooky Sounds
Drew's Famous Kids' Halloween Costume Party by Turn Up the Music. Song: Hedwig's Theme
Toddlers on Parade by Kimbo Educational. Song: Ten Little Goblins

Who Hops?
by Katie Davis

What's the Book About?

This delightful book is filled with illustrations that are colorful and vibrant, and also hilarious. The author asks about the movement of various animals. Children will respond to the repetitive questions and silly suggestions by coming up with their own ideas. The storyline includes a variety of motor movements that children will surely want to try.

Theme Connections

Animals
Colors
Humor

Lesson Objectives

Children will:
1. Experience **predictable text**.
2. Make predictions within the story.
3. Experience a variety of movements.

Action Vocabulary

Crawl
Fly
Hop
Slither
Swim

Concepts Exploration

Animal walks, such as bunny jump, crab walk, crocodile/alligator crawl, dolphin swim, elephant walk, frog jump, giraffe walk, inchworm crawl, kangaroo jump, monkey jump, snake slither, and spider walk

Developing Literacy Skills

Materials: Chart paper • Markers
- Introduce the book's author and illustrator, Katie Davis. Read the title of the book to the children and show them the cover. Ask the children to predict the storyline.
- The cover shows a cow hopping. Ask the children if this seems right to them. Explain that the book asks questions about who can do what!
- Before reading the story, write the five action words (*hop, fly, slither, swim,* and *crawl*) down one side of a large piece of chart paper. On another piece of chart paper, list the animals featured in the story that do not do the five actions (cow, rhino, elephant, anteater, and giraffe). On a third piece of chart paper, write *children* at the top of the paper.
- The story is short, so you will have time to write the names of the animals next to the action words as you read the story. For example, write *frog, rabbit,* and *kangaroo* next to *hop*. Before reading about what the cow does, ask the children to offer their thoughts. List their ideas next to the animals on the second chart and then finish reading what the author wrote. The children will be delighted to learn that they were thinking the same way the author thought!
- When you finish reading the story, invite the children to add more ideas, to the third chart—how children move. They will now be ready for a more active lesson.

Moving to the Story

- Reread the story to the children and suggest that they move like each animal in the story.
- Although the book uses *hop* (a one foot take-off) to describe the movement of the frog, rabbit, and kangaroo, it is actually a *jump* (a two foot take-off). See Animal Walks and Movement Patterns in the Glossary on pages 192-194 for movement descriptions. As the children explore the various animal movements, ask them how they move in ways that animals do not.

Developing Motor Skills

Move to the Beat

Materials: CD player with recommended music (see the following page)
- Put on one of the complementary music selections and invite the children to move like all of the various animals in each of the songs.

Alligator Mountain

Materials: Parachute or large sheet with colored duct tape taped evenly spaced around the perimeter

▶ Most parachutes are divided into colored sections. Instruct the children to space themselves evenly around the parachute so they each line up with a color (more than one child can hold onto the same colored section). If a child has his or her hands on two colors, that child must move to one color or the other.

▶ Count to three with the children and raise and lower the chute three times. When you reach the count of three, everyone quickly pulls the chute to the floor to prevent the air from escaping. The air "captured" under the parachute creates a domed "mountain" for the children to "climb."

▶ Say a color randomly, and all the children with their hands on that color "**alligator crawl**" to the top of the mountain, and touch the center of the parachute. Then they "alligator crawl" backwards down the mountain to their home spot. For example, if you say, "blue," the children touching the color blue on the parachute "alligator crawl" on their tummies to the middle of the parachute and back. Call out each color so all children will have a turn to "alligator crawl."

Note: As the children crawl on their stomachs, the air that is trapped under the parachute will escape through the hole in the center of the parachute. Although the parachute is on the floor, the billowing of the parachute will give the children the sense that they are crawling upward.

▶ After all of the children try the alligator crawl, place the parachute flat on the floor with each child holding his or her color and let the children try snake slithering to the middle of the parachute and back again.

▶ Next, the children go under the parachute to dolphin swim when you call a color. The children holding other colors can raise the parachute up to shoulder height and gently flutter the chute up and down to represent ocean waves. The goal is to go under and swim one time around the perimeter and back to their home place.

Safety Tip: Remind the children to move carefully, especially when moving under the parachute.

More Books to Share

Hop! Hop! Hop! by Ann Whitford Paul

Hop, Skip, Run by Marcia Leonard

Hyacinth Hop Has the Hic-Hops by Tony Kenyon

Music Suggestions

Can a Cherry Pie Wave Goodbye? by Hap Palmer. Songs: Animal Quiz Part One; Animal Quiz Part Two

Can Cockatoos Count by Twos? by Hap Palmer. Song: Magic Scarf

Rowdy Ropes by Dinotrax. Song: I Can Jump Like a Big Green Frog

All terms in bold are explained in greater detail in the Glossary on Appendix pages 188-199.

Wiggle

by Doreen Cronin, illustrated by Scott Menchin

What's the Book About?

If you are looking for a book to energize your class, this is it! From the first line, to the last, there will be non-stop wiggling and giggling. This high-energy book is written in rhyme and includes colorful, zany illustrations of animals taking their lead from a dog that is in perpetual motion.

Theme Connections

Animals
Cooperation
Humor

Lesson Objectives

Children will:
1. Experience rhyming text.
2. Explore a variety of movements.
3. Explore interpretive movement.

Action Vocabulary

Wiggle

Concepts Explored

Movement alone
Movement with a partner

Developing Literacy Skills

▶ Introduce the book's author, Doreen Cronin, and illustrator, Scott Menchin, to the children. Read the title and show the children the cover of the book.
▶ The back cover is also of interest to children as they predict the storyline. Tell the children that the main **character** in the story is a very active dog that wiggles wherever he goes.
▶ Tell the children that the story is written in rhyme and invite them to help you read. Give the children an opportunity to explore rhyming words by reading a phrase and pausing at the end so the children can offer a word that completes the rhyme.
▶ The text and illustrations are hilarious so be sure to allow enough time for the children to take in the illustrations as you read the story.
▶ When you are finished reading the story, the children now have an opportunity to wiggle until they are out of wiggles!

Moving to the Story

▶ Read the book again and invite the children to wiggle along with the story as you read it.

Developing Motor Skills

Hula Hoops

Materials: Hula hoops, 24"–30" in diameter, one for each child
▶ Hula hoops are a great way to get children up and moving in a wiggle.
▶ Show the children the cover again, which shows the dog using a hula hoop. Provide a hoop for each child and encourage them to use the hula hoop around their waist, wrist, ankle, and so on.

Safety Tip: Remind the children to stay within their own personal space and keep the hoop under control when they are trying to use the hoop on their wrist or arm.

Musical Hoops

Materials: Hula hoops, 24"–30" in diameter, one for each child
CD player and music (see suggestions on the right)

▶ Have the children begin by placing their hoop on the floor and standing in it. Tell them that you are going to play music for them to wiggle all around the room. When the music stops, they need to move into a hoop.

▶ Tell the children that you are going to take away several hoops each time you play the music. When the music stops, they should quickly move one part of their body inside a hoop, sharing the hoop with a friend or friends.

▶ When the children have wiggled their way to the end of the song, you will have taken all but one hoop away. All the children need to figure out how to share the one remaining hoop.

▶ This is a cooperative activity for the children. The children must use problem-solving skills to figure out a solution.

More Books to Share

Giggle-Wiggle Wake-Up! by Nancy White Carlstrom
Waggle by Sarah McMenemy
Wiggle Waggle by Jonathan London
Wiggles by Christophe Loupy

Music Suggestions

Hoppin' & Boppin' by Russ InVision. Song: Wiggle & Giggle
Kids in Motion by Greg and Steve. Song: The Freeze
Late Last Night by Joe Scruggs. Songs: Wiggle in My Toe; Ants in My Pants
Sally the Swinging Snake by Hap Palmer. Song: Wiggly Wiggy Wiggles

Yikes!!!
by Robert Florczak

What's the Book About?

Robert Florczak's photo-like illustrations are colorful, detailed, and filled with life. As the boy in the story journeys to wild places, he comes face-to-face with amazing, dangerous creatures. The boy's expressions are so convincing that children will be eager to engage in the simple, one-word expressions on each page. The end of the end of the book is sure to spark a great class discussion! The book includes a visual glossary that will help young learners identify the featured animals, such as mammals, birds, and insects.

Theme Connections

Animals	Imagination
Feelings	Insects and bugs
Habitats	Self-confidence

Lesson Objectives

Children will:

1. Explore interjections in text.
2. Explore a variety of movements.
3. Explore interpretive movement.

Action Vocabulary

Climbing	Running	Tiptoeing
Crawling	Slithering	Walking
Flying	Spinning	Watching
Jumping	Swimming	
Leaping	Swinging	

Concepts Explored

Anticipation	Fear
Apprehension	Fun
Awe	Panic
Excitement	Surprise
Exhilaration	Wonder

Developing Literacy Skills

▶ Introduce the book's author and illustrator, Robert Florczak. Read the title to the children and show them the cover. Show the children the back cover illustration and read the text that accompanies the illustration. This will help them to predict the storyline.

▶ Tell the children that after you read the book, you will ask them if the adventure described in the book was real or not.

▶ Before reading the story, mention that Robert Florczak, the author and illustrator of the book, created strong, colorful pictures to express feelings and emotions.

▶ Tell the children there are few words in the book and that most of the words are *interjections*, which are words that show emotions. In the book, the words tell us how the boy is feeling as he journeys through the wild jungle.

▶ As you read the story, pause and show the children the two-page vivid illustrations. Focus the children's attention on the boy, his interjection, and then the animal. Ask the children to share their thoughts and ideas about how each animal might be feeling when it encounters the boy.

▶ There is also an insect on each page. Ask the children if they can find it. Some are camouflaged. The names of the insects and the pages they are on are listed in the glossary at the back of the book.

▶ After you finish the story, invite the children to answer the question, "Did the boy go on an adventure or did he dream about it?"

▶ If time permits, show each page to the children again and share the glossary information about the animals in the illustrations.

Moving to the Story

▶ Invite the children to have another look at the pages in the book. Help the children identify the 13 interjections in the book by saying the interjections and asking them to show the corresponding emotion. For example, if you say, "trouble," the children will show *trouble* with a facial expression and say, "Uh-oh!"

▶ Next, say each of the interjections on the **page spreads** and ask the children to come up with additional emotions. For example, say, "Uh-oh!" and the children will say "fear."

▶ Explore each of the Action Vocabulary words, such as climbing, slithering, and running, with the children. After the children have had a chance to explore each of the action words and concepts, they will be ready to play the Emotional Statues game.

► Ask the children to stand up. Without using the book, say one of the interjections from the story. The children pose in a statue quickly to demonstrate one of the Concepts Explored (see list on the previous page). Without moving, have them look around at some of their classmates within view to see if their expressions and body language are similar or different.

Developing Motor Skills

Name that Animal
► There are many animals and other wildlife shown in the story. On the previous page are 13 actions (listed in Action Vocabulary on the previous page) in which one or more of the animals or the boy moved. Ask the children to stand on one side of the room.
► Choose one child to be "IT." Whisper one of the 13 actions to IT.
► IT pantomimes the movement and the rest of the children guess the movement, and which animal in the book did it.
► Tell the children if their guess is correct or not. When they guess correctly, all of the children try to get to the other side of the room, doing that same movement, without getting tagged.
► The first child tagged is the next IT. The game continues until the children have explored all 13 action words.

Jungle Gym Obstacle Course
Materials: Items for an obstacle course, such as a climbing rope or ladder or cargo net (climb), cones with a rope between (leap or jump over), hoops (spinning), incline mats (slithering), 12" jump boxes or panel mats (jumping, flying, swimming), jungle gym on the playground (swing, climb), or tunnel (crawling)
► If possible, use objects from the classroom to set up an obstacle course that includes some of the above materials appropriate for an obstacle course.
► Read the book again, and ask the children to find the animals that correspond to each of the Action Vocabulary words listed on the previous page. After they identify the actions to the pictures in the book, invite them to go to the obstacle course area, and discover how many of the actions from the story they can do.
Note: This activity is done most successfully on a playground or in a gym or multipurpose room.

More Books to Share
The Adventures of Abdi by Madonna
The Complete Adventures of Curious George by Margret and H.A. Rey
How I Became a Pirate by Melinda Long
Skippyjon Jones by Judy Schachner

Music Suggestions
Jazz Joint Jump by Jazz Joint Band. Songs: All or any, children/teacher's choice
Jungle Jazz Joint Jam by Jazz Joint Band. Songs: All or any, children/teacher's choice

Safety Tip: Remind the children to be considerate of one another as they explore the movement possibilities on the obstacle course. Turn taking is very important.

Appendixes

APPENDIX A: Glossary

Glossary of Terms

Literacy Terms

Alliteration—The repetition of the same sound in word beginnings, sound clusters, or stressed syllables. Alliteration adds a pleasing sound to sentences, rhymes, and stories. Most children enjoy interacting and "playing" with alliteration in stories.

Author—The person(s) who wrote the story, poem, chant, or other literary work. Children begin to develop a sense of who an author is by repeated interactions with books by the same author. Children learn to recognize a favorite author's style, voice, genre, and illustrations (if the author is also the illustrator). Teachers can help children make connections to authors by sharing information about the author, which is often found on the book's jacket, with the children.

Big books—Big books are large books, about 20" by 30". The large format allows teachers to read to groups, knowing that all of the children will be able to see the illustrations and follow along with the print as the story is read. Many publishers print popular titles in both regular size and big book versions.

Buddy readers—Typically, a buddy reader is an older child who reads to a younger child. Reading with someone helps to foster reading enjoyment and provides learning opportunities.

Characters—Characters may be people, animals, imaginary people, or objects in a story or other literary work. When children relate to characters, the characters become memorable. As children become familiar with stories, they are able to recall the main characters and their importance to the story.

Cover—The outer cover of the book provides children with valuable information. The illustrations, graphics, and print offer important clues about the book's storyline. The back cover often has as much information as the front cover. Some illustrators create a single illustration that wraps around the back and front covers.

Emergent literacy—Through early and repeated exposure to language and print, young children begin to display emerging skills in listening, speaking, reading, and writing. These skills include verbally responding to questions, stating thoughts and ideas, attempting to read words by using letter-sound knowledge, and creating symbols or marks that represent conventional letters.

Environmental print—Signs, symbols, and logos, such as graphics, associated with stores or products that are often "read" before a child pays attention to print.

Illustration—Illustrations are drawings, pictures, or graphics that bring meaning to text. Typically, children focus on illustrations for meaning before looking at print.

Illustrator—This is the person who illustrates a literary work. Through repeated exposure, children begin to identify illustrators because of the illustrator's unique art, style, or technique.

Invented spelling—Invented spelling refers to early attempts to spell words. Emergent writers use letter-sound knowledge, recall of a mental image of a word, or just string together random letters to spell a word. Invented spelling is also referred to as "guess and go" spelling.

KWL chart—The letters K, W, and L represent the words *Know*, *Want*, and *Learned*. Creating a KWL chart before reading to children and referring to it after reading to the children is a teaching strategy used to organize and focus attention to a particular topic. The chart includes three lists: what we know, what we want to know, and what we learned.

Language acquisition—Language acquisition is the process by which children learn to speak their native language and other languages. Humans are born with the capacity to speak all languages. This ability quickly disappears as infants listen and respond to the language they hear. Language-rich environments promote the natural process of acquiring language. This process is continuous, interactive, and takes place in a social context.

Listening—Listening is the auditory process of hearing, for the purpose of taking in information. When children listen with intent, they gather information and begin to process this information, based on prior knowledge. Comprehension of this new information leads to greater knowledge.

Literacy—Broadly defined, literacy is the ability to listen, speak, read, and write. Literacy begins with, and develops in tandem with, language acquisition. Recently, there has been a narrowing of this definition, with a focus on reading and writing. In the early childhood years, it is important to give children rich and varied opportunities to integrate listening, speaking, reading, and writing, guided by best practices in early education.

Literacy continuum—Literacy skills develop along a continuum, in a rather uneven manner, often with skills overlapping. Each child begins school at an individual place on the literacy continuum. This placement is dependent upon prior experiences and development. Exposure and experiences influence children's journey on the continuum.

Literacy-rich environment—Literacy-rich environments are those that allow children exposure to appropriate language, print, and modeled writing. To foster literacy development, children must have opportunities to share their thoughts, ask questions, interact with print, hear stories (oral or read), and participate in functional and creative writing experiences.

Literary elements—All stories have main literary elements: theme, setting, character, main idea or plot, point of view, style, and mood.

Main idea—The main idea of a story refers to the plot. The plot includes the story's problem or activity, conflict or action by the characters, and how the problem was resolved or how the activity ended. Books vary in their complexity of the main idea. It is important to ask children to formulate their ideas about a story as soon as stories are read to them. Over time, children's responses become more complex.

Onomatopoeia—Onomatopoeia refers to words that are formed by imitation of a sound made by, or connected to, its referent. Examples include *boom, ping,* and *zoom.* Many excellent children's books include onomatopoeic language that is fun for children to "play" with during interactive story times.

Oral language—Oral language is the foundation of literacy learning. An extension of oral language is reading and writing, which only become meaningful after children have been read to.

Page spread—Many books contain illustrations that are created on both pages in a book. The two pages are called a page spread. Illustrations designed this way can offer continuity in the storyline and aid in children's comprehension and understanding of a story.

Phonemes—The smallest units of speech sounds are called phonemes. For example, C-A-T has three phonemes. The English language has approximately 41 phonemes.

Phonemic awareness—The ability to hear and segment phonemes in words is called phonemic awareness and develops gradually in young children. It is an important skill in learning to read and write.

Phonological awareness—Phonological awareness includes phonemic awareness but is much broader. It includes that ability to compare and contrast sounds in speech, including syllables, and rhythm and rhyme.

Phrase—A phrase is a sequence of two or more words but missing parts of speech to make the sequence a sentence. Children's picture books are often replete with phrases that rhyme and/or are repeated. This text structure aids in memorization and comprehension.

Picture books—Picture books present stories and information through a combination of text and supporting illustrations. Picture books can be fiction or non-fiction.

Picture cues—Picture cues refer to hints that children gather from pictures and illustrations in a book. The hints help children predict a book's storyline and aid in vocabulary comprehension.

Predict—This is the act of telling or guessing what might happen in a story. Children use prior knowledge to help them predict a storyline. They draw on main ideas and characters from other stories, and events or people from their own lives to visualize and verbalize about the book's storyline.

Predictable text—This refers to text that contains repeated phrases, dialogue, or events. Predictable text helps children learn to read their first words. Predictable text in a big book format is especially helpful during whole class story time.

Pre-reading—Pre-reading is reading a book to a child prior to story time and is a good teaching strategy to use with children who are English language learners or children who require extra time and exposure to books in order to comprehend the text. Pre-reading is usually done with one or two children in a quiet place before story time.

Reading—Reading is the act of decoding text and constructing meaning from what has been read. Reading is a skill that develops over time. When children learn to read, they need support from their environment (home and school), personal motivation, opportunities to interact with text, and an authentic purpose.

Recall—The ability to remember something from the past is recall. Very young children can recall specific items or actions from a story but may not be able to put this information in context.

Retell—Retelling is the ability to hear or read a story and then tell about the story in one's own words. Retelling requires the ability to recall information and verbalize it. When children retell a story, it gives the teacher an opportunity to note a child's progress in literacy development, particularly language development and comprehension.

Rhyme—Words ending in the same sound are said to rhyme. A collection of phrases or verses that end in the same sound are called rhymes.

Rhyming—Experience with rhyming text allows children an opportunity to hear and differentiate sounds.

Rhythm—Text, with a uniformed or patterned beat, has rhythm. Often, this rhythm creates a cadence in text when it is read, making the text enjoyable for young children to experience and to remember. Rhythm in text can provide opportunities for interactive story times by adding hand clapping or rope jumping activities as story is read.

Setting—One of the main literary elements of a story is the setting. The setting introduces the location in which the story takes place, as well as the time period. The setting can also tell us about the characters and the culture in which they live. Settings also help set the mood for the story.

Speaking—Speaking is the ability to vocalize. Speaking begins early in infancy, as illustrated by early sounds called babbling. Vocalizations become meaningful over time. Speaking with purpose develops in children as cognition develops. Children need ample opportunities to share their ideas and thoughts, and to ask questions in order to developing their speaking skills.

Storyline—The book's storyline is the main thread that runs throughout the book. For example, *Hopscotch Around the World* is about hopscotch games played throughout the world. Young children will have an easier time predicting or retelling a book's storyline than the main idea or plot.

Voice inflection—Modulation of the voice by changing the pitch or tone of voice is known as voice inflection. Voice inflection adds excitement to a story, helps to emphasize rhyme or rhythm in text, or draws attention to important aspects of the story.

Wordless books—Wordless books are picture books without text. Wordless books are important in early childhood settings because they provide opportunities for children to use their language to create a story, based on the wordless book's illustrations. Very young children will often label the pictures they see in wordless books. As they become more familiar with the concept of story, children will begin to create a storyline when they interact with wordless books.

Writing—Children's early attempts at making meaningful marks are very unconventional. These early attempts at writing should be supported and encouraged. Conventional writing will develop as children are given opportunities to explore in a safe environment. Writing and reading should be taught in an integrative manner, as one literacy skill promotes development in the other.

Movement Terms and Concepts

Animal Walks and Movement Patterns

Alligator crawl—Child is down on stomach. With left arm and right leg moving in unison and pulling the body forward in a crawl-like pattern, the action is repeated with alternating action of the right arm and left leg.

Bear walk—The child is down on hands and feet, bottom up. The action is unilateral, with the left arm and leg moving simultaneously and alternating with the right arm and leg.

Climb—A vertical crawl.

Crab walk—Child sits on bottom with knees bent, and hand placed to the sides of the bottom. The child then pushes or lifts the bottom off the floor, so that the weight is on the arms and legs.

Crawl—Same as a creeping action, only down on the belly.

Creep—On hands and knees, moving left arm with right leg, right arm with left leg, in a cross-lateral movement pattern.

Crocodile crawl—See alligator crawl, or crawl.

Elephant walk—Child bends over slightly at the waist, and clasps both hands together in front for a trunk. The child moves about with heavy stomping steps. When the elephant gets upset, the child put the hands to the ears and waves the elbows forward and back as elephant ears.

Frog jump—Child is in a squat position with the bottom up. **Important**: Do **not** allow the children to squat all the way down and jump up. This is an explosive type of jump; a knee bend past 90 degrees is not good for the knees. The child stretches the arms upward in the jump, exploding upward with both hands and feet simultaneously.

Giraffe walk—The child extends the arms straight overhead next to the ears with hands clasped, and walks on tiptoe.

Inchworm—The child is in a front bridge, or push up position. The child walks their feet up to their hands, and then walks the hands away from the feet. The action is repeated as the child moves, alternating moving the feet and then the hands.

Kangaroo jump—Child stands with hands in front of body, bent downward at the wrist. The child jumps around the room with the hands held in this position.

Lame puppy dog walk—The child is down on hands and feet, bottom up. The child (dog) pretends to have an "owie" on one of his back feet, so he can't use it. How will he move using only three legs?

Monkey jump—For the monkey jump, place both hands to one side of the preferred foot. Jump the feet over a rope or a scarf that has been placed in front of the feet. Repeat action.

Monkey walk or chimpanzee hip-hop—For the chimpanzee hip-hop, the child is bent over at the hips with knuckles on the floor. Knees are slightly bent. Action is a hip-hop walk on the knuckles of the left hand and foot, alternately with the right hand and foot.

Ostrich walk—The child is bent over at the hip and grasps both ankles. Head is up. The child walks forward keeping a hold of both ankles.

Penguin or duck walk—The child holds arms stiffly at the sides of the body. Feet are turned out, knees are stiff and unbending. Legs are squeezed together. The child takes baby waddle steps with the body weight on the heels.

Rabbit or bunny jump—The child stands in a slight straddle and places hands on floor, reaching forward from the shoulders. The child then jumps the feet up to the outside of the hands and then alternately jumps the hands forward, taking turns jumping the feet and then the hands.

Snake slither—The child lies on his or her tummy with the arms stretched overhead and slides from side to side without using his or her arms or legs.

Spider walks—Similar to a crab walk in which the child sits on bottom with knees bent, and hand placed to the sides of the bottom. The child then pushes or lifts the bottom off the floor, so that the weight is on the arms and legs.

Stork/flamingo stand—A balance walk in which the child first puts their hands on their hips with the elbows out for "wings" and then slides one foot up to the inside of the knee of the standing leg. The child holds that position for a bit and then steps forward, repeating the action on the opposite leg.

Locomotor Skills

Gallop—Also called chasse or foot chaser. One foot stays in front at all times. The back foot chases or follows closely behind the heel of the front foot.

Hop—Land and take-off on the same foot. One foot is held up off the floor. A one-foot take-off from the standing or supporting foot, and landing back on the same take-off foot.

Jump—A two foot take-off, propelling the body upward, followed by a two foot landing, unless a one foot landing is specifically designated. Knees are bent upon landing. Variations to explore are high jumps, side-to-side jumps, long jump, two feet take-off with one foot landing, and scissor jumps.

Leap—an elongated running step in which the body is propelled upward and suspended in the air with the body and the legs doing one or more things. The body stretches up and either the front or the back leg or both may be kept extended straight with one in front and one in back (split), or may be bent (stag).

Other similar leap terms include:

Bound—To move by leaping and jumping,

Frisk—To dance, leap, skip, or frolic about,

Lunge—To place one foot firmly in a long stance, in front of the other, and

Spring—To leap suddenly or swiftly.

Run—similar to the walk, however, the support phase is shortened and the weight transfer is followed by a propulsion of the body through the air. Variations of run include:

Flee—To run away from danger,

Jog—A slow run,

Plunge—To rush or dash with headlong haste,

Race—To run competitively against another,

Scamper—To run playfully, and

Skitter—To run or glide lightly as if skimming along   the surface.

Slide step—A slide step is a sideways gallop with one foot leading and the other foot following. The feet stay perpendicular, or sideways, to the line of direction. Arms are held shoulder high, straight out from the sides of the body, in line of direction of the body. Hips stay sideways to line of direction. Weight is transferred from the ball of the lead foot to the supporting trailing foot.

Skip—a series of alternating step/hops with arms swinging in opposition of foot actions. A way to teach skip: Lift the knees high to tap the hands as in a march, step hop, left side only, right side only, alternate a hop on one foot, then the other.

Walk—alternating transfer of weight from one foot to the other by means of reflexive swing and support action. Walk variations include:

Glide—To move in a smooth, continuous pattern in which body weight is transferred from one foot to the other without the feet leaving the ground,

Hike—To walk, usually through rural or mountainous terrain, a great distance for recreational purposes,

Ice skate or skate—To glide or slide smoothly along (One can use paper plates under the feet to pretend skate, using gliding action of the feet, keeping continuous contact with the floor, by sliding one foot past the other),

March—To walk with a particular measured tread as in a parade,

Plod—To trudge or walk heavily along,

Prance—To dance or move in a lively or spirited manner, or to spring from the hind legs as a horse,

Step—A movement of picking up one foot and putting it down in a new position, usually accompanied by transferring weight to the opposite foot,

Stroll—A rambling, leisurely walk-about,

Strut—To walk proudly and pompously for showing off,

Thump—To walk with heavy steps,

Tiptoe—To lift oneself up on the balls of the feet and walk quietly,

Trample—To tread, stamp, or step heavily and noisily,

Tromp—To tramp or trample,

Trot—To move at a gait between a walk and a run, with one foot always on the ground,

Trundle—To move or walk with a rolling gait,

Waddle—To walk with short steps by swaying from side to side, and

Wade—To walk through water, mud, or something similar with the legs partly immersed.

Other variations: Walk on heels, on inside and outside of the feet, baby steps, giant steps, glide step, and grapevine step.

Body Control Skills

Balance—To not let oneself fall. A state of equilibrium in which the mover has equal distribution of weight.

Bend—To move from a straight line into a curve.

Bicycle—An exercise performed by lying on the back with the hands under the hips and the legs in the air, moving in a circular pattern as if pedaling a bicycle.

Curl-up—A mover brings the upper and lower extremities together into a curved, rounded shape.

Dance—To move the hands and feet around in a rhythmic pattern.

Egg roll—A side roll that begins on the back with the chin tucked in, and knees tucked up into the arms. The mover rolls over sideways like an egg.

Exercise—To exert effort in training the body to increase health and fitness

Extend—To stretch something out to its full length.

Hang—To be suspended so as to allow free movement to swing as from a bar.

Leapfrog—A game in which players take turns straddle jumping over the backs of other players who are bent over into a tucked position.

Log roll—A sideways roll, sometimes called a pencil roll, in which the mover lays down on the back, either with the arms stretched overhead, or in crisscross over the chest and rolls sideways, over and over.

Pike position—A seated "L" position with the legs straight out in front of the body.

Spin—To cause to turn round and round rapidly.

Squiggle—To make short irregular curves.

Squirm—To wriggle, and turn and twist.

Stretch—To reach and extend the body as far as possible in order increase the range of movement.

Sway—To move side to side as in a swinging motion.

Swirl—To move round and round in a twirling motion.

Swim—To propel oneself through the water by pulling with the arms and kicking the feet.

Swing—To smoothly and freely move to and fro when one end is fixed and the other end free.

Tuck—To pull up one's legs tightly under them

Tumble—To fall helplessly down, end over end, or to roll over and over, or to perform gymnastics skills with agility and precision.

Turn-- To stand facing one direction and then move the body to face a different direction, such as left or right side, back or all the way around to front again.

Twist—The act of turning or rotating on an axis, a rotary motion.

Whirl—To spin rapidly.

Wiggle—To move side to side with short, quick irregular movements.

Wriggle—To squirm or twist to and fro.

Space Concepts

General space—A designated movement space in which all movers share without bumping into anyone.

Personal space—A designated individual movement space that encompasses the entire area that a mover can reach from one side to the other and as high or as low as possible while standing in one place, and which no other person should enter unless invited.

Sensorimotor Integrative Skills

Auditory learners—Keenly responsive to sound, whether through rhythmic beat or learning through listening, but always in combination with other means of processing information.

Auditory perception—Pertaining to hearing discrimination, understanding and awareness.

Bilateral—synchronized movements of both sides of the body, such as a jump, with a two foot take-off and a two foot landing.

Body perception—A person's perception of their own body with a mental picture of everything known about their body.

Cross lateral—Also called "cross lateralization." The body is divided into four quadrants: left and right halves and upper and lower halves. Cross lateral activity occurs when synchronized movements of an arm and leg from opposite sides of the body, work together, such as crawling or creeping.

Cognition—the process of learning and knowing.

Cognitive—pertaining to memorizing, judging, and reasoning.

Eye-hand coordination—The ability of the eyes to coordinate distance, speed, and direction to direct the hands to precisely the right place to receive or project an object to the desired location

Kinesthetic learners—Those who learn primarily through doing.

Lateralization—Development of a dominant hand, foot, and eye preference, which indicates that a particular area of the brain has become specialized.

Midline—The dividing space between the left and right hemispheres of the brain that is bridged by the Corpus Callosum.

Midline, horizontal—Dividing the body into upper and lower halves through the waist or bellybutton.

Midline, vertical—Dividing the body lengthwise through the left and right hemispheres of the brain, and continuing all the way down.

Motor planning—The bridge between the sensorimotor and intellectual (cognitive) aspects of brain function. The sensory and motor cortexes work together for a specific coordinated neuromuscular response of two or more sequential tasks.

Movement continuum—Motor skills that develop along a sequential pathway in building block fashion, with more complex and more mature developments occurring with repeated practice.

Proprioception—The skin, joint, muscle response to sensory information.

Sensorimotor integration—Organization of all incoming sensations by the brain for use by the particular individual.

Spatial awareness—Ability to sense where one's body is in space and what it is doing.

Tactile (touch)—To come into contact with something, a tactile sense. The touch system is the largest sensory system of the body, and plays a vital role in physical and mental human development. It is largely controlled by the vestibular system.

Tactile learners—Having a keen sense of specific motor planning and proprioceptive feedback to the body through touching.

Unilateral—One side of the body, (upper and lower) alternate with the opposite side, working in unison to accomplish a movement, such as a bear walk.

Vestibular integration—Having a well developed accurate balance and motor response to gravitational pull.

Vestibular system—The four-way system that informs the individual of changes in the head and body position from gravitational pull activities (spinning, swinging, acceleration/deceleration, sliding, falling), visceral input or stimulation such as peripheral visual cues, tactile or touch information, and proprioceptive (skin/joint/muscle) input.

Visual learners—The ability to accurately process information and learn by seeing an activity done.

Visual motor perception—To be able to accurately discriminate among a variety of moving and non-moving objects, and to determine one's own place in space in relationship to those objects.

Weight-bearing—The joints that support the majority of the body weight. Weight bearing on the hands usually indicates that the weight of the body has been transferred to the hands, arms, and shoulders.

Rhythmic Concept

Steady beat competence—The ability to feel and express the underlying constant, repetitive pulse of a song through clapping or other movement patterns.

APPENDIX B: Resources

Assessment Tools

Test of Gross Motor Development (TGMD-2), Dale Ulrich, 2000
PRO-ED
8700 Shoal Creek Blvd.
Austin, TX 78757-6897
800-897-3202
www.proedinc.com
The TGMD can be used as a teacher resource to gain additional
information about motor development in young children, 3-10 years.
The items contained in the assessment focus on the quality of
movement. Ages and stages of development are discussed.

Music Resources

Abridge Club Entertainment
PO Box 8248
Long Beach, CA 90808
888-421-RIV8
www.AbridgeClub.com

Advanced Brain Technologies
P.O Box 1088
Ogden, Utah 84402
801-622-5676
www.advancedbrain.com

Alleyoop!
Allan Hirsch
2853 21st Ave. W
Seattle, WA. 98199
206-283-3726
alley246@aol.com
www.alleyoop.us

Banana Slug String Band
P.O. Box 2262
Santa Cruz, CA 95063
888-32-SLUGS, 888-327-5847 Phone and Fax
www.bananaslugstringband.com

Dinonastics Music
1919 Avalon Dr.
Nashville, TN 37216
615-226-8162
www.dinonastics.com

Educational Activities
PO Box 87
Baldwin, NY 11510
800-645-3796
516-223-4666
www.edact.com

Greg and Steve Productions, Inc.
P.O. Box 261
Acton, CA 93510
661-269-5407
800-548-4063
www.gregandsteve.com

Hap-Pal Music
Hap Palmer
P.O. Box 8343
Northridge, CA 91364-9998
818-885-0200
www.babysongshp.com
www.happalmer.com

Hug Bug Music Inc
Charlotte Diamond
5005 Vista View Crescent
Nanaimo, B.C.
CANADA V9V 1L6
www.charlottediamond.com

Joe Scruggs
Shadow Play Records
PO Box 180476
Austin, TX 78718
800-274-8804
www.hellojoe.com

KIMBO Educational
PO Box 477
Long Branch, NJ 07740
800-631-2187
www.KIMBOEd.com

Kindermusik International
PO Box 26575
Greensboro, NC 27415
336-273-3363
www.kindermusik.com

KinderTunes
PO Box 169
Corbett, Oregon 97019
503-695-5975
www.kindertunes.net

Music with Mar
149 Garland Circle
Palm Harbor, FL 34683
727-781-4MAR
www.musicwithmar.com

Songs for Teaching, Using Music to
    Promote Learning
6632 Telegraph Rd. #242
Bloomfield Hills, MI 48301
Orders: 800-649-5514
Information: 800-901-1060
www.SongsforTeaching.com

The Brain Store
4202 Sorrento Valley Blvd. Ste. B
San Diego, CA 92121
800-325-4769
www.thebrainstore.com

The Learning Station
Don Monopoli Productions
3950 Bristol Court
Melbourne, FL 32904

800-789-9990
321-728-8773
www.learningstationmusic.com

Wagon Wheel Records and Books
Paul James
16812 Pembrook Lane
Huntington Beach, CA 92649
Phone/Fax 714-846-8169
www.wagonwheelrecords.net

Professional Early Childhood Organizations with Publications

Association for Childhood Education International (ACEI)
    17904 Georgia Avenue, Suite 215
    Olney, MD 20832
    800-423-3563
    Publication: Childhood Education
    www.acei.org

National Association for Sport and Physical Education (NASPE)
    American Alliance for Health, Physical Education, Recreation, and Dance
    1900 Association Drive
    Reston, VA 20191-1598
    703-476-3400
    800-213-7193
    Publication: Journal of Physical Education, Recreation, and Dance
    www.aahperd.org/NASPE/

Early Childhood Music Association
    2110 27th Avenue
    Greeley, CO 80631
    Publication: Early Childhood Connections: The Journal of Music and Movement Based Learning
    336-272-5303
    www.ecconnections.org

Early Childhood Music and Movement Association (ECMMA)
    805 Mill Avenue
    Snohomish, WA 98290-2238
    Telephone/fax: 360 568-5635
    www.ecmma.org

High/Scope Educational Research Foundation
    600 North River Street
    Ypsilanti, MI 48198-2898
    734-485-2000
    www.highscope.com

International Reading Association (IRA)
    International Reading Association
    Headquarters Office
    800 Barksdale Road
    PO Box 8139
    Newark, DE 19714-8139
    800-336-7323
    www.reading.org

National Association for the Education of Young Children (NAEYC)
    1313L Street, NW, Suite 500
    Washington, DC 20005-4101
    800-424-2460
    Publication: Young Children
    www.naeyc.org

National Institute for Early Education Research (NIEER)
    Rutgers, The State University of New Jersey
    120 Albany Street, Suite 500
    New Brunswick, New Jersey 08901
    732-932-4350
    www.nieer.org

PACE (Professional Association for Childhood Development)
    114 Sansome Street, Suite 300
    San Francisco, CA 94104
    800-924-2460
    www.pacenet.org

References and Resources

American Heart Association. 2005. "Exercise (Physical Activity) and Children." [Online]. Available: http://www.americanheart.org/presenter.jhtml?identifier=4596

American Heart Association. 2005. "Overweight in Children." [Online]. Available: http://americanheart.org/presenter.jhtml?identifier=4760

American Medical Association. 2005, Oct. 4. "News From the AMA: Fitness-Oriented Gym Classes Demonstrate Measurable Health Benefits for Overweight Children." [Online]. Available: http://www.medem.com/medlb/article_detaillb.cfm?article_ID=ZZZ0OWDSIEE&sub_cat=0

Block, B.A. 2001. Literacy through movement: An organizational approach. *Journal of Physical Education, Recreation & Dance*, 72(1), 39-48.

Carmona, R. 2005. "The Value and Promise of Every Child." United States Department of Health & Human Services. [Online]. Available: http://www.surgeongeneral.gov/news/speeches/02072005.html

Carmona, R. 2005. United States Department of Human Health Services. 2005. The Surgeon General's Call To Action To Prevent and Decrease Overweight and Obesity [Online]. Available: http://www.surgeongeneral.gov/topics/obesity/calltoaction/fact_adolescents.html

Center for Disease Control. 2005. "Physical Activity and Good Nutrition: Essential Elements to Prevent Chronic Diseases and Obesity." [Online]. Available: http://www.cdc.gov/nccdphp/aag/aag_dnpa.htm

Elkind, D. 2000-01. Cosmopolitan school. *Educational Leadership*, 58(4), 12-17.

Elliott, E. & Sanders, S. 2005. "The Issues: Children and physical activity." PBS Teacher Source. [Online]. Available: http://www.pbs.org/teachersource/prek2/issues/202issue.shtm

Gopher Sport, Active and Healthy Schools, 2006. [Online]. Available http://activeandhealthyschools.com/index.cfm?PAGE_ID=2

Hammett, C. Republished, 2006. *Movement activities for early childhood*. PE Central. [Online] Available: http:/emerchant.aciwebs.com/stores/pecentral/

Jensn, E. 2000. *Learning with the body in mind*. San Diego, CA: The Brain Store.

Kranowitz, C. 1998. *The out-of-sync child: Recognizing and coping with sensory integration dysfunction*. New York, NY: The Berkley Publishing Group.

McGee, L. M. & Richgels, D. J. 2000. *Literacy's beginnings: Supporting young readers and writers*. Needham Heights, MA: Allyn and Bacon.

Medical News Today. June 28, 2006. "Bill Clinton in drive to tackle childhood obesity." [Online] Available: http://www.medicalnewstoday.com/medicalnews.php?newsid=23813

National Association of Sport and Physical Education. 2002. *Active start: A statement of physical activity guidelines for children birth to five years.* Reston, VA.AAHPERD Publications.

National Association of Sport and Physical Education. 2004. *Physical activity for children: A statement of guidelines for children ages 5-12.* Second Edition. Reston, VA. AAHPERD Publications.

National Institute for Health Care Management (NIHCM) Foundation. August, 2004. "New Research Shows More Physical Education Time Sharply Reduces Overweight in Children. Being Overweight Also Has Implications for Behavior and Academic Performance". [Online]. Available: http://www.nihcm.org/OYCpress.html

Nesmith, J. Sunday, November 6, 2005. Childhood tummy fat predicts diabetes and heart trouble for girls." *New York Times Syndicate.* [Online]. Available: http://www.nlm.nih.gov/medlineplus/news/fullstory_27877.html

Nestle, M. 2006. "Food marketing and childhood obesity—a matter of policy." *New England Journal of Medicine.* 354:2527-2529 Available: http://www.foodpolitics.com/pdf/foodmktg.pdf

News in Health, July 2005, "National Institutes of Health: Preventing Childhood Obesity." [Online]. Available: http://newsinhealth.nih.gov/PastIssue/July2005/docs/01features_02.htm

Nichols, K. 2001. *Music moment to teach academics.* Lacey, WA. Tree Frog Productions/Kerri-oke Publications

Owacki, G. 2001. *Make way for literacy! Teaching the way young children learn.* Portsmouth, NH: Heinemann and Washington, CD: National Association for the Education of Young Children.

Pica, R. 2006. *Great games for young children.* Beltsville, MD: Gryphon House, Inc.

Routman, R. 2003. *Reading essentials: The specifics you need to teach reading well.* Portsmouth, NH: Heinemann.

Russ, A. 2004. *Action Angie's activity guide.* Long Beach, CA: A Russ InVision Company.

Saltz, G. 2005. Five ways to get your child moving. *Parade Magazine* September 9, 2005. [Online]. Available: http://archive.parade.com/2005/0925/0925_get_moving.html

Sanders, S. 2002. *Active for life: Developmentally appropriate movement programs for young children.* Washington, D.C: National Association for Young Children (NAEYC).

Sawyer, W. E. 2000. *Growing up with literature*. Albany, NY: Delmar Thompson Learning.

Snow, C., Burns, M.S., & Griffin, M. 1998. *Preventing reading difficulties in young children*. Washington, DC: National Academies Press.

Strickland, D. S. 2006. Language and literacy in kindergarten. *K Today: Teaching and Learning in the Kindergarten*. Washington, DC: National Association for the Education of Young Children, 73-84.

Trelease, J. 2001. *The read-aloud handbook*. New York: Penguin Books.

Weikart, P. 2003. *Movement in steady beat*. Second Edition. Ypsilanti, M.D. High/Scope Press.

Yopp, H., & Yopp, R. 2000, October. Supporting phonemic awareness development in the classroom. *The Reading Teacher*, 54(2), 130-143.

Websites of Interest

Action for Healthy Kids
www.actionforhealthykids.org/

Active and Healthy Schools
www.activeandhealthyschools.com

Childcare Exchange
www.childcareexchange.com

Dr. Koop, former Surgeon General
www.drkoop.com

Learning Brain Newsletter
www.learningbrain.com

PE Central
www.pecentral.org

Physical Education Links
www.pelinks4u.org

Rethinking School Lunch
www.ecoliteracy.org/programs/rsl.html

SPARK
www.sparkpe.org

Appendix C: Materials

As with classroom materials and supplies, all items used for movement sessions should be checked regularly to maintain safe use. Discard equipment materials that are worn or have missing parts. Making repairs, in a timely manner, allows you to maintain a wide inventory of materials for a variety of purposes. It also reduces the risk of the broken items being used by unsuspecting teachers. You will find it helpful to develop a system for organizing and storing your materials. Labeling cabinets and closets and bins with a list enables you to access items at a moments notice.

Equipping an early childhood classroom with materials can be very expensive. If you are just beginning to acquire items, make a list of what would be the most versatile for the children in your class and your classroom or your movement environment. Develop a method of rotating materials on a weekly or monthly basis. Enlist the help of parents by creating a "wish list" of items you would like to have for your program. Be sure to list how the materials will be used. Parents appreciate the opportunity to help out, especially when they know materials and supplies will be used. We have included directions for making simple materials. You will find this especially helpful if you are on a limited budget. Don't forget to invite parents to participate in making simple items. You may also want to consider visiting local thrift shops. You can find things such as milk crates to be used as jumping boxes, nylon scarves for dancing, and wooden badminton racquets that can be shortened and re-gripped, using electricians tape. You may also want to approach businesses in your community for donations of closeout items. For example, your local variety store may be willing to donate beach balls left over at the end of the summer season. With a little creativity, you can begin to build an inventory of materials.

Alphabetical listing of materials with suggested uses:

Balls, types of:
    Beach balls, 12"–16"
    Fleece balls 4"
    Fluff balls, 90 mm
    Foam balls, 3.5" and 6"
    Koosh balls, 3.5"
    Playground balls 8"
    Punch balls 26"
    Soccer balls, vinyl coated and regular
    Yarn balls 4"
Suggested uses include bouncing, dribbling, tossing, kicking, hand/eye coordination, eye/foot coordination, target play, parachute play, games, and partner activities.

Safety Considerations:
Choose materials that are appropriate for the age, size, and skill level of your children. For example, using a full-size football would not be suitable for young children. It is difficult to throw and catch and the hardness and size of the ball might injure or intimidate youngsters. Early childhood supply stores and catalogs have materials that are designed with safety in mind and are appropriate for children's developing motor skills. Most early childhood equipment materials are brightly colored and available in a variety of sizes and weights. These qualities help capture children's interests, encourage exploration of the materials and various skills, and meet the developmental needs of children.

Balloons, types of:
- Round 12", bright colors
- Balloons covered with duct tape

Suggested uses include for eye/hand and eye/foot coordination, tracking skills, nutrition games and activities, bouncing (balloon/duct tape balls), and partner activities.

Balance strips, types of:
- Velcro for carpeted floors
- Nonskid for wood, asphalt, cement, linoleum, and other smooth surfaces
- In 4' and 8' lengths, set of 6 in a variety of colors

Suggested uses include for locomotor skills, balance activities, games, and indoor and outdoor use.

Bars, types of:
- Jungle gym bars
- Monkey bars
- Over/under bars (1" PVC pipe)
- Single hanging bars

Suggested uses include for climbing, hanging, and learning about space concepts, such as *over*, *under*, and *around*.

Beanbags, types of:
- Cloth
- Nylon
- Variety of shapes and colors, sizes and textures

Suggested uses include for eye/hand coordination, catching, throwing, tossing, target throwing, kicking, games, balance activities, and passing. Try to make or purchase larger, textured beanbags for children to have more success in catching and balance activities.

Cones, types of:
- Dome markers
- Foam cones
- Inflatable cones
- Marker cones, 8", 18", 28"
- Weighted cones

Suggested uses include for soccer goal area, class organization, boundary markers, activity/obstacle course, and activity stations.

Hoops, 24", types of:
> Flat hoops
> Hollow tubed hoops
> PVC homemade hoops

Suggested uses include for balance activities, locomotor activities, inside/outside concepts, personal space markers, and games.

Jump Ropes, types of:
> No handle-nylon/cotton/poly ropes 7' length, homemade
> Long double Dutch ropes, 16'–24' long
> Speed ropes, 7'
> Tug of war 1" diameter, either professional or homemade construction

Suggested uses include for flat rope jumping (non-turning), individual rope jumping, partner rope jumping, long rope jumping, tug of war, and personal space markers.

Mats, types of:
> Fold-up, 2" thick
> Incline, all sizes
> Landing, 4"–8" thick
> Stairs
> Tumbling, 2" thick

Suggested uses include for rolling, crawling, dancing, sitting or lying down activities, landing, or any activity that requires a soft surface. Always use manufacturer's guidelines for proper use.

Paddles, types of:
> Foam
> Paper plates/paint stick, nonprofessional construction

Suggested uses include for striking games, eye/hand coordination, and partner activities.

Parachute, types of:
> Rainbow colored nylon 6', 12', 20' round
> Parasheets, 4' x 4' and 6' x 6' feet
> Bed sheets

Suggested uses include for cooperative play, rhythmic activities, vigorous games, and upper body strength development.

Personal space markers, types of:
- Activity mats, 9" round
- Carpet squares
- Foam cut-out shapes
- Hoops
- Nonskid place mats
- Poly spots

Suggested uses include for each child to determine his or her own personal space, without running into another child.

Scarves, types of:
- Nylon, see-through activity 17" x 17" rainbow-colored
- Juggling 17" x 17"
  - Nonprofessional made from lightweight fabric 18" x 18"

Suggested uses include for eye/hand coordination development, games, juggling, waving, tossing, twirling, and rhythmic and dance activities.

Scooters, types of:
- Safety grip scooters
- Laminated wood scooters
- All terrain scooters
- Easy link up scooters

Suggested uses include for cooperative activities, rowing activities, games, strength development, and vestibular stimulation.

Streamers, types of:
- Wand with attached ribbon
- Looped handle with 4 attached ribbons
- Nonprofessional made with dowel, eye hook, fish
- swivel, and satin ribbon

Suggested uses include for rhythmic and dance activities, to create designs, and for twirling, swirling, waving, and circling.

Tunnel, types of:
- Connecting tunnels
- Play tunnels
- Arched tunnels
- Inflatable crawl-through shapes

Suggested uses include for obstacle courses, crawling activities, and games.

Ideas for Making Selected Materials

1. **Beanbags**: Use textured polyester fabric, denim, or sail cloth. Cut into 5" x 6" rectangles. Sew and zigzag stitch on all four sides leaving a 2" opening to fill with dried beans, corn, peas or rice. Use a wide-mouth funnel. Top stitch across the opening.

2. **Chin or hanging bar**: These can be purchased at a sport store, and secured in a doorway at your chosen height for children to experience over/under concepts, strength development, hanging, and so on.

3. **Directional signs**: These can be made from cardboard or bulletin board paper and laminated to provide arrows for directional signs or station identification with symbols, numbers or anything you choose.

4. **Duct tape balls**: Blow up a round, thick 12" party balloon. After tying a knot in the end, place a piece of duct tape over the knot. Take strips of duct tape and, beginning at the bottom of the balloon, tape over the top and down the opposite side. Do the same with a second piece of duct tape so that the balloon is now taped into a quadrant. Fill in with shorter pieces so that the entire balloon has been taped. It will bounce like a ball.

5. **Personal space markers**: Foam sheets cut into a variety of geometric shapes.

6. **Parachute**: Use a regular queen-sized sheet and cut the corners off to make it round. Sew a hem in raw edges.

7. **Ribbon streamers**: Tear or cut crepe paper into 4' lengths and tie two lengths together by knotting the end. Option 2: Purchase: ⅜" diameter dowels, cut into 12' length; small eye hook; fishing swivel; thick nylon thread; and 4' satin ribbon. Fold one end into a triangle shape, tack it and attach to the fish swivel with nylon thread or fishing line. Attach to the eye hook on the dowel.

8. **Ropes for flat rope jumping**: Purchase 100 feet length of ⅜" "diamond-braid" cotton/poly rope from a hardware store or home improvement store. The rope comes in a wide variety of bright fun colors. Cut into 7' lengths and burn the ends to melt them. Wrap the ends with duct tape, or other.

9. **Scarves**: Purchase inexpensive chiffon-type fabric from your local fabric store. Cut into 18" x 18" squares. Hem to avoid unraveling.

10. **Scoops for catching**: Use plastic gallon jugs. Cut off the bottom and one side. Use electrical tape on the cut edges to prevent scrapes.

11. **Shakers**: Add to the music by filling film containers with pebbles. Tape the end so that children will not open them.

12. **Skates**: Purchase styrene type paper plates for maximum slideability on carpeted floors. Option 2: For wood or linoleum floors, ask parents to bring in old thick cotton or wool socks for children to put on over their own shoes or socks.

13. **Tunnels**: Large cardboard boxes from appliance stores make good tunnels, as do sheets or blankets over tables.

14. **Yarn balls**: Cut a 4.5" x 6" piece of heavy cardboard. Wrap length of yarn 200–250 times around the 4.5" length. Bend cardboard slightly to remove yarn, holding tightly onto the middle of the yarn. With a helping hand, secure yarn very tightly in the middle with zip tie. Cut extra zip tie length off. Cut looped ends. Fluff out.

Indexes

Title Index

Author Index

Recorded Music Index

Theme Connections Index

Index

Tunnels, 177, 185, 210
    making, 212
Turning, 38, 40–41, 78, 94, 98, 119, 136, 136, 154, 160
    defined, 197
Twirling, 74, 80, 84, 94, 108, 132, 140, 178
Twisting, 94, 98, 116
    defined, 197

U

U.S. Department of Education, 20
Unilateral movement
    defined, 199
Uniqueness, 62
Up/down movements, 119
Utility balls, 83

V

Vestibular integration, 119
    defined, 199
Vestibular system, 29, 99, 198
    defined, 199
Visual cuing, 23
Visual learners, 30
    defined, 199
Visual motor perception, 30
    defined, 199
Visual stimulation, 29
Voice inflection, 25, 60, 68, 108, 110
    defined, 192

W

Waddling, 64–65, 108, 122, 168
    defined, 196
Wading, 178
    defined, 196
Walking, 20, 30–31, 53, 82, 88, 118, 122, 124, 138, 150, 152, 154, 170, 184
    defined, 195
Watts, S., 95
Websites, 206

Weight-bearing activities, 20
    defined, 199
Weighted cones, 208
Weikart, P., 75, 103
Whirling, 44, 94, 126, 176
    defined, 197
Wiggling, 31, 46, 50, 62, 78, 108, 116, 132, 162, 182–183
    defined, 197
Winter, 64–65
Wood, D., 134
Word meaning, 26
Wordless books, 192
Wriggling, 78, 108, 116
    defined, 197
Writing, 22, 25, 27–28, 188–190
    defined, 192

Y

Yarn, 83, 154, 159, 212
    balls, 33, 42, 64–65, 207, 212
    ropes, 130–131, 142
Yopp, H., 26, 35, 206
Yopp, R., 26, 35, 206

Z

Zebra walk, 174
Zip ties, 212